Information Technology in Educational Management for the Schools of the Future

IFIP – The International Federation for Information Processing

IFIP was founded in 1960 under the auspices of UNESCO, following the First World Computer Congress held in Paris the previous year. An umbrella organization for societies working in information processing, IFIP's aim is two-fold: to support information processing within its member countries and to encourage technology transfer to developing nations. As its mission statement clearly states,

> IFIP's mission is to be the leading, truly international, apolitical organization which encourages and assists in the development, exploitation and application of information technology for the benefit of all people.

IFIP is a non-profitmaking organization, run almost solely by 2500 volunteers. It operates through a number of technical committees, which organize events and publications. IFIP's events range from an international congress to local seminars, but the most important are:

- the IFIP World Computer Congress, held every second year;
- open conferences;
- working conferences.

The flagship event is the IFIP World Computer Congress, at which both invited and contributed papers are presented. Contributed papers are rigorously refereed and the rejection rate is high.

As with the Congress, participation in the open conferences is open to all and papers may be invited or submitted. Again, submitted papers are stringently refereed.

The working conferences are structured differently. They are usually run by a working group and attendance is small and by invitation only. Their purpose is to create an atmosphere conducive to innovation and development. Refereeing is less rigorous and papers are subjected to extensive group discussion.

Publications arising from IFIP events vary. The papers presented at the IFIP World Computer Congress and at open conferences are published as conference proceedings, while the results of the working conferences are often published as collections of selected and edited papers.

Any national society whose primary activity is in information may apply to become a full member of IFIP, although full membership is restricted to one society per country. Full members are entitled to vote at the annual General Assembly, National societies preferring a less committed involvement may apply for associate or corresponding membership. Associate members enjoy the same benefits as full members, but without voting rights. Corresponding members are not represented in IFIP bodies. Affiliated membership is open to non-national societies, and individual and honorary membership schemes are also offered.

Information Technology in Educational Management for the Schools of the Future

IFIP TC3/ WG 3.4 International Conference on Information Technology in Educational Management (ITEM), 22–26 July 1996, Hong Kong

Edited by

Alex C.W. Fung
Department of Education Studies
Hong Kong Baptist University
Hong Kong

Adrie J. Visscher
Faculty of Educational Science and Technology
University of Twente
Enschede, The Netherlands

Ben-Zion Barta
Ministry of Education
Jerusalem, Israel

David C. B. Teather
Faculty of Social Sciences
Hong Kong Baptist University
Hong Kong

SPRINGER-SCIENCE+BUSINESS MEDIA, B.V.

First edition 1997

Originally published by Chapman & Hall in 1997
MyCopy version of the original edition 1997

DOI 10.1007/978-0-387-35090-5

A catalogue record for this book is available from the British Library

Printed on permanent acid-free text paper, manufactured in accordance with ANSI/NISO Z39.48-1992 and ANSI/NISO Z39.48-1984 (Permanence of Paper).

www.springer.com/mycopy

CONTENTS

Part 3: Organisational Culture

Part 4: Evaluation & Implementation

Part 5: Systems Development

INTERNATIONAL PROGRAM COMMITTEE

Dr. Ben-Zion Barta (Chair)	Israel
Dr. Alex C.W. Fung (Co-chair)	Hong Kong
Dr. Moshe Telem (Co-chair)	Israel
Mr. Gordon Davies	UK
Mrs. Betty Ip	Hong Kong
Mr. Y.Y. Ng	Hong Kong
Prof. Patrick Nolan	New Zealand
Mr. Brian Samways	UK
Prof. Dennis Spuck	USA
Prof. Raymond Taylor	USA
Dr. Adrie Visscher	Netherlands
Dr. Phil Wild	UK
Prof. Harald Yndestad	Norway

CONFERENCE ORGANISING COMMITTEE

Dr. Alex C.W. Fung (Chair)	Hong Kong Baptist University
Dr. Jack Chan	Hong Kong Baptist University
Mr. Jerome Day	Hong Kong Baptist University
Mr. W.K. Kwok	Hong Kong Education Department
Mr. M.S. Lau	Hong Kong Education Department
Mr. Jacky Pow (Secretary)	Hong Kong Baptist University
Mr. S.W. Pun	Hong Kong Institute of Education
Dr. Atara Sivan	Hong Kong Baptist University
Prof. David Teather	Hong Kong Baptist University

SPONSORS

International Federation for Information Processing, T.C. 3, W.G. 3.4
Department of Education, Hong Kong Government
Hong Kong Baptist University

THE WORKING CONFERENCE HAS BEEN SUPPORTED BY

Epson Foundation, Hong Kong
Novell Hong Kong Ltd

PREFACE

This book is for both specialist and generalist. For Information Technology (IT) and Educational Management (EM) researchers, it brings together the latest information and analysis of ITEM projects in eleven countries. But the issues raised by this collection of papers are so important for schools, school systems and the future of education that it is essential reading not only for researchers but also for teachers, administrators and all concerned with the planning and governance of our education systems.

New technologies may improve our lives in two ways: by enabling us to do things better (accomplishing what we do already more efficiently) and by enabling us to do better things (accomplishing new things that we were not able to do before).

Sometimes "doing things better" merges into "doing better things". Thus in the 19th century the coming of the railway enabled our forbears to accomplish their existing journies in less time and in greater comfort. But it also opened up the prospect of new journies to more distant places, and led ultimately to far-reaching changes in lifestyles in new, commuter settlements far from the old city centres.

So it is in the present day with Information Technology in Educational Management. Some of the papers in this volume focus on specialist tasks, for example how to develop a computer-based decision-support system to help those drawing up school timetables. Others address situations in which the power of the technology offers us the potential to change radically what we do.

The papers in this volume have been selected from those presented at the second International Working Conference on ITEM, held in Hong Kong in July 1996. Participation in the Conference was by invitation only, to leaders in the ITEM field from around the world.

The first International Working Conference on ITEM, held two years previously in Israel, was aware that "a massive and rapid computerisation process in schools, school districts, and throughout the other levels of the educational system" was then going on. Delegates were well aware that successful implementation of ITEM depends not only on hardware, but also on adequate software - mainly Management Information Systems (MIS)/Decision Support Systems (DSS) - and on human factors.

Two years later the context has moved on, but similar issues are still with us. Thus in the abstract of his paper, Matti Mäkelä states: "Information Technology will cause continuous changes in our technology environment. The general impression is that the digital age will improve our lives and societies. Huge national strategies and programmes are underpinned by this belief. They do not properly take into account the human dimension."

The main theme of the second Conference on ITEM caused us to focus on the schools of the future. What do schools and education systems of the future have to face in the wave of information and communication technology? What is the current state of the art, and experience that can be shared from different places on the globe? What can we learn from research about ITEM? What are the cultural, organisational, managerial, and technological issues needing to be addressed? These questions are answered, in this volume, from the different perspectives of researchers, administrators, and teachers themseThis second Conference on ITEM, from which these papers are drawn, was sponsored by the Technology Committee on Computers in Education of the International Federation for Information Processing (IFIP), by the Education Department of the Hong Kong Government, and by the School Administration and Management Systems (SAMS) Training and Research Unit of the Hong Kong Baptist University. Thanks are also due to the members of the International Programme Committee and of the Organising Committee of the Conference, and to all who participated in the role of presenters, chairs or delegates.

Through this book, selected papers from this Conference are brought to a wider readership. In these pages you will find pointers to the identification of what are the really significant issues for the schools of the future. You will find also a wealth of information which will help to realise the potential of information technology for the benefit of pupils and teachers in the years to come.

The Editors.

Key Note Speech

1

Quo Vadis? --- Internet

Elizabeth Wong
Legislative Councilor, Hong Kong

I am deeply honoured to be invited as the key-note speaker of the ITEM '96 conference today. It is also a pleasure to be here with so many people of achievement and importance in the field of information processing and technology. I am particularly privileged in sharing the same platform as Mr. Joseph Wong, Secretary for Education and Manpower and Dr. Daniel Tse, President and Vice-chancellor of the Hong Kong Baptist University and Dr. Alex Fung, Chairman of the Organizing Committee for this conference.

As the title for the conference itself denotes, information technology in educational management for the schools of the future is important.

I have therefore deliberately chosen for my talk a topic which yet has to evolve answers. I should like to discuss with you the question of processing information, having regard to dramatic advancements in modern technology which allows quick access to information and which has yet to evolve a set of acceptable and universally understood standards of behaviour. This, indeed, is where educational management for the schools of the Future is central to the issue.

For many years, I have felt that computer studies are not only part of science but part of humanity. To understand the use of the computer, and to understand the morality involved in the computing business and the use of the internet, we need people who can communicate and we need teachers and students alike who will help to address the moral aspects of handling information technology, the use of the internet and access to information.

We all know that at affordable prices, and with incredible speed, people from a diversity of ethnic and cultural backgrounds can visit people in far away places. They can exchange information on line and need not worry about getting out of line.

Although already some 60 million people, spanning over some 150 countries, are already surfers on the Web, many of them may feel that they are at sea or are managing to keep themselves from being bitten by sharks on the Net, so to speak.

But, let us face it, though the Internet is still an inchoate technology, it is here to stay. Its possibilities for exploding into a global market in information, in commerce and trade, are enormous, though the risks of the Net being used and abused by shady sharks in cyberspace are also there.

Reality being what it is, I think the key to information technology and to the future relationship between the Government, the individual and the international community rests with evolving a universal modus operandi: a code of practice, if you like, for acceptable standards of behaviour for us to act locally and interact globally in a coherent manner.

The question is how to arrive at a situation where there is truly egalitarian interaction between the peoples of the world on the Net. How to get the full benefit from this technology; how to get the right balance between the rights of an individual and the responsibilities of the State; and how to set the right level of control, if we need controls at all, to preserve the integrity of the technology and promote individual choice: all these are questions to which we do not have ready answers yet. There is at present no consensus. Neither is consensus something that can be cursorily arrived at or carelessly agreed upon.

But it is important to arrive at some commonality of view since having some connectivity is better than having no connectivity at all. I put it to you that we need to come together and to evolve a new universal consensus to that we are all on the same intellectual and moral wave-length to deal with access to information and to deal with the information technology in educational management for the schools in the future.

For a start, I think not enough resources are being deployed to promote in schools a cyberconsciousness in the use of the new technology. While we recognize the good work done in schools and while we acknowledge that the Government is trying to introduce computer literacy in schools, I put it to you that not enough is being done in schools to educate students with a view to understanding not only the mechanical side but also the ethical side of information technology.

The use of computer requires as much knowledge in ethics as any other science. For example, in medicine, we have laws to guide practitioners and we have self-regulating councils that govern the behaviour of practitioners in that profession.

But even as I speak, there is an absence of a universal consensus in setting a framework for some commonly acceptable multilateral and multinational parameters within which each country is free to determine rules governing the deployment and use of information technology.

Here I am of the view that the deliberations of this conference are of immense importance to the future educational management of information technology. And it would be a good thing to have every contentious view and important issue identified and thrashed out; and to have available options evolved and developed for adoption. It is important that the right sort of questions are asked. The pros and cons must be debated. All the twists and turns of each argument, albeit all inevitably interlinked, must be ironed out, negotiated and resolved on a world wide basis. In this technology, we need to develop a tripartite relationship between the cyber-mind, the cyber-brawn and the cyberheart --- I hope you will forgive me in coining these words to reflect exactly what I mean.

Thus, I have a vision that very soon, there will be a set of internationally understood and acceptable framework to guide us through the years.

To develop a comprehensive and coherent policy for providing information on the Net, we should develop a coherent approach. There should be provided the necessary resources for this strategy. In this public domain, we must move with the times. I hope too that at the end of the day, before the dawning of the next century, international internet agreements could be negotiated and agreed upon just as trade treaties or agreements on intellectual property are negotiated and signed to govern acceptable standards of behaviour between countries.

When this happens, concerned individuals, communities and Governments will be on the same wave length. When this happens we'll have good reason to celebrate.

Let me therefore extend my best wishes to you and hope you have a successful conference. Let me also say that I shall look forward to the outcome of your deliberations which will have far reaching implications in the years to come.

Your individual contribution and collective wisdom will be long remembered and appreciated in the years to come.

PART ONE

Tomorrow Schools

2

Internet support to school innovation management

B.Z. Barta
Ministry of Education
Jerusalem, Israel,51 Disraeli Str. Haifa 34333, Israel.
Phone: (972)-4-8345845
e-mail: ben@actcom.co.il

M. Telem
School of Education, Tel-Aviv University, Tel-Aviv, Israel
Phone: (972)-3-6407123 *Fax: (972)-3-6409477,*
e-mail: telem@post.tau.ac.il

Abstract

Internet services that support the introduction of innovations in teaching and management in the educational system are: access to global information resources, communication among peer-teams and improved communication links between individuals and team members. Internet's support for teaching, management and supervision is elaborated. A pilot project in Israel presently involving five user groups, including curriculum developers and supervisors, working in the field of Informatics and Information Technologies is presented. Preliminary recommendations are formulated.

Keywords

Educational management, professional development, curriculum development, internet, user groups, teleconferencing

1 INTRODUCTION

In recent years, Internet has developed into a reliable, accessible, large-scale communication medium. Various educational initiatives use its services to support a variety of activities (Johnson, 1995; Hughes, 1993; Protheroe and Wilson, 1994; West, 1993). However, only few publications refer to Internet applications supporting curricular development and innovation, implementation of new curricula and approaches (Doyle, 1995; Hert, 1994; Seguin, 1994).

Schools are loosely coupled organizations (Weick 1976, 1982). As a result the information flow among a school's functionaries and between it and other schools is very often slow or even hardly exists at all. In the case of innovation projects, very often in a given school only a few teachers and their subject coordinators are involved in the project, and they work on identical or similar issues and deal with similar problems. Other teams in other schools, though geographically apart, also deal with similar issues and face similar problems. The groups at the different schools do not cooperate due to communication difficulties, thus impending exchange of ideas and accumulation of experience.

Updated and accessible information, including effective tools for easy information retrieval and exchange of ideas, constitute a fundamental requirement for a variety of activities related to education in general and teaching in particular. This is especially so as regards innovative activities leading to school change and renewal (Telem, 1990a). Efficient communication is extremely important for dealing with implementation of educational innovation, which usually involves one or several development teams, as well as implementation teams who are variously located. The importance of effective communication grows with the size of the project (e.g., number and size of teams involved).

The project described in this paper is at a very early stage of development. It is intended to investigate the use of Internet in supporting curricular innovation. As a byproduct, the project also considers Internet contribution to school employees' routine work and educational staff in-service development.

2 THE RATIONALE OF THE INTERNET PROJECT

The Israeli school system is a rather dynamic one, with respect to curricular and methodological changes and updates. Specifically, in the field of Information Technology and Informatics, significant innovations have been continuously fostered during recent years (Gal-Ezer et al., 1995; Telem and Barta 1993; Barta and Telem, 1992, Barta 1990).

While curricular development projects deal with a variety of subjects, a common line of activity typifies most of them. Each project is composed of several stages, each one with its particular communications needs and "classical" communication means (e.g., meetings, telephone). The Internet may constitute a powerful additional communication component to these means, in each of the following main stages:

Design and planning. The main communication needs at this stage relate to the gathering of information on similar work done or being carried out by other teams and, perhaps, setting-up contacts and cooperation with them. Classical communication means for this stage are libraries with their abstracts data bases (e.g., ERIC), published journals, correspondence by mail or fax, telephone, personal visits and/or meetings.

Internet may contribute to this stage by the search and "surfing" tools provided by the World Wide Web (WWW) and by electronic-mail (e-mail) services. The WWW system may help in gathering updated information much faster and easier than any of the above mentioned means. The e-mail facility may provide means for team-to-team information exchange, preferable to ordinary mail or fax because of its ease of access and use, speed, cost, accuracy of data transfer and the variety of the types of information that can be transferred (texts, graphics, computer files).

Development and small scale implementation and evaluation. This stage is usually achieved by a small team who can get together and who communicate mainly in meetings, through brainstorming and through the direct transfer of documents. Internet may make only a minor contribution at this stage.

Partial implementation and evaluation. At this stage a larger group of people is involved. For instance, development team members and teachers in different schools spread out over several regions, and they all implement the new curriculum in their classrooms. Distribution of learning materials and aids, support and advice provided by the developers to the implementors, feedback from the implementors and collection of data for ongoing evaluation, are the major communications-based activities at this stage of development. The classical means of communication at this stage, consist of regular pre-scheduled group meetings, in-service training and seminars (development team with teachers), visits of development team members to the participating schools, peer-to-peer contacts at meetings and by phone, transfer of documents (by mail, fax or diskettes), ad-hoc solving of problems that occur during implementation - mainly by telephonic contacts.

In addition to the above mentioned classical means, Internet constitutes a valuable tool for achieving the project's communication needs at this stage. The main goal of the project described in this paper is to develop and make available the additional Internet communication tools needed at this stage, such as information exchange and discussions between groups of people without forcing teams and team members to be present at the same place (e.g., scheduled meetings) at the same time (e.g., telephone, video-conferencing); transfer of messages, documents and files; on-line access to information banks containing well organized items relevant to the group. Emphasis is on approaching large groups of people, on dealing with large amounts of information in an efficient and cost effective way, and on efficient methods used to update, modify, transfer, search and retrieve information.

Full scale implementation. This stage involves hundreds of teachers, members of the development teams and teams of supervisors and advisors. At the end of this stage the innovation changes into routine. At this stage, the information in information banks is less dynamic (i.e., changes are less frequent and of a minor nature) but the size of the group using them and requiring communication facilities grows significantly. Coordination issues may have an important role (e.g., within the supervising team, between the supervising and the development teams).

Internet may play the same roles as in the partial implementation stage, the main change being the size of the group using the services.

Summing up, the main goals of the Internet project are:

- Definition of Internet services and applications that are valuable to curricular innovation in each stage of a project.
- Identification of problems and difficulties to be overcome in order to assimilate and support the services, as defined.
- Development of the specific Internet application and its operation and maintainence, both technically and content wise.
- Establishment of an evaluation mechanism that will provide ongoing feedback needed for introducing changes and improvements both to the new curricula and to the use of the Internet services.

3 INTERNET SERVICES - SUPPORT TO INNOVATION

A good overview of Internet's potential contribution to education and educational management is presented by Fung and Pun (1996). The following, Internet-based services have been considered suitable for satisfying the requirements mentioned in Section 2:

3.1 Global Communication Services

"Reinventing the Wheel", i.e., repetition of achievements (or mistakes) already made by others, may hinder the development and implementation of innovative educational projects and research. "Bridging" between members of the development team, between the intraschool and interschool information "islands", and between the school and the other levels of the educational systems, constitutes a challenge faced by the educational system (Telem, 1990b). Internet's networks of live, active interest-groups, may help in this bridging process. Internet allows direct and iteractive contact with colleagues and teams dealing with similar issues. It enables users to actively participate in live discussion groups, i.e., it makes possible inter-team cooperation. The use of these tools in educational settings may be of crucial importance at international, national and regional levels.

3.2 Link to Global Information Resources

Internet's on-line availability of relevant and significant information and its search, browsing and retrieval tools provide easy access to local and international educational library catalogues and databases.

3.3 Support to Educational Innovation

Implementation and success of new curricula, teaching methods and approaches, very often depend, among other factors, on a sound infrastructure of information exchange. Promising ideas and means may fail when not effectively conveyed, brainstormed and supported. A curriculum development team may use Internet as an effective tool for distributing its thesaurus of resources, for an on-going updating of teaching materials, syllabi, bibliography and sources of information relevant to the subject matter. It may also present and/or explain didactics, strategies, doubts and difficulties, as well as on-site innovations related to the teaching process. Problems, exercises with their solutions, teaching materials, graphics, demonstrations and multimedia are available through the Internet. Moreover information and resources can be organized by using multiple links among the information items by hypertext techniques, which provide tools for access and selection unique to the computerized media. Internet's down-loading and up-loading capability enable fast transfer of information among users. Internet enhances active human communications, ideas transfer, feedback, discussion and elaboration. However, it requires written - though not too formal - communication, which is slower and, from some aspects, less convenient than speaking (as long as voice transfer will not be used on a large scale).

Internet facilitates several communication modes, each of them with its rationale for innovation support. The one-to-many mode is the most common mode for conveying information from a development team to the groups of teachers implementing the new curriculum. Similarly, Internet provides a path from any group member to each of the other group members. Thus, the one-to-many mode can easily be used also in a many-to-many mode - when all members of the group are allowed to provide input and make it available to the entire group. The many-to-many mode allows group discussions when all members refer to a specific issue, raised by any member of the group, including its leader/s. This may take the shape of a synchronous process ("chat"), when all participants provide their inputs and receive others' inputs - all together at the same time. Or, it may be asynchronous - when each member accesses the system at any convenient time, reads the other group members' inputs and provides his/her own. The one-to-one mode provides a personal, confidential communication link between any two persons, specifically between peers, members of the group, or between the leader and group members. The many-to-one mode is effective for data collection and for answering a specific individual query.

When innovation is the issue, Internet's services and its information infrastructure may be of crucial importance for its success. This in addition to its similar valuable support to routine teaching and educational activities, Internet can provide similar services to both innovative and routine work of managers and supervisors. Managers and supervisors may use Internet tools for helping them to manage, communicate, supervise and advise their peers, subordinates and superiors. For example, the principal can use Internet to improve information exchange and communication between her/himself and various school employees and school management teams (e.g., deputy-principals, councelors, subject-coordinators). The Internet may support her/him, in communicating with his/her peers (i.e., other principals) and with various employees in the school district and central educational authorities. School districts and central educational authorities can use Internet services in similar ways.

4 A PILOT PROJECT: THE ISRAELI INFORMATICS TEACHERS' NET

In line with the general approach presented in Section 3, the Israeli Ministry of Education established during 1995/6 school year an Informatics teachers' Internet service. Its target population is Informatics and Information Technologies (IT) teachers, supervisors and curriculum development teams. The establishment of the net is considered as a pilot project, starting with a few scores of teachers and other functionaries, which will hopefully develop to cover several hundreds in the next school-year, and finally, about 2000 participants, i.e., the entire community of Informatics teachers and related team-members in Israel.

Priority was given to teachers who are implementing new curricula and new approaches, with the aim that the net should support this innovation process. A group teaching the regular curricula and all supervisors and advisors related to Informatics teaching were also included.

4.1 Basic Services on the Net

Currently, the net provides the following basic types of services:

Personal Mail is ordinary e-mail allowing exchange of messages between users on the net, including forwarding the same message to several/all users.

Bulletin Boards contain current information provided by a user and addressed to a defined group of users, who subscribe to a specific board. Each bulletin board has a leader, in charge of the board's activity. The board can be either moderated or un-moderated. The leader of a moderated bulletin board is responsible for its contents. The board will contain information provided only by him/her or by a member of the group as approved by the leader. The leader has the sole right to write and/or remove information from the moderated board. An unmoderated board contains information posted freely by any of its subscribing users - i.e., the initial information or message as provided by its initiator and group members' reactions. Still, the leader is responsible for looking after the activity on the board, and in extreme cases s/he may restrict or even remove information posted.

Discussion Groups are in fact unmoderated bulletin boards dedicated to a specific subject/s that a group of users is concerned about. It contains all the exchanged messages, relevant to the selected subject/s.

Information Banks contain large amounts of well structured and organized information. Access to the information banks is possible in a hierarchical way using adequate menus, by hypertext techniques using multiple links between files and a variety of key-word search techniques. The information banks are created, augmented and updated by teams of experts in a specific subject-matter. An information bank coordinator is in charge of the updateness of the data. Information banks are not replaced very frequently. Appreciable effort is invested to adequately design, establish and update them. In many cases information initially published in a bulletin board is later included in the information bank.

Information banks are either general, i.e., used by the whole community of users on the net, or specific to some group of users. Existing information banks, still under construction include: syllabi, bibliography, didactic advice, learning materials, problems and exercises, hints and tips, and general instructions related to the organization and contents of teaching. Access to existing national and international information banks is available with adequate guidance.

News Bulletins. The net provides several news bulletins, implemented as moderated bulleting boards: A monthly "Newspaper", reviewing main news and current developments in Informatics and IT - i.e., software, hardware, applications. The "newspaper" is based on professional journals and IT industry announcements, and provides references to those wishing to read the entire article rather than its abstract. Its main goals are to convey important and updated information to the teaching community. The "System News" and "General Information" are additional news bulletins for announcements which are of interest to all users on the net.

4.2 Groups on the Net

The following five user groups are presently active on the pilot net. Each of them uses e-mail services and both moderated and unmoderated bulletin boards. Each group on the net has its own specific information bank. As the activity of each group goes on, it produces new items to be added to the information bank.

Software Design: A group of Informatics teachers implementing a new curriculum in advanced Informatics in 12th grade. The curriculum was developed by a team of experts at the Hebrew University in Jerusalem. There are some 20 teachers in the group, located in different parts of Israel.

Computer and Communications Literacy: A group of teachers teaching the subject at junior high school level, organized as a didactic workshop with Internet communication support. The group deals mainly with didactic problems pertaining to the development of adequate learning materials and approaches. Each member develops materials and transfers them for trial and comments to the other group members. The final product consists of modules of educational materials available to any interested teacher. The group is moderated by a supervisor at the Ministry of Education.

Logic Programming in Prolog: This is one of the modules of the introductory part in the Informatics curricula. It was developed by a team of experts of the Weizman Institute of Science in Rehovot and was released for general use towards the 1996/7 school year.

Southern Group: A group of teachers in south Israel, all related to one supervisor-advisor who acts as the group moderator. In contrast to the formerly mentioned subject-oriented groups, this group includes teachers of any subject within the broad field of Informatics and IT. This group was formed with the intention to investigate the help that can be provided by Internet to the work of a member of a supervising team.

Supervisors' Group: All its members are supervisors/advisors active within the Ministry of Education and dealing with teaching of Information and IT. The group is moderated by one of the supervisors, having a central position within the group's activities. It supports all information exchange required to support the activity of this group.

5 CONCLUSION

Though the pilot project is in its initial stage, it is apparent that a well functioning and information-rich system provides a valuable tool to support the managerial, educational and instructional activities in the educational system, both for innovative activities and routine work. However, some recommendation can be clearly formulated:

- The system has to be reliable and accessible. If it is not, users will not access it.
- Appreciable effort is needed to set up an information bank of attractive size and contents, well formatted for easy and convenient access.
- Good information banks and a good news service do attract users to access the system and they then try its communications services as well.
- It takes time and effort to convince people to use the net. It seems to be hard to get used to a new tool. The groups' leaders have to find means to promote the system and encourage its users, until a critical mass of contents and users is reached.

6 REFERENCES

Barta, B.Z. (1990) End users education at high school level: a preliminary report. *Education and Computing,* **6(1, 2)**, 63-68.

Barta, B.Z. and Telem, M. (1992) New trends within the basic training of I.T. professionals in Israel, in *Professional Development of Information Technology Professionals* (eds. B.Z. Barta et al.), North-Holland, Amsterdam.

Doyle, S.C. (1995) Telementoring takes off in California: the Telemation project develops integrated curriculum. *Internet Research,* **5 (1)**, 40-45.

Fung, A.C.W. and Pun, S.W. (1996) The impact of Internet on ITEM: educational management in preparation for the future, in *Proceedings of the 2nd IFIP International Working Conference on ITEM*, Hong Kong Baptist University, Hong Kong.

Gal-Ezer, J., Beeri, C., Harel, D. and Yehudai, A. (1995) A high school program in computer science. *Computer*, **28(10)**, 73-80.

Hert, A.C. (1994) A learning organization perspective on training: critical success factors for Internet implementation. *Internet Research,* **4(3)**, 36-44.

Hughes, R.D. (1993) Appropriate and distributed networks: a model for K-12 educational telecommunications. *Internet Research,* **3(4)**, 22-29.

Johnson, A.D. (1995) The Mankato schools Internet project. *Internet Research,* **5(1)**, 40-45.

Protheroe, N. and Wilson, E. (1994) *The Internet handbook for school users.* Educational research services, Arlington, VA.

Seguin, A. (1994) Using the Internet in professional development. Paper presented at the American Vocational Association Convention, Dallas.

Telem, M. (1990a) DSS in educational organizations, *Computers and Educations,* **14 (1)**, 61-69.

Telem, M. (1990b) Educational DSS: Potential services, benefits, difficulties, and dangers. *Computers and Educations,* **14 (1)**, 71-80.

Telem, M. and Barta, B.Z. (1993) Case tools in the basic training of I.T. professionals in Israeli high schools, in *Software Engineering Education* (eds. B.Z. Barta et al.), North-Holland, Amsterdam, 263-272.

Weick, K.E. (1976) Educational organizations as loosely coupled systems. *Administrative Science Quarterly*, **21(1)**, 1-19.

Weick, K.E. (1982) Administering education in loosely coupled schools. *Phi Delta Kappan*, **63**, (673-76)

West, P. (1993) The mother of all networks. *Teacher Magazine,* **4 (4)**, 19-22.

7 BIOGRAPHIES

Ben-Zion Barta, Ph.D. from Technion Israel, Chief Inspector for Computers in Education in the Ministry of Education, Israel, in charge of the coordination of R&D projects and the implementation of computer education activities in the Israeli school system. Chaired IFIP's Working Group on Training and Education of IT Professionals. Chaired several Working Conferences, published and edited in the areas of Informatics' teaching and of computers in education.

Moshe Telem, Chair of the educational administration program in the School of Education, Tel-Aviv University, received his doctorate from the Hebrew University in Jerusalem. He specializes in MIS in education and educational administration. He has published widely on a variety of computerized educational issues.

3

The impact of internet on ITEM: educational management in preparation for the future

A.C.W. Fung
Department of Education Studies, Hong Kong Baptist University
Kowloon Tong, Hong Kong
Phone: (852)-23395679 *Fax: (852)-23397894*
e-mail: alexfung@hkbu.edu.hk

S.W. Pun
Hong Kong Institute of Education
Grantham Campus, 42 Gascoigne Road, Kowloon, Hong Kong
e-mail: swpun@gc.ied.edu.hk

Abstract
Schools of the future will no longer be islands on their own. The common saying that "it takes a village to educate a child" might have to be re-worded as "it takes the globe to educate a child"! The world is shrinking, metaphorically speaking, in space and time as IT advances. Recent studies suggest that there are now in USA alone more than 100,000 E-mail accounts on state educational networks, and approximately 600,000 networking students in private and grassroots initiatives. With the expansion of global networking, educators have many pressing issues to reconsider. How different, for instance, will the schooling process become in the next decade? This paper is no attempt to give any positive answer. It is an attempt instead to give a snapshot of the current state of affairs on the Internet in connection with education and ITEM in particular. Prospects are discussed and questions are raised. The intent is to generate interest from participants in the '2nd IFIP International Working Conference on ITEM' in developing a vision for which educational administrators need to prepare.

Keywords
Educational management, communications, future developments, infrastructure, internet, networks, visions

1 INTRODUCTION

Nineteen ninety-six will be dominated by the Internet. This is the opinion of the US-based research company, IDC, in a recent report in Asia Computer Weekly, 1996. This report also forecasts for 1996 that 80 percent of PC shipments will be to the home market and that the number of on-line users will rise to more than one billion. Recent studies also suggest that there are now in USA alone more than 100,000 E-mail accounts on state educational networks, and approximately 600,000 networking students in private and grassroots initiatives (Itzkan, 1995). Expert opinion estimates that by the end of the decade, there will be 3 to 5 million networking students in the U.S. With the expansion of global networking, educators have many pressing issues to reconsider. How different, for instance, will the schooling process become in the next decade? What are the impacts of the Internet on teaching and learning, and on educational management? This paper is not an attempt to give a definitive answer. It is an attempt instead to give a snapshot of the current state of affairs on the Internet in connection with education broadly, and ITEM in particular.

2 THE TECHNOLOGICAL REVOLUTION

Technological advances in computing and telecommunication have in the past few years set off at an unprecedented pace developments in information networking and sharing. New ideas and applications are generated everyday, if not every hour, around the world. New terminologies are created that soon become old - Internet, World Wide Web (WWW), Emailing, Video conferencing, high speed RAS (remote access services), Integrated Services Digital Network (ISDN), modems, multimedia, hypertext, Internet phone, WebPC, WebTV, cable modems, etc. While this list will continually lengthen, there is a convergent view that speed and price in datacomm is no more the major issue and the information network will soon be penetrating into homes. The US-based cable television industry, for example, will begin offering datacomm on cable television channels to home-users with cable modems to enable access at speeds up to a thousand times faster than the 28.8 kbits/s of the analog telephone lines (Asami & Kato, 1996). It is asserted that this US-based cable television network is emerging as the ultimate home information infrastructure, mainly because about 96 percent of all households can subscribe to cable television in USA.

In this information era, schools can choose to react passively and reluctantly to technological changes, or they can proactively learn to harness the power to the benefit of their pupils. Taking the latter stance, for example, the Lake Oswego District in Oregon has a vision for the 21st century "to provide a learning environment in which the use of technology is just as natural to students as the use of a pen or pencil is to most adults" (Lake Oswego District Web Server, 1996).

3 THE IMPACT ON BOOKS AS INFORMATION VEHICLES

Books, whether of reference, non-fiction, or novels, have been around with us for years. We have all been accustomed to the traditional way of obtaining information through them and the paper medium. We all know the good things about such vehicles: they are compact and cheap, they are quite accessible and easy to carry, and they can be reproduced conveniently. We can write notes on them, and we certainly know how to browse our way through books. However, searching with an index or table of contents in a book is somehow quite limited. Finding a specific piece of information within a book can be very tedious, or sometimes impossible although the data is there.

Intrinsically, information is confined to each individual book. When more related information is needed and libraries or archives are taken into consideration, books are not economical in terms of time, costs and space. Costs of keeping paper documents in libraries increases in this information age. Maintenance is difficult and expensive, especially when the documents become dated. And, perhaps most importantly from a publisher's point of view, writings on papers are static and their revisions are costly.

From a user's point of view, knowledge and information are best to be up to date and meeting their needs. When a certain piece of information falls short of users' expectation or satisfaction, it would be ideal to have further or related information immediately available on demand. It would also be much more useful and attractive if such information is not just in plain text, but in different forms of sound, pictures, and videos, as the user desires. Such hyperlinking and multimedia capabilities are, of course, beyond the capabilities of the traditional book, but are realities in electronic ones, and on web-pages now available on the Internet. Besides, there is no limit to the number of users simultaneously reading the page, and there is no problem with deterioration of the paper !

Books and papers will not of course be abandoned. But they will not be the dominant source or vehicle of knowledge and information as in the past. They can only coexist with their electronic counterpart in future.

4 THE IMPACT ON TEACHING & LEARNING

In the course of preparing for this paper, we have visited a number of educational Websites on the Internet. The number of educational bodies getting onto Internet is definitely multiplying, including government departments, research institutes, commercial vendors, universities, and schools. A few emerging uses of Internet are identifiable for educational purposes:

- informing the public;
- providing research findings;
- providing resources;
- promoting image;
- providing support to teachers;
- providing support to pupils;
- providing support to school administrators and managers.

The wealth of information now available on the Internet in these seven areas, though not necessarily categorized as such, is simply amazing. In fact the number of resources on the WWW has grown at such an incredible rate that some Websites are specially dedicated to provide meta-indexes (indexes to other indexes) for educators. Examples of these meta-indexes are found in the USA at websites such as the "http://www.yahoo.com/Education/ K_12/", or "http://hillside.coled.umn.edu/others.html"; and in the UK such as the 'pathways Home Page' of "http://www.ifl.rmplc.co.uk/".

Apparently there is also the converging opinion from writings in different Websites (e.g. NCREL, Horizon, EdWeb) that the Internet Age will open up a scenario in teaching and learning significantly different from the traditional process:

1. In allowing teachers and pupils immediate connection to the outside world, the Internet has broken down in some sense, if not entirely, the boundary of the traditional classroom;
2. Collaborative teaching and learning, between schools and external partners, becomes feasible at the district, national, and international levels;
3. Students can learn by doing in a more authentic sense, using real life situations and simulations at times;
4. In becoming both a publisher and a browser on the Internet, as simple as just joining a discussion group with emailing, pupils are learning not just from their classroom teachers but also from many others.

We all accept that active and expressive learning means a shift from teachers' traditional information-giving to pupils' participation in information-gathering, interpretation and use. Nothing in history has provided a medium with power comparable to that of the WWW for this purpose. Wallis (1995) has described the wondrous things that occur at the Dalton School in New York City and the way it is using technology " to change the traditional roles of the teacher as oracle and the student as passive receptacle for hand-me-down knowledge".

"The Internet provides a vehicle for teachers" says Giordano (1996), "to create high-performance learning environments through which the goals of the various dimensions of schooling can be accomplished. Through resources available via the Internet, students may be provided opportunities to engage in authentic, challenging activities. Teachers can set meaningful, challenging activities as the center of instruction. Classroom approaches that support such a paradigm might include collaborative learning, heterogeneous groupings, teacher as facilitator, performance-based assessment, peer-to-peer mentoring, multidisciplinary curriculum, interactive modes of instruction, student exploration, and extended blocks of time." (ibid: 360)

The Internet will not only change classroom processes, it will also radically change pupils' learning when an ultimate home information infrastructure is in place. In the commercial arena, many companies are already marketing their products and services on a home page. The Web technology has opened a new channel for direct sales to customers. To-day, electronic publishers are selling thousands of edutainment CD-ROM titles to families with after-sales services and support (e.g. Microsoft's Encarta and Bookshelf 96-97). Tomorrow, such sales will not be just edutainments. The IFL (Internet for Learning) pages at the Rmplc Website in UK is but one example, among many existing sites around the world and numerous more to come, competing to provide learning materials to pupils and students directly. The spectrum of subject contents, and their design and attractiveness to pupils, will be beyond the competition of the curriculum in any single school. Such knowledge providers on the Internet are definitely keen to take a share in education that has been dominated by schools for centuries!

5 THE IMPACT ON 'SCHOOLING'

In 'Planning for the 21st Century', the Lake Oswego District (1996) declares:

> *"We recognize the learning environment is tied to the real world, that we serve a wide variety of learners, and that learning extends beyond the traditional time and space concepts of School."*

We have also described in the above section that our pupils, sooner or later, will be acquiring their own communication links for exploring topics beyond the boundaries of the traditional concept of School. While access to subject experts (teachers) and resources are limited by time and space at school, pupils in future (some already now) studying at home, or in a library, or any place with Internet connection can quickly access learning resources at any hour of the day. This raises a fundamental question then of what 'Schooling' is for? When the school is no longer the only place to acquire knowledge and information, is it where pupils go for socialization? for physical development? for intellectual group interaction? for learning how to learn? for learning how to think? for learning how to communicate? for learning how to create? These are questions that we would like to seek answers to.

Education cannot stay isolated from the electronic world. The entire educational system, from K-12 to universities, will most likely be re-engineered in the Internet age. We attempt to present in Figure 1 such a transformation. In the traditional system, teachers and students interact mostly within a school which has linkage to publishers and libraries. Such subsystems work within the rather tight boundary of a single nation with a certain cultural environment. The whole system is often under government control of varying degrees. In the 'Internet Age', students are more detached from a single school and the teachers therein. They are opened to more opportunities of interacting directly with other schools and with other 'knowledge providers' on the Internet. These organisations possibly will have their own intranet (see below) boundaries while working under a multi-national and multi-cultural environment. Government control over these subsystems will become much looser than that of today.

In view of such a transformation, there are three related issues educators have to reconsider:

1. Empowering the students ?

The key characteristic of Web technology is its ability to shift to the users the control of information flow from the information provider. When students have the pathway easily to access what information or instruction materials they prefer, as well as choose when they want to have them, no single school or text-book publisher can dominate or confine anymore the students' learning style or contents. Students are empowered in their learning on the one hand, but just the thought of it could be threatening to many teachers on the other.

2. School as a knowledge broker ?

Web technology has made both publishing and retrieval of information easily accessible to many. What will not be easy is finding the relevant information that is created in this loosely controlled and independent environment of the Internet.

The school, as a curriculum planner and a gatekeeper, might possibly have to take up in future an additional role - serving as a kind of 'knowledge broker'. Teachers will probably have to shortlist not only books for students to read, as they do now, but also educational Websites to be visited.

The Traditional System:

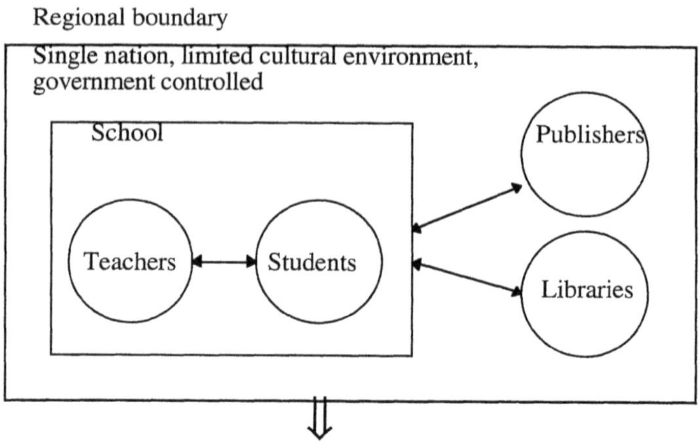

The Paradigm Shift:

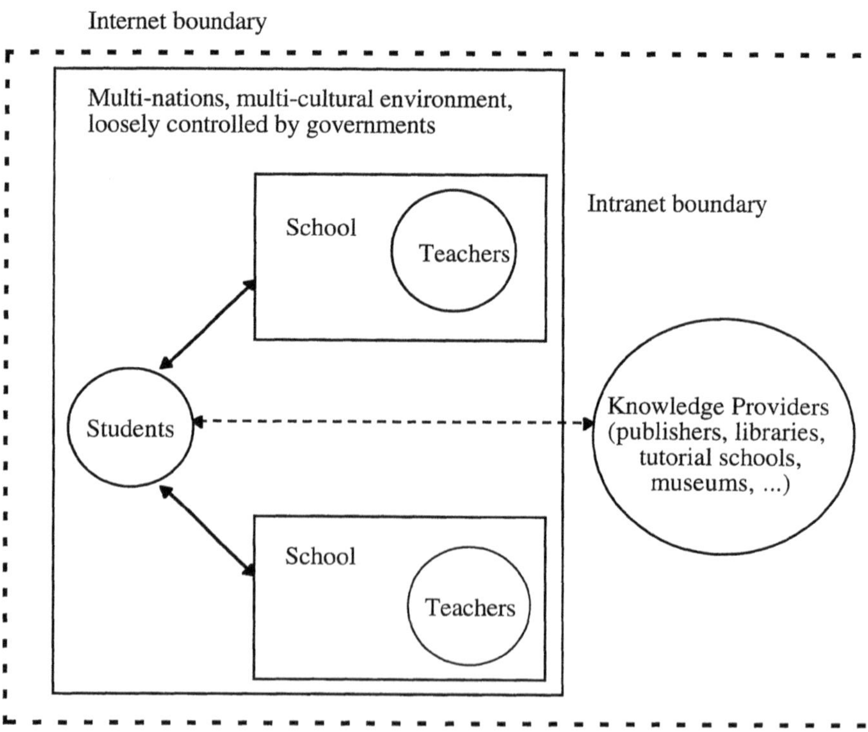

Figure 1. 'Schooling' in the Internet Age.

3. A controlled anarchy ?
Internet is anarchic in that it is accessible by anyone anywhere in the world and anyone anywhere can publish anything. Without proper management, the Internet could become a potential threat to the well-being of a school and its pupils when they are internetconnected. In the business and IT sectors, the concept of 'Intranet' is currently evolving (Amdahl Coporation, 1995). This is the implementation of Internet technologies within a corporate organization which can be applied in an individual school. Instead of directly connecting the school library or classrooms to the global Internet, access first goes on an Intranet within the school. The implementation is performed in such a way as to permit only communication with selected and authorised Websites of educational value to students and teachers. In such a controlled anarchy, anyone on the Intranet can still access or publish anything and benefit educationally from the Internet.

6 CONCLUSION

Schools of the future will no longer be islands on their own. The common saying that "it takes a village to educate a child" might have to be re-worded as "it takes the globe to educate a child"! Educational administrators conscious of the rapid developments in the field of IT, and in particular of Internet, will probably agree with this. The world is shrinking, metaphorically speaking, in space and time as IT advances.

Today, technology is not the issue. It is a matter of hardware performance (costs dropping and speed increasing) to realise what we have discussed and see the pieces put in place as a reality. ITEM (Information Technology in Educational Management) should no longer be confined to the scope of School Information Systems or Computer Assisted School Administration. Educational management is, after all, for the support of learning and teaching, to make "the best schools, teachers, and courses available to all students without regard to gender, distance, resources, or disabilities" (Lake Oswego District Web Server, 1996). Confucius, thousands of years ago, had already highlighted such an educational ideal of "Teaching without discrimination". IT should be able to contribute in making this dream come true. Towards this goal, educational administrators and transformational leaders have to learn to ride with the wave of IT, and one can be sure that IT will not halt with just the Internet. Managing IT in education and for education will be a continual challenge to leaders in the schools of the future.

7 REFERENCES

Amdahl Corporation (1995) Intranet planning and management. On the *WWW* at http://www. amdahl. com/

Asami, N. & Kato, M. (1996) Cable TV begins 30-Mbit/s datacomm service. *Nikkei Electronics Asia*, May 1996.

IDC (1996) 1996: Year of the Internet ? *Asia Computer Weekly*, Jan 29 - Feb 4, 11-12.

EdWeb (1995) EdWeb Homeroom. On the *WWW* at http://k12.cnidr.org:90/

Giordano, V. (1996) The Internet: tool for transforming teaching and learning. *Proceedings of the Thirteenth International Conference on Technology and Education*, **1**, 359-361.

Horizon (1996) Horizon Homepage. On the *WWW* at http://sunsite.unc.edu/horizon/

Itzkan, J. S. (1995) Assessing the future of telecomputing environments: Implications for instruction and administration. *The Computing Teacher*, Dec/Jan 1994-95, 60-64.

Lake Oswego District (1996) On the *WWW* at gopher://gopher.nrel.org:70/00/programs/ technology/plans/lakeoswego_plan

NCREL (1966) Pathways to school improvement. On the *WWW* at http://cedar.cic.net/ncrel/sdrs/ pathwayg.htm
Wallis, C. (1995) The learning revolution. *Times*, Spring 1995, 49-51.

8 BIOGRAPHIES

Alex C.W. Fung received a B.Sc. in 1970 from the University of Hong Kong and Cert.Ed., Adv.Dip.Ed., and M.Ed. in subsequent years from the same university. He received his Ph.D. in educational management and administration in 1992 from the London University Institute of Education. He was a secondary school principal in Hong Kong for more than twenty years before he joined the Department of Education Studies of the Hong Kong Baptist University as senior lecturer in 1994. He is currently an associate professor and also Director of the School Administration and Management System Training & Research Unit at the Hong Kong Baptist University.

S.W. Pun received a B.Sc. in 1972 from the Chinese University of Hong Kong and Dip. Ed. in subsequent years from the same university. He received his M.Ed. (Math Ed) in 1976 from the University of Georgia, USA and M.Sc.(Computing) in 1996 from the City University of Hong Kong. He was a secondary school computer teacher and principal in Hong Kong before he joined the Department of Science and Mathematics, Hong Kong Institute of Education in 1995. He is currently a senior lecturer in computer education and computer studies.

4

Information technology - a tool and an obstacle in the education of the future

M. Mäkelä
Department of Computer Science, University of Helsinki, Box 26 (Teollisuuskatu 23), FIN-00014, Finland
e-mail: matti.makela@helsinki.fi

Abstract
Information technology will cause continuous rapid changes in our technological environment. The general impression is that the digital age will improve our lives and our society. Huge national strategies and programs are underpinned by this belief. They do not properly take into account the human dimension. The information society started principally when writing was invented, but the past technological inventions have not driven major changes in education. Challenges to the education of the future arise when the issues of cognition and human information processing are combined with the future technology. This offers an environment for rapid communication and search for information but especially the means to deepen thinking and understanding. This will set new objectives for education. Permanent skills such as learning to learn in changing environments are more important than rapidly deteriorating content. Visual literacy should be promoted in the future. The educational management must be flexible, react quickly and be able to anticipate change. A proper management information system is needed.

Keywords
Educational management, visions, creativity, literacy, human/social sciences

1 MOTTO

Richard Hamming: *"The purpose of computing is insight, not numbers."*

Hamming's idea is often neglected. Technology is an end in itself. I have been engaged in computers and university teaching since 1961 and have experienced the tremendous development during the past 35 years. Is it possible to learn something from the past progress? Even though we are not able to foresee the future from our experience, we may learn something from the history and the present trends. If so, we might better steer computer uses in education at present, and perhaps prepare ourselves to compete in the 21st century. I will consider casual histories that are important.

2 ACCELERATED CHANGE IN INFORMATION TECHNOLOGY

When the first commercially made computer, an IBM-650, was started in 1958 in Finland, experts in the country thought that it was sufficient for all future computing needed in the country. The situation has changed dramatically. Finland is now one of the little countries around the world whose development of, and uses for, IT are out of proportion to their sizes and natural resource endowments (Dedrick et al., 1995). It has become one of the major IT producers and sophisticated users. Historically, Finland has been among the poorest of the Nordic countries, but now has one of the highest per-capita consumption of IT in the world. It has its own multibillion IT manufacturer in Nokia, which is second to Motorola as a world supplier of mobile phones. The rapid development will continue producing increasingly complex and sophisticated working environments. Computers will soon be in every home, too.
Your personal computer has replaced your typewriter, it connects you to other computers, to other people all around the world. It gives you access to libraries and data banks. It allows you to draw pictures, make animations, compile multimedia, design hypermedia documents and deliver them in the Internet. All this is available only if you are willing to learn repeatedly new computer equipment, new programs and operating systems, new peripherical devices, new types of applications. New skills are required every day in an ever changing environment. It is necessary to enhance worker productivity. Technology has become such an integral part of our life that we have to learn to integrate it into our nature.

The new technology has obvious benefits. It will also cause a growing mental burden of lifelong learning required by the continuous changes inherent in a working life based on computers and world wide networks. The educational authorities and organizations must promote networking of the educational system and create open learning environments to support the development from "once-and-for-all" training towards lifelong learning. Individual study opportunities must be improved at all levels of education, and study methods, teaching material, as well as the required information services need to be developed. New types of "information products" for lifelong learning purposes must be developed.

The principle of lifelong learning is not possible if people are not willing to learn. It is not sufficient that we have professionally skilled teachers. They know how to manage and to communicate information in their own fields and moreover to teach methods of obtaining and using information to enable learners to work independently. They also can use media necessary for open and flexible learning and be able to modify and develop material for the electronic media. The most crucial point is to develop the learning environment and the materials and contents so that learners are motivated to learn, can do it efficiently and not repeating the same things every second year. Learning to learn is the future key issue. Those who will master this in the rapidly changing world will survive.

The key component of most product designs is the human being. This idea must be taken most seriously in any information product serving education. There are parallels to the design of any good computer application and its user interface. Difficult user interfaces are no longer tolerable. Everything must start with the requirements definition for the product. We may learn from the experiences in general customer oriented product planning (Holzblatt et al., 1995). The problem is to know enough about ourselves, our brains, our learning psychology, our ability to learn continuously new things.

3 PUBLIC ENTHUSIASM AND INTENSIVE PROGRAMMES

It is a general impression that the digital age will change our lives and our society. Individuals will deal with all aspects of information-based technology. The new digital age focuses on the synthesis and availability of data from a variety of disparate sources. Every day we can see and hear in the media news about the networked information society. A complete Internet strategy is increasingly a requirement for doing business and marketing and tapping its vast information stores as a critical resource, etc. The goal is to learn to manage, manipulate, and effectively utilize information in the next decade. Recently, in most industrialized countries, extensive programmes are being carried out to further accelerate the development and use of information technology and its applications in the different layers and functions of society. Information technology is expected to clear the way for profound improvements in education, health care, communications, telework, and administration. As an example, in January 1995, the Finnish Government decided the principles for the development of Finland as an information society.

According to this decision the Ministry of Education is responsible for achieving a long list of goals in its sector concerning education, research and development, national information resources and culture. For the fulfillment of these goals, the Ministry of Education has published in 1995 a national strategy for education, training and research in the information society. The Finnish goals for education are the following:

- All levels of education and training from comprehensive school upwards must teach the necessary basic skills in information technology (IT), management of information, and communication. Teacher training is a key development area, especially in the adoption of new competencies and skills.
- Training of professionals for information technology and information industries will be developed to reflect the diversity of changing professional roles. Students in vocational and higher education should learn information technology, information management, and communication skills that meet the needs of fast-changing and increasingly networked working life.
- Education and training of the information sectors at universities and vocational education will be increased. Continuing professional education and training will be developed to stay abreast of technological advances and to meet the needs of the information industry.
- Adults will be given opportunities to learn basic information technology skills by expanding the range of training available and by improving library services. Exclusion from the labour market must not occur because of a lack of these basic skills.
- The whole education system will be brought within the reach of information network services, ensuring that educational establishments can use these services. Open and distance learning will be promoted at all levels of education and training.

Many questions arise but they are not popular. Why is an information society so important? Why is all this information needed? Is it really necessary and useful? What is its value? Is it reliable? Can we see the difference between facts and fiction, between natural phenomena and computer simulation models, between real life and virtual reality? Do we really need an exponentially growing amount of information? Do we enjoy the limitless research opportunities the Web offers? What are our long term goals and does information technology offer proper tools to achieve them?

4 INFLUENCE OF PAST TECHNOLOGICAL INVENTIONS

We tend to pretend that the present information revolution is something new and original, but is it? It is advisable to take a look at some earlier inventions and their implications to mankind and education.
Actually the information society started when people invented writing and it was possible to store and manipulate information. At the same time thinking, or at least the results of it, started to have more literal forms. This led to the present linear way of coding our expressions character by character. This kind of result is easy for the computer to process. The whole history has taken thousands of years and the diversity of different developments is astonishing (Haarmann, 1990). Seeing and making pictures was left aside.

So far the inventions like pen, pencil, paper, and printing have had more influence on the mental development of mankind than the computer. These past technological discoveries have not driven major changes in education, however. We observe similarities when we look at mailing letters by post, printing press, microscope, telescope, stereoscopic pictures, electricity, telegraph, photography, movies, telephone, radio, TV, video, etc. Once a new invention has been made it is proposed that it will change radically our views and habits and a great enthusiasm exists for a while. However, the lack of impact of camera, radio or TV in the classroom is clear.

Marshall McLuhan (McLuhan et al., 1967) wrote in 1967 about the role of media: "The medium, or process, of our time - electric technology - is reshaping and restructuring patterns of social independence and every aspect of our personal life. It is forcing us to reconsider and re-evaluate practically every thought, every action, and every institution formerly taken for granted. Everything is changing - your family, your government, your relation to "the others". And they're changing dramatically." It is remarkable that he did not have the computer revolution in his mind. It started to influence the general public much later. Similar opinions can be found in the literature in the middle of the 19th century concerning the stereoscope. Very little has changed. Conservatism is the key issue in the history.

A more recent example is the changing history of computer aided instruction. The behavioristic view of learning was dominant when the computer era started in the sixties. The key idea was to prepare programmed learning material so that the computer can replace teachers. Then gradually the technology was shown to be inefficient. Our views on learning have changed. Now the dominant paradigm is based on cognitive psychology and constructive learning theories neglecting subconscious processes. Computer systems are considered as good learning tools and environments for the active learner. The problem is to make learners active.

The computer based labs are recommended as they support "learning by doing" (although in a virtual environment) (Soloway, 1994). Computers should be present in the classroom (Shneiderman et al., 1995). Most of these ideas are in a preliminary and experimental stage and not commonly used because of the lack of knowledge and equipment. I myself have not followed my propositions for computer uses in the university classroom (Mäkelä et al., 1990) although I think they are still valid. The reason is that the technology is too complicated and rapidly changing. It is fairly difficult to invent novel applications as the old tradition is in your mind all the time. It takes time to adapt oneself to the changing world of new ideas and concepts. Learning is a hard job even for the teachers. A good advice is to take only small steps. A few of them are perhaps giant leaps for mankind.

Anyway we must remember what Alfred Bork (1989) has written:

"Unfortunately where technology is involved people often start by asking questions about how to use a particular technology. This seldom leads to the best. . . ";

"No matter whether technology is involved or not, our primary concern should be with learning, and this must be strongly emphasized from the very beginning. . . . ";

"The notion that we start from learning problems has a strong corollary: The people in charge of the development should not be the technologists, but extremely competent teachers and educational researchers in the area involved. I emphasize too that it is not the subject matter experts, and not the educational psychologists that we want, as is often suggested; these people can be very helpful but they should not be in charge. Rather we want people who are experts in helping people to learn the subject matter, different individuals than subject matter experts, or psychologists. There is no substitute for the intuition of a skilled teacher!"

5 CHALLENGES FOR THE FUTURE EDUCATIONAL SYSTEM

We must see education as a whole and combine the technological advantages with the human aspects of computing. They will be central in the future. Educational computer systems must offer contents, tools and environments for rich and efficient personal accomplishment.

Perhaps the most exciting and threatening challenge is the continuous change in our working environment. We must study and learn permanent skills instead of changing facts which will deteriorate. Teaching must be as much as possible independent of the present technology and well suited to the human brains.

How to achieve this? Do we understand computer systems and the media they represent? What are the relevant and lasting features? The ideas and doubts of C. Stoll (Stoll, 1995) are worth studying. Understanding the situation and learning to learn and to adapt oneself without frustration in the rapidly changing environment are the basic goals. More than the basic skills to use computers are needed.

The history of e-mail shows that simple solutions work fine though they may require a fairly long time to be accepted and widely used. More powerful and sophisticated applications will need more time and elaboration before they are used world wide outside the professional circles. A deeper interactivity will be a standard part of modern communications. We can already study interactive multimedia collaborative processes and use complex, global, real-time multipoint collaborative and videoconferencing systems (Ishii et al., 1994).

In these systems it is necessary to understand the partners' ways of thinking and talking immediately. The cultural and semantic problems must be recognized. The technology is not an answer even though one may expect a real time language translation during a telephone call to be reality in the future. Smells, flavours, gestures, touches, feelings and emotions are still nearly impossible to convey electronically.

The vast information stores on electronic media must have a proper structure and assisting tools. They help search for relevant and valuable information so that users do not become lost in the information space. People should learn to know their needs and to understand and evaluate the information available. They should construct their own knowledge from the scattered pieces of information they are receiving all the time. Contents production should be a more important part of the information industry than the production of hardware and software. Who is responsible for the subject matter and its reliability? What should be the information content of the material?

Multimedia and hypermedia materials will be the usual forms of information. Two types of problems will arise. When deep understanding and learning are required, the information product (e.g. hyperdocument) must intentionally guide readers through an information space, controlling their exploration along the lines of predefined structure (Thüring et al., 1995). The information structure should be tailored for a specified group of readers. So, the readers' reactions and expectations should be known.

Another problem is to convert an expert's knowledge to a readable form. The increased use of pictures and images, instead of words, in everyday life needs consideration by everybody. The producers and users of information should learn to communicate by producing and scrutinizing pictures of our ideas and activities. The second computer revolution is visualization (Friedhoff et al., 1991), not only as a scientific tool but also for nonprofessionals. The ability to produce and read pictures will be vital. A flexible way to generate pictures by the computer, and to visualize abstract objects and difficult structures, are central challenges for technical development and education.

Thoughts and images are intimately connected in our brains as about one half of our brain neurons are connected to the human visual system. Visual input is the most efficient way to feed data in, and pictures and images are the natural data formats. The main difficulty lies in the output from the brains. Traditional education does not support picture production and the corresponding output channel is missing. Perhaps computers can help us in this. Education will be both a problem and a solution. A recent issue of Computer Graphics (Special Focus, 1995) paid attention to visual literacy. It should be added to the list of basic skills and seriously promoted and supported at every level of education.

Issues of cognition and human information processing are widely neglected. Interesting are the changing balance between pictures and words in the technological age. (see e.g. Davies et al., 1990), and flexible thinking that uses both the left and right hemispheres of the brain (McKim, 1980). Flexible thinkers have easy access to both subconscious and conscious levels of thinking. They have many vehicles for the representation of thought. Some of them as language rely on logical reasoning using linear operations. The visual vehicle facilitates holistic, spatial, metaphoric and transformational operations providing a vital and creative complement to logical reasoning. Another vehicle is the emotional intelligence.

Computer systems will differ from our physical environments. Virtual reality as a 3-D interactive series of pictures will destroy our ability to see the difference between real life and simulations. Real world circumstances and social norms are not recognized in the computing situations. This will give rise to ethical problems as explained in Conger et al. (1995). Ethical education (Huff et al., 1995) must be integrated to the basic skills not only for tomorrow's professionals but also for nonprofessionals.

Teacher education should be reshaped to match the new demands. The new skills of visual and computer literacy and ethical subjects should be added to the curricula at all levels of education.

Education is one of the key issues in the adaptation to the rapid changes. Blonder (1995) thinks that it is not enough and puts forward another scenario: Computers' capacity will exceed that of human brains' in about hundred years. Machines will be intelligent enough to be independent of human operators. The human genetic development is very slow. Hence, the only possibility to adapt ourselves into the development is the use of genetic manipulations to compete with the computers. As continuous exponential growth is not natural, I expect that Blonder's scenario is not real. The growth will smooth down as the usual S-curve shape shows in many natural phenomena. This will happen before we are ruled by computers!

6 CHALLENGES FOR EDUCATIONAL MANAGEMENT

Networked computers will be the most important tool in education within the next few years. Computers and networking are available in every school and the schools are integrated with their local environment. There are links between schools and educational establishments at different levels and operating in different fields, and links with community and business life. Information network services are available to all schools and libraries. The educational management will be a part of the networking.

The management of the material resources such as hardware and software including networks and communication systems, and especially their delivery and replacement with new versions, forms a difficult OR-problem. Cost-effectiveness analysis and adjustment of different conflicting goals may use the modern computational decision support systems with fuzzy logic. Another problem is establishing the links between the new partners to increase the level of interaction between the public and the private sectors of society.

Modern concepts of learning emphasize the students' responsibility for their own learning and their active role in seeking and using information. The basic skills to find and manage information and to communicate using the new information technology are central. Teachers are no longer distributors of information but change to be tutors guiding the students and helping them in their work and working together as companions. Schools become learning centers which offer open learning environments for different activities. Distance learning and teaching will be a natural part of the education.

The spatial and time distribution of the equipment and persons involved in the education will be dynamic. New types of scheduling problems will arise. The teachers and the students are working sometimes at different places and in different groups. The working habits and conditions will be different. Buildings must be more flexible. Control and evaluation of the activities will change.

The educational system is faced by continuous challenges in the rapidly changing society. Decision making which affects the educational system must be flexible, must react quickly to changing circumstances, and must be able to anticipate change. The management should understand the modern learning theories and teaching based on them, and should support them to fulfill the central goals of the educational system.

Management by results and evaluations are the essential tools for steering the educational system. A proper management information system is needed. It needs to have an adequate information and data base and telecommunication links necessary to collect and transmit information. It must be flexible and anticipate changes. It should be available for both central and local decisions. It should contain all essential data and knowledge about the educational system.

7 REFERENCES

Blonder, G. (1995) Faded Genes. On the *WWW* at http://www.att.com /youwill/blonder.html

Bork, A. (1989) Suggestions for developing technology based learning material. *Interactive Learning International*, **5**, 25-30.
Conger, S. and Loch, K. (1995) Ethics and computer use. *Communications of the ACM*, **38(12)**, 30-32.
Davies, D., Bathurst, D. and Bathurst, R. (1990) *The telling image: the changing balance between pictures and words in a technological age.* Clarendon Press, Oxford.
Dedrick, J.L., Goodman, S.E. and Kraemer, K.L. (1995) Little engines that could: computing in small energetic countries. *Communications of the ACM*, **38(5)**, 21-26.
Friedhoff, R.M. and Benzon, W. (1991) *The second computer revolution visualization.* Freeman and Co., New York.
Haarmann, H. (1990) *Universalgeschichte der Schrift.* Campus Verlag, Frankfurt/Main.
Holzblatt, K. and Beyer, H.R. (1995) Requirements gathering: the human factor. *Communications of the ACM*, **38(5)**, 30-32.
Huff, C. and Martin, C.D. (1995) Computing consequences: a framework for teaching ethical computing. *Communications of the ACM*, **38(12)**, 75-84.
Ishii, H., Kobayashi, M. and Arita, K. (1994) Iterative design of seamless collaboration media. *Communications of the ACM*, **37(8)**, 83-97.
McKim, R.H. (1980) *Experiences in visual thinking.* PWS Engineering, Boston Massachusetts, 2nd ed.
McLuhan, M. and Fiore, Q. (1967) *The medium is the message.* Bantam Books, New York.
Mäkelä, M., Huovinen, L. and Nummelin, P. (1990) Computer uses in the university classroom. *Education & Computing*, **6**, 191-197.
Ministry of Education (1995) *Education, training and research in the information society: a national strategy.* Helsinki. Also available on the *WWW* at http://www.mined.fi /infostrategy.html
Shneiderman, B. *et al.* (1995) Windows of opportunity in electronic classrooms. *Communications of the ACM*, **38(11)**, 19-24.
Soloway, E. (1994) Log on education: ways of seeing. *Communications of the ACM*, **37(2)**, 15-20.
Special Focus (1995) Visual literacy. *Computer Graphics*, **29(4)**, 11-47.
Stoll, C. (1995) *Silicon Snake Oil - second thoughts on the information highway.* Macmillan, London.
Thüring, M., Hannemann, J. and Haake, J.M. (1995) Hypermedia and cognition: designing for comprehension. *Communications of the ACM*, **38(8)**, 57-66.

8 BIOGRAPHY

Matti Mäkelä, born 1941, graduated from Helsinki University of Technology. Since 1974, he has been Associate Professor of Computer Science (Numerical Algorithms of Applied Mathematics) at the Department of Computer Science, University of Helsinki, and also lectured in Numerical Analysis at the Helsinki University of Technology. His main research interest has been numerical analysis, and he is currently engaged in scientific visualization and computer uses in education.

5

Information technology in educational management of tomorrow's school

M. Telem
School of Education, Tel Aviv University, Tel Aviv, Israel
Phone: (972)-3-6407123
Fax: (972)-3-6409477
e-mail: telem@post.tau.ac.il

B.Z. Barta
Ministry of Education
Culture and Sports, Jerusalem, Israel
Phone: (972)-4-353755 *Fax: (972)-4-353754*
e-mail: ben@actcom.co.il

K.D. Levin
College of Management, Tel Aviv, Israel
Phone: (972)-3-6990444 *Fax: (972)-3-6990454*
e-mail: levind@technion.ac.il

Abstract

The main principles of Sizer's "Coalition of essential schools" project in the US, and Chen's "Kramim school" project in Israel, two "school of the future" projects, are presented. ITEM's possible contribution to each of their principles is exemplified. It is argued that ITEM is indispensable in the school of the future, especially as a tool for enhancing school leadership, change introduction and management and, for teaching and learning evaluation. The "school of the future" still has to evolve and current ITEM systems will have to be redesigend to serve its emerging pedagogical and administrative needs.

Keywords

Educational management, information technology, evaluation, school leadership

1 INTRODUCTION

The current dissatisfaction with the way schools operate (Goodlad, 1991; Sarason, 1990; Sizer, 1984, 1993) has resulted in a search for a new type of school - the "school of the future". So far however there is no agreement on the nature and structure of this school. For example, some information technology oriented scholars envision a "virtual school", very unlike today's school. Students in this school would not have (partly or at all) to attend classes the way they do now. They will study at their own pace, mainly from their homes, via computers linked up with educational databases. Currently we have a long way to go to this disputable "virtual school" model. Rather than looking this far out into the future, this paper discusses the role of information technology in educational management (ITEM) in the school of the future by relating to two innovative projects: a) Professor Theodor Sizer's "Coalition of essential schools" project, already encompassing about 180 high-schools, whose principles are widely accepted in the USA, and b) the "Kramim school" project, headed by Professor David Chen (1995), established as part of the school of the future project in Israel.

2 MAIN PRINCIPLES WITH EXAMPLES OF ITEM'S POSSIBLE ROLE

According to Sharan (1995) Sizer's project has the following five main features:

1. The school is viewed as a community in which systematic teamwork and teachers' collaboration should contribute to both students and teachers on the instructional as well as the social level, (Bryk and Driscoll, 1988; Little, 1987; Murphy, 1991; Sarason, 1993). Many school decisions are group-based (Telem, 1990a). For instance, reviewing a particular student's achievements throughout the term, a decision on students' transfer between "houses" (see ahead). Instructional strategies should be tailored to the needs of the student.
   Examples of ITEM's role: 1. Groupware software packages (e.g., Lotus "Notes") which enable collaborative work among teachers and/or various other school employees (e.g., principal, counselor, subject-matter coordinators, home-room teachers, grade-level coordinators), by creating and sharing various types of data (such as relational databases, word processing documents, spreadsheets, e-mail) in a shared database, hold significant promise for improving teamwork in schools. 2. In a high-school where ITEM operated successfully it was found to encourage teamwork among teachers teaching the same subject, collaboration in preparing lesson-plans, teaching materials and tests, and in dealing jointly with issues arising from ITEM's reports (Telem and Avidov, 1996).

2. An integrative curriculum with a reduced number of subjects in three to four knowledge areas of significance to students' life.

3. Tighter interrelations between school and community. Part of the learning should take place at various community sites (such as government agencies, district public services, industry, commerce, banking, transportation). For example, in Sizer's project, students serve in such community sites half a day, once per week.
   Example of ITEM's role: Handling, follow-up and evaluation of student-community interrelations as well as the management and control of the non-school sites (i.e., in the community) learning activities, should be effectively undertaken by ITEM.

4. Frontal instruction should be minimized and replaced by activities such as project preparation, social systems simulations, etc. For example, in Sizer's project students investigate phenomena in nature, society and the world, and simulate situations in which they act as professionals.
   Example of ITEM's role: When needed, the school's database should be expanded to enable handling, follow-up and evaluation of these activities.

5. Tighter teacher-student relations, where each student is personally recognized by at least one teacher.
   Example of ITEM's role: Present schools' database should be expanded to provide information on these tightened student-teacher relations including "soft information" (i.e., non-factual information such as counselor's opinions, reports and explanations expressed in text form), for instance, teachers' opinions on students, students explanations for their absenteeism.

According to Chen (1995), the following basic assumptions underlying the traditional school (**T**) should be replaced in the school of the future (**F**):

1. **T**: Human knowledge is linear, and hence both structure and organization of learning should be linear too.
   F: Human knowledge is complex (e.g., network, tree-shaped). The learning organization should match this.
   Example of ITEM's role: ITEM's computer managed instruction (CMI) module (Telem, 1982) should be developed to serve these complex structures of learning.

2. **T**: Human knowledge is universal and relatively static. A curriculum that represents the study "discipline" is therefore needed.
   F: Knowledge is dynamic and inter-disciplinary. As a result, curricula keep rapidly changing quantitatively and qualitatively.
   Example of ITEM's role: When needed, ITEM's CMI module should be adjusted to support this on-going rapid quantitative and qualitative change.

3. **T**: Human knowledge is standard. Therefore, all students should use the same textbooks in order to achieve this knowledge.
   F: Human knowledge is pluralistic and relative and therefore should be adjusted to each student's personality.
   Examples of ITEM's role: ITEM's CMI module should be expanded to monitor each student's progress in any course/subject of study, providing him/her with a pluralistic choice of textbooks, exercises, etc.

4. **T**: The site of learning is exclusively the school.
   F: Students encounter new knowledge and learn anywhere.
   Example of ITEM's role: An effective management of the non-school sites learning activities.

5. **T**: A fixed relation exists between time and learning: The more the student studies the more knowledge s/he gains. Therefore, fixed time units such as a class, study day, semester, academic year, etc. are used. As a result, time resources are inefficiently used. According to Chen (1995, p. 93), only about 12% of the time resources are allocated to institutionalized, controlled studies.
   F: Time resources should be used in a more effective manner.

Example of ITEM's role: ITEM should be redesigend to provide school employees with information on "time consumption", thus enabling a more flexible/effective use of time. For instance, changes in the length of the school day, changes in the structure of studies.

6. **T**: The class, i.e., 30 to 40 students and one teacher, constitutes the basic organizational unit. Classes are assembled into age levels which are assembled into a school.
   F: The school should support a flexible and differential study group structure. For example, Sizer overruled the existing conception of "one class one teacher". In his project the high-school encompasses up to 1350 students, divided into "houses" of 210 students with 13 teachers each: Three mathematics and science teachers, three teachers of history and philosophy, three for arts, three general teachers and one additional teacher. They are divided into three sub-groups consisting of one teacher of each of the above disciplines. This structure eliminates organizational barriers between teachers and encourages teamwork and teaching and learning coordination.
   Example of ITEM's role: In order to assist both in effective class mapping and construction, and in students' and teachers' placement and on-going evaluation, expert systems and models should be developed and extensively used.

7. **T**: Policy management and control are carried out according to inputs (e.g., class hours, classes, teachers, teacher training). A direct relation exists between inputs and outputs so that an increase in the former will result in an increase in the latter.
   F: Cybernetic management control, i.e., maintaining a course towards a goal through on-going communication, feedback, control and regulation.
   Example of ITEM's role: An effective cybernetic management control is virtually impossible without a computerized mechanism, i.e., an ITEM. Real-time feedback on, for example, student/teacher/"home"/etc. achievements, is one of ITEM's strongest advantages.

8. **T**: Partial development policy i.e., introduction of change/s in one subsystem (e.g., teaching, discipline, evaluation) while ignoring the others.
   F: A systems development policy approach should be adopted, implying that a change in one of the school's subsystems affects its other subsystems.
   Example of ITEM's role: Since ITEM should be designed a-priori from a systems approach perspective, its contribution toward this aim is paramount. Its integrated, school database as well as its easily and instantly retrieved information, disseminated concurrently to the school's various functionaries, serve both as a systems development approach and as follow up tools. Reliable evaluation in a systems approach mode is possible only through ITEM.

9. **T**: Reformist strategy of change, seeking to achieve immediate change/s through administrative measures.
   F: Experimental along time strategy of change.
   Example of ITEM's role: Built in to the experimental strategy is the notion of both on-going data collection and instant feedback mechanisms. ITEM is an ideal tool for achieving this strategy in various domains such as "home" construction, student/teacher evaluation, etc.

3 LEADERSHIP, LEARNING AND INSTRUCTION EVALUATION

In the "school of the future" the principal's role as a school leader is of major importance. Taking into account Sizer's and Chen's above mentioned assumptions, teaching and learning evaluation will be shaped differently in this school. Therefore, ITEM should be designed "to match the structure, management tasks, instructional processes and special needs of the school [of the future] ... [It] is not a means in itself. It is a computer-based artificial technological system ... providing decision support to the decision system that is a regular part of organizational management" (Telem, 1994, p. 2828). According to Telem (1990a,b) ITEM provides information on "what has happened" and on "what would happen". It incorporates model formation, expert systems, text manipulation, and soft information handling. However, to comply with the emerging needs of the school of the future, ITEM's information needs should be redefined and its database redesign. ITEM is an indispensable mechanism for both pedagogical and administrative decision making and leadership.

3.1 ITEM and the principal as a school leader

Special emphasis is allocated in the school of the future to the principal as a school and change leader. As such, s/he should be capable of leading individuals and groups and of planning change projects. S/he has to set objectives, fix priorities (relating to students, teachers and the community), present objectives and change plans to school employees, identify discrepancies between present and required situations, and allocate resources for achieving school objectives and change (Sharan, 1995). The information provided by ITEM is a tool for achieving these tasks. It has already been found that in high-schools where ITEM operates effectively, principals use it as a pedagogical leadership tool (Telem and Buvilski, 1995; Telem and Avidov, 1994, 1996).

The problem solving process includes the identification of relevant information and its analysis. Information retrieved from ITEM's integrative, overall and updated database should serve the principal in his/her systematic analysis of problems and achievement of good solutions, as well as for strategic school planning. As Telem and Buvilski (1995) showed, principals do use ITEM for making strategic decisions and for physical and human resource allocation. They also showed that ITEM provides the principal with on-going feedback (i.e., a cybernetic process) on the pedagogical and administrative activities taking place in school. In Sizer's project the team in each house is authorized to make most of the organizational and pedagogical decisions related to the work in their house. This team is also responsible for controlling performance and for closing gaps between plans and performance. The information provided by ITEM should serve as a major tool for this purpose too.

3.2 Evaluation

On-going evaluation is of major importance in the school of the future. According to Sizer, external examinations (e.g., matriculation examinations) should be eliminated, while the amount of internal examination should also be reduced to a minimum. Evaluation of students' cognitive skills over long periods of time in different situations and by different tools, will replace answers to test questions at a given date and time. Written examinations will be replaced by evaluation of students' exhibits and portfolios (cf. Barone, 1991). Lectures will be minimized and replaced by students' involvement in the process of learning, mainly by self-achievement and use of knowledge. As such, evaluation will become significantly more complex than the evaluation of written tests which is currently common. According to Sharan (1995) evaluation in the school of the future should encompass qualities such as clear oral and written presentation (through various means e.g., drawing), sophistication (e.g., well informed and perceptive use of sources) logic, organization and congruence between the various parts of the presentation. ITEM should be developed to constitute a major tool in the reshaped evaluation process. It has already been found that principals and subject-coordinators do use ITEM for evaluating student/class's achievements and teachers' work (Telem and Buvilski, 1995; Telem and Avidov, 1994, 1996).

4 CONCLUSION

ITEM will constitute an indispensable tool in the school of the future. Whatever form and structure the school will take, on-going information retrieval and distribution (on learning, teaching, school site and finance, plan versus performance etc.) to school community members, is of major importance. As future schools will metamorphose, present ITEMs will have to be redesign to serve their new pedagogical and administrative needs, while also adapting themselves to on-going hardware and software innovations.

5 REFERENCES

Barone, T. (1991) Assessment as theater: staging an exposition. *Educational Leadership,* February, 47-59.

Bryk, A. and Driscoll, M. (1988) The high school as community: contextual influences and consequences for students and teachers. National Center on Effective Schools, Madison, Wisconsin.

Chen, D. (1995) "Kramim" school in Rishon-Lezion: principles and planning of an innovative model in education, in *Education Toward the Twenty First Century* (ed. D. Chen), Ramot, Tel-Aviv (Hebrew)

Goodlad, J. (1991) Why we need a complete redesign of teacher education. *Educational Leadership,* **49**, 4-6.

Little, J.W. (1987) Teachers as colleagues, in *Educators' handbook: A research perspective* (ed. V. Richardson-Koehler), Longman, New York.

Murphy, J. (1991) *Restructuring schools.* Teachers College, New York.

Sarason, S. (1990) *The predictable failure of educational reform.* Jossey-Bass, San Francisco.

Sarason, S. (1993) *The case for change: rethinking the preparation of educators.* Jossey-Bass, San Francisco.

Sharan, S. (1995) The innovative high school: structure, administration and teaching, in *Education toward the twenty first century* (ed. D. Chen), Ramot, Tel-Aviv (Hebrew).

Sizer, T. (1984) Horace's compromise: The dilemma of the American high school. Houghton-Mifflin, Boston.

Sizer, T. (1993) Horace's school: redesigning the American high school. Houghton-Mifflin, Boston.

Telem, M. (1982) The CMI and the MIS - an integration needed. *AEDS Journal*, **16(1)**, 48-55.

Telem, M. (1990a) DSS in educational organizations. *Computers and Education*, **14(1)**, 61-69.

Telem, M. (1990b) Educational DSS: potential services, benefits, difficulties, and dangers. *Computers and Education*, **14(1)**, 71-80.

Telem, M. (1994) Information technology use in educational management systems. *The International Encyclopedia of Education* (2nd Ed), **5**, 2828-2831.

Telem, M., and Avidov, O. (1994) Management information system (MIS) impact on the loosely coupled nature of a high-school: a case study. *Planning & Changing*, **25(3/4)**, 192-205.

Telem, M., and Avidov, O. (1996) School management information systems and the loosely coupled nature of a high-school instruction administration subsystem - a preliminary study. *Journal of Research on Computing in Education,* **28(2)**, 258-269.

Telem, M., and Buvilski, T. (1995) The potential impact of information technology on the high-school principal's role - a preliminary exploration. *Journal of Research on Computing in Education*, **27(3)**, 281-296.

6 BIOGRAPHIES

Moshe Telem, Chair of the educational administration program in the School of Education, Tel Aviv University, received his doctorate from the Hebrew University in Jerusalem. He specializes in MIS in education and educational administration.

Ben Zion Barta received his Ph.D. from Technion Israel. As Chief Inspector for Computers in Education in the Ministry of Education, he is in charge of the coordination of R&D projects and the implementation of computer education activities in the Israeli school system.

K. Dan Levin has served on the faculties of the Wharton School of Business at the University of Pennsylvania and at the School of Management of Tel Aviv University. He is currently at Tel Aviv College of Management.

PART TWO

Computer-assisted Decision-making

6

Technological facilitation for decision-making in education

D.W. Spuck, A.J. MacNeil, D.L. Prater, and D.B. Palumbo
University of Houston
Clear Lake, 2700 Bay Area Boulevard, Houston, Texas 77058
USA
Phone: 713-283-3501 *Fax: 713-283-3509*
e-mail: SPUCK@CL.UH.EDU

Abstract

An alternative form of meeting environment known as Electronic Meeting Systems (EMS) is now possible through the application of information technology that attempts to make meetings more productive. Group involvement in decision making is consistent with current trends toward site-based management and total quality management. The movement toward collaborative decision making and group consensus building requires facilitation. Through the use of this technology, administrators have the opportunity and the support for issue identification and prioritization procedures, which facilitates achievement of group consensus.

Keywords

Educational management, electronic meeting systems, policy, problem solving

1 INTRODUCTION

Group decision making is very much a part of the democratic process and culture. Restructuring organizations by decentralization to site-based decision making is now the emerging management and organization model in both the public and private sectors (Barzelay, 1992; Katzenbach & Smith, 1993; Lawler, 1986, 1992; Wohlstetter, Smyer, & Mohrman, 1994). As our society evolves technologically, the work world increasingly becomes more complex, requires teamwork, and exists in a rapidly changing environment. Work that is simple, individual, and always predictable needs a hierarchical structure. Work that is complex, collegial, and uncertain tends to be decentralized and requires employee involvement, and commitment. The collective wisdom of a group can, in many instances, improve the quality of decision making. Conventional wisdom also advocates that participation in the decision process increases commitment for the decision. In a recent longitudinal study comparing group decisions to individual decisions, Watson, Michaelson and Sharp (1991) showed that groups scored higher than their best member by 70 percent at each point in time. The study also showed that as the group gained experience, best members became less important to the group's success.

Traditional meeting methods are currently under review, particularly in their ability to effectively and efficiently bring groups to consensus (Hitchings & Cox, 1992; Paulus, Dzindolte, Poletes, & Camacho, 1993). Educational leaders are constantly in search of the most efficient and effective meeting techniques and computer-based technologies have begun to provide effective tools to effect more productive meetings. These hardware/software combinations, commonly known as electronic meeting systems (EMS) have begun to find their way into a variety of educational environments (Aiken & Riggs, 1993). Some strategies for group decision support are patterned after the nominal group process models of Delbecq and Van de Ven (1971; see also Spuck, 1976). EMS provides computer support for issue identification and prioritization procedures, which facilitates achievement of group consensus. Nunamaker and Briggs (1991) suggested that the major advantage is more time free from the demands of frequent - and often frustrating - meetings. Technology-mediated environments are designed to improve the productivity of many collaborative planning and decision making processes (RICIS, 1994).

Current practice increasingly involves collaborative methods and group consensus building in educational decision making. Nunamaker and his colleagues (Nunamaker, Dennis, Valacich, Vogel, & George, 1991) have proposed that EMS improves group work in the following ways:

1. All participants can input their ideas simultaneously.
2. Opportunity for equal participation of all group members is provided.
3. Behavior that can impact negatively on group productivity is discouraged.
4. Large groups can work together effectively to provide more information, knowledge and skills to work on the task.
5. More techniques and methods are available for large groups to perform tasks.
6. External information is accessible for the group members.
7. An organizational memory is developed from meeting to meeting.

Nunamaker et al. (1991) also have presented a strategy for understanding EMS processes, focusing on the characteristics of the group to be involved in the process, the tasks to be completed, the context of the organization and culture, and the outcome to be achieved. These items provide a framework for evaluating and understanding this and other examples of EMS and establish an organization for a research agenda on system use (Spuck, Prater & Palumbo, 1995).

Examples of issues for which EMS can provide assistance are defining school district planning priorities, identifying strategies for resolving specific problems such as improving school drop-out rates, setting priorities, formulating school policy, and designing curriculum. This paper describes the purpose and function of EMS as used to support decision making in respect of two different problems. The first is the redefinition of the graduate core curriculum for master's degree programs in a school of education and the second is an analysis of a case study used in the instructional program for school administrators.

2 IMPORTANCE OF GROUP DECISION MAKING

The continuing efforts toward decentralization and making the public schools more accountable and responsible, focus on the need for improved group decision making processes. Recently there have been studies that show that site-based management efforts have not resulted in the predicted change. Bimber's (1994) study for the Rand Corporation predicted that the decentralization movement will continue even though there is little success to show with decentralization to date. Bimber (1994) noted that the theory is appropriate but the process has been inadequate. Site-based management relocates the power, authority, and accountability of the organization to the people directly involved with providing the service or making the product. Mohrman, Lawler, and Mohrman (1992) argued that teachers do intellectually complex tasks, are most effective when working collegially or in teams, and face uncertainty in their day-to-day work. Therefore, a high-involvement and decentralized management strategy is appropriate for schools. Failure of the decentralization movement is rooted in the lack of empowerment of the mass of educators. Fullan (1996) focused attention on the failure of reform as a failure to involve enough people in the process. "This is why attempting to change the system directly, through regulation and structural reform does not work. It is people who change systems, through the development of new critical masses." (Fullan, 1996, p. 423). The use of EMS would be a direct and pervasive means of involving greater numbers in the process of deciding.

Given the importance of good decisions and good decision making and the increasing numbers and groups of people who will now be involved in the decision process (e.g., site based decision making), facilitation is necessary. It is important to minimize poor decisions and poor decision making practices. There are and have been many times when groups have made bad decisions or when the conditions of information would warrant a different decision than the one made. Educators often tell stories that attest to the befuddled and bizarre decisions that come from school boards throughout North America. Listing examples of building design and location problems, personnel selection decisions or policy decisions that would boggle the mind are often the sport of educators as they gather in social situations at professional development meetings. There is no end to the stories and situations that have been the result of flawed decision making practices of groups responsible for educating our youth. There is also well documented evidence of poor decision making by other decision making groups that have fallen victims of "group think" and "escalating commitment" such as the Bay of Pigs fiasco of the Kennedy administration and the NASA Challenger Disaster.

3 ELECTRONIC MEETING SYSTEMS

Computer programs specifically designed to help in the group decision making process are now available. Best and prevailing practice increasingly involves collaborative methods and group consensus building. It also includes involvement of various interest groups, or representatives, of groups, in educational decision making.

EMS environments can be characterized by three essential components: (a) the meeting facility, (b) the electronic meeting software, and (c) the facilitation method used. This electronic meeting system works on a network of personal computers, usually one for each participant. Computers are arranged around a meeting table with each computer connected directly to a central computer that serves to coordinate and store data about the meeting. EMS facilities often also contain one or more large display screens for group viewing during discussion, brainstorming ideas and decision making (Nunamaker, et al., 1991).

There are a variety of EMS software tools currently available to support EMS environments. According to Johansen (1994), there currently are more than 100 software vendors developing more than 300 products that support some form of electronic meeting environments. Some examples of the meeting environments are Lotus Notes that distributes to many group members a variety of information quickly and easily. Examples of more collaborative environments are: Option Finder, Group Systems V, Vision Quest, and The Meeting Room.

While EMS environments offer the possibility of large productivity gains, such gains are not easily obtained and require a fundamental shift in the thinking of a group. The shift is linked to the manner in which the EMS are facilitated. A variety of meeting methods have been adapted to these EMS environments. Most EMS activities follow a common sequence:

1. A group leader meets with a facilitator to develop an agenda and to select Groupware tools.
2. Meetings generally begin with an idea generating activity using the electronic brainstorming tool.
3. Comments from idea generation are organized into a list of key issues using the idea organization tool.
4. The vote tool is used to prioritize the key issues.
5. The topic commenter tool is used to discuss the top issues (Nunamaker & Briggs, 1991).

While the adoption of EMS technologies has not advanced much beyond the technology development and implementation stage, initial analysis indicated that in these environments there appears to be: (a) more attention placed on pre-meeting planning, (b) more material generated, (c) somewhat less verbal discussion, (d) more focus and intensity from both the group leaders and participants, (e) less "wasted" non-productive time, and (f) higher degrees of participant satisfaction with both the process and the decisions taken (Greene, DiPette, Palumbo, & Wijesinghe, 1994).

4 TWO RECENT EXPERIENCES USING EMS

Given the need to involve the participants and those affected by decisions in the decision making process, as well as the inherent capability of erring in group decisions, the following studies were undertaken at the University of Houston - Clear Lake (UHCL). The EMS lab was used with educators for two very different types of decisions that demonstrate the diversity of situations in which EMS has capability for facilitating decision making. These two examples involve the use of EMS in redefining the master's-level graduate core, and student use in reaching consensus in a case study analysis.

4.1 EMS Use in Redefining the Master's Degree Core

For more than a decade, master's degree programs in education at the University of Houston -Clear Lake have included a set of four core courses that remained relatively stable over that time. The only significant change was that a computer literacy course replaced an educational psychology requirement about five years ago. While the content of specific courses was revised over time, the basic structure and philosophy of the core was not.

The task the faculty had was to undertake a complete reassessment of the graduate core; reopening the questions of whether a set of core experiences, to be included in all master's degree programs in the School of Education, still made sense, and if so, what outcomes should be included. A task force of seven faculty members, representing current core areas, as well as faculty members from master's degree programs served by the core, were appointed. The charge given to the task force requested: (a) a recommendation for courses and experiences that would be common to all graduate programs and therefore required of each master's degree student, (b) that the committee ensure that broad-based input was solicited, and (c) that they consider the use of the EMS lab in gathering input and reaching consensus.

While the actual plan to be followed evolved over time, the process that emerged may be seen as containing ten steps. These ten steps are outlined in Figure 1. Included as initial input, Step 1, was that gained from forums with the faculty in each of our master's degree programs and with the faculty who currently taught courses in the present core. Faculty associated with each of the master's degree programs were asked to meet as a group prior to the open form and to identify for their program eight to ten major outcomes or challenges for future graduates; as a result 155 items were submitted.

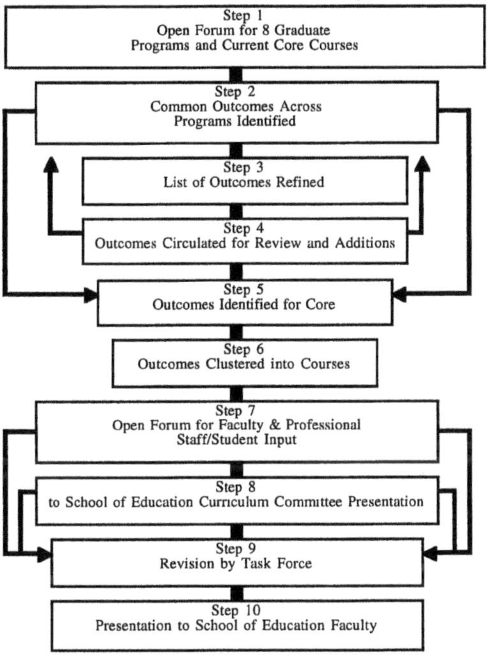

Figure 1
Graduate Core Review Process.

The following two steps, utilizing the EMS lab, identified those outcomes and challenges that were believed to be common to three or more of the master's degree programs, reducing the list to 91 items. Following discussion and comment, a vote was taken and items that four or more committee members identified as common to three or more programs were retained. Items that did not receive this level of committee support were deleted.

Next the list of common outcomes was refined to combine similar and eliminate duplicate items, to expand narrow items and become more specific about broad items, and try to begin to achieve a measure of consistency and parallelism in item statements; this process resulted in a reduction of the outcome list to a total of 41 items. For example, the items "issues related to understanding multicultural populations" and "understanding microcultures (e.g., gender, religion, exceptionality)" were seen by the committee as being included in another item, "model and encourage appreciation for students' cultural heritage, unique endowments, learning styles, interests and needs," and the former two items were eliminated from the list.

All faculty members in the School of Education were then invited to review the 41 items and to provide suggestions for additions, deletions, and rewordings to the list. Most of the suggestions provided rewordings of the outcomes and generally were incorporated. The other more substantive suggestions were discussed at length and the EMS lab was used by the task force to achieve agreement as to whether or not to add items to the list; as a result, one new item was included, for a total of 42 outcomes. In step five, the EMS lab was utilized to gain consensus from the task force as to which of the 42 outcomes were core responsibilities, and which were responsibilities of individual programs; 31 items remained on the list of core outcomes.

Until step six the idea of combining objectives into courses had been avoided, as it was clear that this is when the process would become highly political, as academic territory emerged as an issue. Even here, the term course was not used, as the committee was asked to create content "chunks", placing those outcomes together which seemed to share a similarity of content; but following the chunking of outcomes, the combining of these chunks into four clusters defined the structure of the courses to be proposed. Consensus of the task force members was achieved around these courses.

Step seven provided an opportunity for students and faculty to comment on the proposed master's degree core courses. Step eight formally presented the task force recommendation to the curriculum committee of the School of Education. Also in step eight, the task force considered various comments and suggestions that had been received and made final revisions in the recommendation. The task force recommendation was presented to the entire faculty for consideration and was approved unanimously for implementation.

Comments and observation on EMS processes

Typically academic considerations, such as defining a core, are ripe for political agendas and conflict; while these forces were apparent in this case, too, the graduate core recommended by the task force was approved overwhelmingly by the faculty as-a-whole, and with a high level of esprit and camaraderie - a remarkable result and one in part attributable to the process followed.

The EMS lab was used to supplement activities that transpired over a period of seven months. While EMS software was helpful, it was used only at selected intervals within the process. The major EMS program features that were employed were voting, sorting, and the use of comment cards. Voting is used to gain group consensus (for example, this outcome should be the responsibility of the core). Sorting is the identification of items of similar content, that is, the grouping of outcomes into similar categories (for example, similar dusters of outcomes were sorted into courses). Comment cards allowed task force members to describe their interpretation of the meaning of a particular outcome and to explain why each outcome was a core responsibility or why it would be best delivered by an individual program.

Key things learned from the process revolve around the following issues

Issue #1: The Facilitator. The facilitator must understand both the issue to be considered as well as the process to be followed in addressing the issue. It is important that the facilitator not get involved in the discussion and not be, or even be perceived, as having a position on the issues addressed. It is best that the facilitator not be well known by the program participants.

Issue #2: The Importance of a Well-Developed Agenda. The participants were intrigued with the software. The initial visit to the lab was fascinating and the group looked forward to the sessions in the lab. There was a tendency, however, to want to move too quickly through the process (e.g., Let's take a straw poll since we can do it so easily). If you vote too quickly on issues, positions get polarized. It also seems that you can get too reductive in your thinking, moving too quickly to resolution. Due to the novelty of the software, there was a tendency to want to try all the options. It is important that the agenda be thoughtfully worked out in advance; which we did, as the task force chair met with the facilitator prior to each meeting and prepared the agenda. This agenda was shared at the onset and participants knew what to expect.

Issue #3: Comment Cards. The comment cards were one of the most useful parts of the process, particularly those comments that participants directed back to each other's input. There were instances where comments continued to build and branch off an original comment, pointing out a "hot- issue that needed to be worked through." The comments also illustrated that we sometimes discover our own position about an issue through collective thinking (i.e., your idea triggers an idea in me that I might not otherwise have considered). The process was very generative in nature.

Issue #4: Use the Lab as a Supplement. Carefully plan how and when you can benefit from using the lab. Don't be seduced into thinking it does all things for you. At some stages traditional group deliberations are better. Make it work for you, but don't get too enamored of the software and lab setting.

4.2 Graduate Students Case Study: The process

This investigation used a case study as the basis for creating a decision making situation. The case concerned an experienced high school principal newly assigned to a school that lacked leadership. The case focused on the difficulty he had in dealing with a recalcitrant secretary. A group of graduate students in the educational leadership program that were familiar with a case study approach used the EMS lab. Other students, also familiar with the case study approach, followed a traditional analysis approach to case studies.

The educational leadership class had 39 students; 13 students used the EMS, while the other 26 students stayed in their usual groups of five or six students. These five groups had the same case and were to follow the traditional case study approach. These groups were studied to determine whether problem identification would be similar.

The EMS used an approach based on the Nominal Group Technique. This approach is a refinement of brainstorming that focuses on generating alternatives and choosing one. This approach is recommended where group members fear criticism. The following steps were used: members silently list their ideas, all ideas are listed on chart with discussion allowed for clarification but no criticism, finally a written vote is taken (Van de Ven & Delbecq, 1974). This process encourages members to pool their judgments in order to solve the problem and then determine a satisfactory course of action.

Using the EMS system students followed this agenda:

5:15 PM	Introduction to the Case
5:20 PM	Introduction to the EMS lab
5:50 PM	Generate problems (Categorizer). Identify the problems faced by the Kingsville High School, & the principal
6:20 PM	Determine Agreement (Vote). Identify the crucial/important problems. (Multiple choice: top 15 problems)
7:20 PM	Determine Agreement (Vote). The Rank order list of top 14 problems.
7:50 PM	Generate Solutions (Categorizer). Generate suggestions/solutions to overcome problems [for the top five problems]
8:20 PM	Identify the top most important problems (Vote). Identify the two most important problems [reviewing the solutions]
8:50 PM	Identify Advantages/Disadvantages (Categorizer). Identify the advantages/ disadvantages of implementing each solution.

The process is one of brainstorming to identify the problem. The group of thirteen graduate students identified 61 problems. To succeed and get agreement on the identification of the problem that the case presented, the students were asked to vote to

narrow the selection to the top fifteen. The sixty-one possible problems had many similarities about them and an attempt to group them together was not successful.
The group was then asked to vote and prioritize the fourteen selections. The sum of the rank ordering and the mean are calculated and the standard deviation from the mean is also provided. The ballot showed that most of the students identified the main problem as the lack of support from the Superintendent, but this result was not significantly more important that the other problems identified. The significance level is found by the program calculating the consensus threshold using Ventana's coefficient of consensus (VCC). The value of 1.00 represents complete consensus and the value of 0.00 represents no consensus. The VCC = 1.00-((STD / (high Limit - low limit)) * 2). The significance 0.18 showed very little consensus, as a result of 0.65 would be considered significant. The lab assistant then narrowed the choices to five and the students voted. This time the VCC was calculated at 0.26 which again showed non significant agreement among the decision makers.

The next step in the process is to generate solutions. The most top five identified problems were presented for solutions. Problem one created forty-five solutions. Problem 2-15, solution, problem 3 -11. problem 4-11, problem 5-9. After identifying solutions for the problems they were asked to vote again on the critical problem. The students were then directed to predict by brainstorming the advantages and disadvantages of the solutions for the problems. Again there was a great deal of data that needed to be sorted.

The outcome

The identification of the problem with the EMS system focused on the Superintendent and his/her lack of support for the principal in handling the difficulty with the secretary. The other five groups of five or six students identified the problem as being a difficult secretary and the need for the principal to proceed with progressive discipline. The EMS students focused more on the problem of lack of leadership in the organization and the relationship between the principal and the superintendent. There is no one correct answer to case studies because a case reports the author's bias and all detail cannot be given; as well, the assumptions that the students make in determining the analysis cannot be controlled. Given these considerations it can still be seen that the use of EMS has a great deal of potential for overcoming problems with decision making. The fact that the EMS group identified the problem differently points to the potential of creativity in the decision-making process.

5 THE ADVANTAGES OF USING EMS

There is an overwhelming amount of data produced and easily sorted using the EMS system. The variety of ideas makes the group's work more focused on solving the problem rather than defending a solution. Olaniran (1994) made the observation that using electronic brainstorming produces significantly more fresh ideas. The use of EMS allows the calculation of the data to be produced by the system and the results are available throughout the meeting as well as in summary at the end of the session. A complete record of the meeting is available for analysis at the end of the meeting.

Using the EMS removes a major barrier of members seeing and hearing which ideas are whose. It encourages members of the decision making team to think and create solutions rather than to play the politics of supporting an ally or friend. Nelson & Quick (1994) reported that the Boeing Company study of its meetings found that 20 percent of the team members did 80 percent of the talking. Using EMS frees members' participation and relationships become less important as the focus is on determining a best result. While the time taken to reach consensus on the case study took longer than it did for the traditional case study group, the number of problems identified and the number of solutions generated was much greater. In the traditional group, a member of the group emerged as a leader and shaped the work of the group in order to move to closure and likely shaped the conclusions in a direction acceptable to hime/her. Nelson & Quick (1994) also reported from the Boeing study that the time needed to complete team projects was reduced by an average of 91 percent with an average cost saving in employee time of $6700. The fact that there can be simultaneous input is a time saver. Members of the decision-making group are not having to stop their own inputs or observations because another member has the floor; all members of the group can talk at once and still be heard and recognized.

6 SOME PROBLEMS USING EMS

Using the EMS can be more time consuming than using the traditional method of working in a group on a case study. As noted, the groups not using the EMS reached their conclusions more quickly than the EMS student group. The anonymous nature of the meeting can also encourage frivolity and distract others from the task, although some humor may add to the meeting. Another problem with anonymity is that it encourages irresponsibility and the accountability for one's actions can be lost. Educational settings, because they often require public accountability, cannot always be anonymous.

7 CONCLUSION

Just as some decisions are best made by individuals and some by teams or groups; some decisions are better suited to the use of the EMS. Decisions that tend to be emotional, controversial or complex would best be served by the EMS. Decisions that will result in hurt feelings and poor relationships that can cause an organization to become dysfunctional could be best served by the EMS. Decisions that need to be made avoiding the groupthink phenomena can be well served by EMS. Meetings that require creative or better solutions can be enhanced through the use of EMS. Decisions that can be helped with quick results through rapid polling and immediate feedback with real time results can be enriched through EMS. The importance of having a complete record of the meeting also is a distinct advantage of the EMS. The entries as well as the process are recorded and able to be analyzed.

One purpose of encouraging the use of the EMS lab for the reconceptualization of the master's degree core was to provide a useful example of lab use which represented a real problem to our faculty; it was hoped that the outcome would be positive, both in process and result, which it was. It also was hoped that use of the EMS process would encourage the faculty to make use of the lab for other purposes, and in particular encourage its use with problems and issues affecting their field-based constituencies. This goal is beginning to be realized as the EMS lab has since been used in a local school district, and is now scheduled by a superintendent and school board to be used in establishing priorities for the coming year.

In summary, the EMS lab provides a viable option for securing broad-based group involvement in decision making. Medium-sized groups can work together efficiently, ideas can be generated, and highly charged or sensitive issues can be aired in relative anonymity. Voting and prioritization of ideas are facilitated. While we should be cautious not to overstate the benefits of EMS use, it appears that group problem solving and consensus building may be particularly appropriate areas in which to take advantage of this technology.

8 REFERENCES

Aiken, M., & Riggs, M. (1993) Using a group decision support system for creativity. *Journal of Creative Behavior*, **27**, 28-35.

Barzelay, M. (1992) *Breaking through bureaucracy: a new way for managing in government.* University of California Press, Berkeley, CA.

Bimber, B. (1994) *The de-centralization mirage: comparing decision-making arrangements in four high schools.* Rand, Santa Monica, CA.

Delbecq, A.L., & Van de Ven, A.H. (1971) A group process model for problem identification and program planning. *Journal of Applied Behavioral Science*, **7**.

Fullan, M. G. (1996) Turning systematic thinking on its head. *Phi Delta Kappan*, **77(6)**, 420-423.

Greene, L., DiPette, P., Palumbo, D.B. and Wijesinghe, R. (1994) *Electronic meeting systems.* Paper presented at the Phi Delta Kappa Eighth Annual Research Conference, Houston.

Hitchings, G. and Cox, S. (1992) Generating ideas using randomized search methods: a method of managed convergence. *Management Decision*, **30**, 58-61.

Johansen, R. (1994) Is there life after reengineering? Continuity: The organizational desire for the 1990s, in *Conference proceedings from the Fifth Annual Groupsystems Users' Conference* (ed. J. Ceridwen), Ventana Corporation, Tucson, AZ.

Katzenbach, J.R. and Smith, D.K. (1993) *The wisdom of teams: creating the high-performance organization.* Harvard Business School Press, Boston.

Lawler, E. III (1986) *High involvement management.* Jossey-Bass, San Francisco.

Lawler, E. III (1992) *The ultimate advantage: creating the high involvement organization.* Jossey-Bass, San Francisco.

Mohrman, S.A., Lawler, E. III, & Mohrman, A.M. Jr. (1992) Applying employee involvement in schools. *Education Evaluation and Policy Analysis,* **14(4)**, 347-360.

Nelson, D.L. and Quick, J.C. (1994) *Organizational behavior: foundations realities and challenges.* West Publishing Company: St. Paul, MN.

Nunamaker, J.F. and Briggs, R.O. (1991) *Groupware user experience: ten years of lessons with Group Systems.* Center for the Management of Information, University of Arizona, Tucson, AZ.

Nunamaker, J.F., Dennis, A.R., Valacich, J.S., Vogel, D.R. and George, J.F. (1991) Electronic meeting systems to support group work. *Communications of the ACM,* **34(7)**, 40-61.

Olaniran, B.A. (1994) Group performance in computer-mediated and face-to-face communication media. *Management Communication Quarterly,* **7(3)**, 256-281.

Paulus, P.B., Dzindolte, M.T., Poletes, G. and Camacho, L.M. (1993) Perception of performance in group brainstorming: The illusion of group productivity. *Personality and Social Psychology Bulletin,* **19(1)**, 78-89.

RICIS (Research Institute for Computing and Information Systems) (1994) GSS Research Lab furthers the spirit of collaborative effort. *RICIS Review,* **6(1)**, 4-5,8.

Spuck, D.W. (1976) Evaluation for effective decision making, in *The principal and individually guided education* (eds. J.M. Lipham & M.J. Fruth), Addison Wesley, Reading, MA.

Spuck, D.W., Prater, D.L. and Palumbo, D.B. (1995) Using electronic meeting system support in the design of the graduate core curriculum. *Educational Technology: Research and Development,* **43(2)**, 71-78.

Van de Van, A. and Delbecq, A. (1974) The effectiveness of nominal, Delhi and intergroup decision-making processes. *Academy of Management Journal,* **17(4)**, 605-621.

Watson, W., Michaelson, L. K. and Sharp, W. (1991) Member competence, group interaction and group decision making: a longitudinal study. *Journal of Applied Psychology,* **76(6)**, 803-809.
Wohlstetter, P., Smyer, R. and Mohrman, S.A. (1994) New boundaries for school-based management: the high involvement model. *Educational Evaluation and Policy Analysis,* **16(3)**, 268-286.

9 BIOGRAPHIES

Dennis W. Spuck is dean of the School of Education and professor of foundations and educational leadership.
Angus J. MacNeil is an assistant professor of educational leadership.
Doris L. Prater is associate dean and professor of educational foundations.
David B. Palumbo is an associate professor of instructional technology.

All are at the University of Houston - Clear Lake and interested in applications of group decision support systems to problems and issues in teaching and policy development.

7

Potential contributions of management science to expert information systems in schools

R.G. Taylor
North Carolina State University
Campus Box 7801, NCSU, Raleigh, NC 28695, USA
Phone: 919-745-5544 Fax: 919-745-5771
e-mail: nidrgt2@unity.ncsu.edu

Abstract

In this paper the author claims that a mature expert information system within educational management must incorporate the contributions of management science completely within the information system and transparent to the user/manager. Only by such a complete incorporation can the manager have the benefit of sophisticated underlying mathematical models in the analysis of data without first having to become well-schooled in the mathematics or fully aware of the questions that need to be asked. The marriage between management science and expert systems can thus allow the manager to concentrate on the problems of pedagogy, knowing that the information system will "automatically" provide the information he/she needs to make good decisions.

Keywords

Management information systems, operations research, expert systems

1 INTRODUCTION

Management science uses a group of mathematically-oriented methods to help managers make good decisions. These methods apply to two large categories of problems. The first pertains to optimization, wherein, limited resources must be allocated in such a way as to maximize or minimize one or more specified objectives. The second pertains to the reduction of risk and uncertainty -- making the best decision when some or all of the information needed for that decision is probabilistic. Management science is now well-developed and is widely used in business, industry and banking, as well as in certain large public-sector agencies such as the military. It is less often employed in state and regional governmental agencies and almost never in the management of educational systems. The few examples of management science in education which appeared in the literature from 1968 to the early 90s have been documented, commented upon, and expanded by Taylor (1992).

The present author has been involved in teaching management science in education through workshops, lectures, and publications since 1985 and has observed some of the reasons why management science has not claimed the attention of educational administrators. First, it is inherently mathematical, and most school administrators are not well schooled in the mathematics. Although classical inferential statistics is often included in the training of educators, the standard mathematical tools upon which management science are based are generally omitted -- linear algebra, linear programming, calculus, and topics in statistics such as stochastic processes. Secondly, until recently, management science models were solved using mainframe computers -- a tool that was generally unavailable or not easily mastered by those in educational decision-making roles.

2 EMERGING POSSIBILITIES

Notwithstanding these historic constraints to the advancement of management science in education, the science and its underlying computer hardware technology are on the edge of a breakthrough that could substantially improve the rate of adoption and the utility of the tools for educational administrators. More specifically, the capacity of microcomputers to solve full-sized realistic management science problems is now available and inexpensive, as are robust computer programs designed to handle such problems without fully involving their users in the underlying mathematical complications. Even more importantly, the growing interest in decision support systems and expert systems within educational management, suggests a marriage between management science and decision support which could be far more beneficial than either set of tools used alone.

The remainder of this paper makes a case for having certain management science models "live within the bowels" of the decision support system, constantly updating themselves and yielding information that the educational manager needs but may not have the prerequisite skills or awareness to ask for. Readers who are familiar with expert systems and exception reporting may well regard the suggestions made here as a mere elaboration on what has been promulgated by others. Similarly, readers who are familiar with the tools of management science may well conclude that the suggestions made here are elementary or obvious. What both readers need to appreciate is that the technologies of management science and expert systems have not been integrated within the field of educational management, and that both technologies have limitations that the other can remove.

3 EXAMPLES

Consider an example recently studied by a doctoral student at North Carolina State University. Working within an industrial education environment, she built a Markov model based on how trainees moved through the skill levels of a certain Computer Assisted Instruction (CAI) module. There were, perhaps, eight skill levels, seven needed for certification. Every so many minutes, a snapshot was taken within the CAI system. The snapshot updated the Markov matrix (probability of moving from any one skill level to any other). After enough persons had been through the CAI module, several analytical possibilities emerged. The instructor could make optimal interventions, because s/he would know who was functioning at or below any given percentile in terms of past (normative) performance. S/he could also tell, based on the first passage time analysis within the model, how long it would be before some given percentage of the total group would reach mastery. Or, put differently, s/he could tell how much longer the present group would have to work before 80 percent of the machines would be available to a new group.

The above illustration is heavy on the management science side of the marriage. Now, let us suppose that the instructor or CAI systems manager were not required to make any of the inquiries suggested above, but that the Markov system was automatically created and updated for every CAI module. And, further, that a small electronic alarm would tell the instructor (on the instructor's screen) that the person at machine 14 was well outside the band of normative performance and needed help. And let us suppose that every half-hour a forecast for the group and a forecast for the future availability of the resource was made and a suggested schedule for the next group was produced. These auto-reporting mechanisms could occur without the CAI manager knowing any of the underlying mathematics or without even knowing that s/he should seek such information.

Consider one more illustration based on an entirely different management science model. In many cities in the United States, there is, either voluntarily or as a result of court intervention, an effort to racially balance the enrollments within public schools. This is done by creating attendance boundaries that capture, for each school, a certain proportion of children from each pertinent race. The goal is to have the balance within each school similar to the balance within the overall system. Some students and their parents resist such assignments by changing their place of residence. Thus, "flight" and other demographic phenomena require that attendance lines need to be periodically changed. The danger is that one or more schools will get too far out of balance before administrators are aware of what is happening. If the system is under a court decree, such imbalance can cause considerable economic and political problems for the administration, as well as a sudden disruption in the educational program of children who must change schools with little notice.

Now, let us suppose that the transportation information system (a GIS [Geographic Information System]-based system used in many school systems which can convert addresses to X-Y coordinates as well as performing many routing and scheduling functions) and the student information system (which includes race and address) were automatically linked together along with a forecasting model. The model would make forecasts based on small areas within the system's perimeter, monitoring and projecting numbers of students and their racial composition. As these small areas change demographically, a forecast for the schools to which those areas are assigned could likewise be forecast and could yield warning that certain schools would, within one year, be beyond a tolerable balance. A binary linear program could then annually find the optimal assignment of areas to schools, balancing race and minimizing distance. In April or May of each year, the system would automatically report recommended changes in boundaries for the coming fall. Again, the underlying mathematics would not need to be understood by the user, nor would the user have to ask all the right questions in order to receive the recommendation.

4 SUGGESTIONS FOR FUTURE DIRECTION

There are countless possible examples of how management science and decision support systems could inform each other and exponentially increase their respective values for school administrators. A very brief description of each of several possibilities follows:

• Merit pay systems could employ linear programming to make an optimal distribution of funds. In such a system, the objective would be to maximize the amount of salary money awarded to each teacher for performance on each merit compensation variable, subject to all the constraints of the employing institution and the agreement between the employer and employees. Such variables might include teaching performance, professional development activities, school citizenship, extra duties, and so on. The constraints would include merit money available, and limits on the amount of merit pay that can be obtained by any one teacher.

• Systems for the analysis of impending teacher shortages could use Markov analysis, a well-known tool within the world of engineering. Markov analysis helps managers understand the behavior of dynamic systems, in which the elements being studied are constantly in the process of changing states. In terms of the teacher shortage problem, those states might include: a) being enrolled in a teacher training program in a particular field, b) being a first year teacher in that field, c) continuing beyond the first year, d) taking an unpaid leave from teaching, and so on. By tracking the movement of individuals once every year with respect to these states, an overall understanding of the way teachers move through career paths can be determined. This determination yields answers to many policy questions and, in addition, allows the school manager to gauge impending shortages.

• General scheduling problems (rooms, teachers, courses, times of day) can, if the scale is small enough, use binary programming, or for large scale scheduling problems, some sort of matrix/conflict system. In any case, much of the work commonly associated with the use of these methods could be automated within the management information system so that annual or semi-annual schedule-building would not be daunting.

• One of the critical problems in scheduling, especially in higher education, is finding an optimal sequence of teachers for given students. Based on the absence of any indication in the commonly available literature, the present author believes that this problem has never been studied or controlled scientifically. As an example, consider what happens in a large university that specializes in engineering. Students might be expected to take a sequence of four mathematics courses during their freshman and sophomore years. Now, for the best students, this sequence presents no serious threat. Such students will earn high grades regardless of which combination of instructors they draw. At the other extreme, the poorest students are likely to have difficulty passing even the first course. For the large majority of students, however, how the courses are taught will make a big difference in how well they perform. A student who was able to earn a low "B" in the first course from an instructor who used many examples and graphic illustrations, might have great difficulty if, in the second course, he is scheduled with an instructor who uses only abstract mathematical symbolization. Since there are many possible approaches to the subject and many teaching styles, the dozens of sections of each course that are available each semester are not truly interchangeable. Instead, there are combinations of instructors that provide a "best path" through the four courses for each student. Instead of letting students register for sections without "intelligence," it would maximize overall success for students and productivity for the university to compute the best paths based on what is known about the student or based on his/her success or failure in the first course or two. This is a classic dynamic programming problem, with well-documented parallels in industrial job-shop optimization.

• Enrollment projections have long relied on the cohort survival method of forecasting. Recent elaborations of this model have made such forecasts even more accurate. Since the method and its improvements rely on annual grade-by-grade data, and such data should be easily available from the student information system, such forecasts should be provided automatically.

• The use of nonlinear programming for finding the optimal locations for new schools in growing school systems was impractical until recently. Now, however, the presence of powerful nonlinear solvers for PCs has made the use of this tool very cost efficient. By properly sizing and placing new facilities, substantial reductions in long-term transportation costs can be achieved. This is especially true when such problems are constrained by racial or other social balance requirements as in the United States.

• There are many policy analyses issues that can best be studied using management science techniques. For example, it is impractical to determine the outcome of certain facility or transportation policies by experimentation. The school system cannot build multiple structures or set up multiple transportation networks just to see which works best. Likewise, it may be immoral to study other policies by experimentation. Can a system in good conscience try several different personnel management policies (such as retirement rules) just to see which works best? By simulating the physical or social environment on the computer, many such policies can be tested without dire consequence. In other cases, instead of simulations, it may be possible to compute the probabilistic outcome of each policy alternative using Bayesian analysis. In the literature there are a few examples in which this approach was successfully employed.

In all of these cases, the tools are unlikely to be widely used if they retain their present status as stand-alone management science methods. Educational managers simply do not have the time, and in many cases do not have the skills, to use precise mathematical methods to inform their practice. However, if the information scientists were to use the same tools deep within the structure of the Management Information System and make them transparent to the user, then such systems would take on an "expert systems" quality and would yield extremely useful results.

Information Technology in Educational Management for the 21st Century will be missing a major opportunity unless the marriage between management science and information systems is encouraged.

5 REFERENCES

Taylor, R. (1992) *Decision science in the public sector: emphasis on applications to educational administration*. Felicity Press, North Whitefield, ME, USA.

6 BIOGRAPHY

Prof. Raymond G. Taylor is the president of OR/Ed Laboratories and professor of educational administration at North Carolina State University. He also holds appointments as an associate faculty member in Operations Research at NCSU and as a visiting associate to the Moscow Institute of Economics, Politics and Law.

8

Facilities for computer-supported decision-making in schools: explanations for lack of use and proposals for improvement

A.J. Visscher
University of Twente, Faculty of Educational Science and Technology
P.O. Box 217, 7500 AE Enschede, The Netherlands
Phone: (31)-53-4893609 *Fax: (31)-53-4893791*
e-mail: Visscher@edte.utwente.nl

Abstract
In this paper an attempt is made to explain the fact that the power of computer-assisted school information systems to support decision-making is wasted. This is done on the basis of research findings regarding the characteristics of information handling by school managers and on the decision-making capacity of schools. In addition, some ways to promote the use of school information systems (SISs) for decision-support are presented.

Keywords
Educational management, information handling, problem solving

1 INTRODUCTION

This paper focuses on the support that School Information Systems (SISs) can provide when school staff make decisions and develop school policy to solve ill-structured, 'open' problems. The attempt to find solutions for structured, 'closed' problems (e.g. allocation problems like composing student lesson groups) are outside the scope of this paper.

SISs can provide various types of information that can contribute to solving unstructured school problems requiring policy-development. SIS-information can for example show:

- patterns in school results, absenteeism rates, costs, etc. and as such indicate that something needs to be done in a specific policy area.

- relationships between phenomena (e.g. between absenteeism and student achievement, or between admission criteria and passing the final examinations).
- the probable implications of alternative policy measures (e.g. the impact of changes in student promotion criteria on student promotion).
- results of policy measures.

Although the value of computerized school information systems is being recognized worldwide, these systems are still mainly used for clerical activities carried out by school office staff and other school personnel. The extent of system usage in support of school decision-making proves to be very limited, even when sophisticated and powerful SISs are available in schools (Visscher, 1991; 1992; 1995).

In this paper explanations for this phenomenon are sought as follows. The research on information management by school managers is reviewed to give an impression of the kind of information they like and use. In addition, some general features of decision-making processes in educational organizations are presented that are relevant to computer-assisted decision-making. The information resulting from both activities is used for answering the two central questions of this paper: 'Why is decision-making support in schools so limited in magnitude?' and 'How can this be changed?'

2 CHARACTERISTICS OF INFORMATION HANDLING BY SCHOOL MANAGERS

In the view of Mintzberg (1989) managers are the nerve centres of organizational information who look for relevant internal and external information and who manipulate and disseminate the obtained information.

The information they collect concerns, among others, organizational operations, external events, ideas and trends information on pressures from consumers and interest groups. They especially look for information that is current, ('hot') and comes in the form of triggers (no aggregations but details, stimuli that illuminate). Since they communicate verbally 70-80 percent of their time, they especially like verbally transmitted information (e.g. by telephone, in meetings). Managers manipulate and restructure the information they receive, to build their own models on organizational functioning, and to benefit from it in decision-making.

The stereotype, rational, problem solving manager who takes smart decisions on the basis of all relevant information is a fairy tale (McPherson et al., 1986). Profound problem analysis and problem solving by managers are rarely found.

On the basis of a review of the literature on information handling by principals, Riehl et al. (1992) argue that the nature of the conditions under which principals work (many brief episodes of unpredictable interactions) affects their information use. Since school managers have to pay attention to so many different topics, they do not spend much time to each topic. They must react rapidly and therefore need information quickly. The objective quality of information, in terms of reliability and validity, is less important for its usage than the *perceived* information quality and the speed with which information becomes available. School managers prefer simple information they understand and think they can rely on and therefore like informal, verbal information. Collecting and processing formal information (e.g. information from SISs) often takes too much time and for that reason is not done very intensively (Sproull, 1981). As a consequence managers frequently take decisions without a solid information basis.

Although principals do not use computer-output very intensively, Leighwood and Montgomery (1982) in their research found that principals who frequently analyse student and teacher performance quantitatively (which nowadays is usually done in computer-assisted ways) run more effective schools. However, it is also known that school managers in general experience difficulties in using quantitative/statistical data because they are untrained and inexperienced in this respect (Riehl et al., 1992). The latter makes it difficult for them to determine the quality of this type of data, and to interpret and use it.

According to Mintzberg (1989) the characteristics of the information managers rely on differs from that with most formal ISs produce. The latter is aggregated, precise, internal and historical. In his opinion the formal information ISs generate is only partially used because that information is poor: it does not include qualitative information like politics, personality features, and formally non-transferrable information like gestures and tone. Formal information is too general, and since its processing takes considerable time it makes the required quick responses impossible.

A second reason for the partial use of IS-information is that political reasons may result in the distortion of IS-information, e.g. organizational staff may only provide that piece of information that strengthens their own position.

The last reason concerns the fact that human beings, when taking decisions, can only take into account a limited number of information elements as a result of their limited information processing capacity.

It can be concluded that computer-supported ISs contain only a small part of all relevant information, of which the manager receives a subset, of which the brain absorbs a subset and of which only part is precise and relevant! Much of the relevant information is in human instead of in computerized memories. This implies that printed/written as well as verbal information channels have to be used (see Sproull and Zubrow, 1981).

The research on information management by school managers may be summarized as follows:

School managers take many decisions, are burdened with information and have little time to process all information and to reflect on it. Full rational behaviour in terms of choosing the best action to achieve a goal, after processing all relevant information, is exceptional. As a result information processing is reduced and information is only used selectively. Many school management actions are uninformed or based on inaccurate information. School managers have a strong preference for information that comes quickly, is informal, understood and that triggers action. The perceived information quality, rather than its objective quality, determines the extent to which certain information is used.

3 THE DECISION-MAKING CAPACITY OF SCHOOLS

How schools function as organizations before a SIS is available, especially in terms of their decision-making capacity, also affects their SIS-usage in support of school policy-making.

In the literature on decision-making in educational organizations it is often argued that policy-making at school level is limited as a result of the political interests of those who participate in decision-making processes. In non-profit organizations decision-making situations are often used as 'garbage cans' in which participants throw their own, instead of organizational problems and goals (Cohen et al., 1972). This political process makes taking decisions very difficult, and in many instances leads to decisions that neither threaten any participant nor solve a problem.

Another factor weakening the decision-making power of schools concerns the difficulty to determine cause of and remedy for observed problems. The latter is due to the fact that so many factors play a role (e.g. in case of poor educational results the features of students, teachers, home features, societal patterns) and that their precise influence is uncertain. 'What causes what?' and 'What should be done to achieve or prevent something?' is therefore very difficult to say.

The partial or non-execution of decisions made (Weick, 1982) concerns another feature of school policy-making frequently mentioned in the literature.

Until now we have spoken about schools in general terms, and we have determined some features that schools on average possess with respect to school decision-making. Although these school characteristics may be true for many schools, Marx (1975) has indicated that 'the' school does not exist. Schools vary in their policy-making capacity as a whole (school A on average is more capable in developing school policy than school B) as well as in specific areas of policy-making (school B may be a better policy-developer in policy-making field X than school A, which performs better in field Y).

The degree to which a school benefits from the facilities for computer-assisted policy-making will vary in concordance with the extent to which the prerequisites for policy-making are fulfilled in that school. Thus, if a school's policy-making capacity is small a first prerequisite for benefiting intensively from the power of SISs concerns organizational development in that school.

4 IMPLICATIONS FOR COMPUTER-SUPPORTED DECISION-MAKING

Although SIS-output can be very useful for school policy-making, benefiting from this form of computer-support proves to be far from easy. Information does not directly lead to decisions since decisions are the product of enormous numbers of interacting variables besides pure information (Weiss in Alkin, 1990).

That school managers do not inform their decision-making activities, by analysing trends in and relations between data or by simulating or evaluating the effects of their policy-making, may be caused by their work conditions which do not permit informed decisions, thorough reflection and evaluation (Goodlad, 1975). Using mainly information that is informal, simple, verbal, hot, quickly available and that triggers actions, they take non- or partially informed decisions as a response to this constraint in their working conditions.

Although it will not be easy to change the ways in which school managers operate, given the potential of SISs it is certainly worth trying to let them, and the schools they work in, benefit more from these tools. We should try to make their decisions as informed as possible. However, we are aware that more computer-supported school policy-making will not bring universal happiness. Computers are powerful but also have their limitations. The information they supply can for instance be too general, too old and/or inaccessible (Wild et al., 1992). SIS-information is valuable, but at the same time it is only one kind of information, and this has to be used in combination with other, more informal, types of information. Moreover, even when SISs are used in the desired ways, other school features will make full rational behaviour impossible: the role of political processes, the difficulty to find causes of and remedies for organizational problems, the non/partial execution of problems, the limited human information processing capacity, and the work conditions that make profound, informed problem analysis and problem solving impossible because managers must act quickly.

Despite all these restrictions SISs can be valuable for managing schools and therefore we will now present some proposals for increasing the degree of computer-supported decision-making.

a. The subjective perception of users of the value of information proves to be crucial for the degree to which a certain type of information is used.

   For that reason we must try to influence the perception of school managers, by letting them experience how useful SIS-information can be in the policy-making processes they are involved in. Just as millions of people use computers for their office work because they are aware of the advantages of doing so, experiencing the added-value of computer-supported decision-making most probably will stimulate school staff to use SISs for this goal more. The best strategy to work towards that goal is probably to start with small projects with a high success probability. If school improvement has proven to be possible as a consequence of using computer-generated information, this most probably encourages school staff to invest more in using decision-support systems.

b. School staff do not receive too little information: the problem is that human attention and information processing capacity are scarce relative to the information available (Simon, 1993). SISs must therefore operate intelligently and do something interesting' by outputing information that is useful (e.g. because it helps to improve schools).
   The nature of information influences information usage also in another way. The information SISs generate must not require time consuming retrieval and analysis, but be appealing and invite action. Modern SISs do not meet these demands yet. We therefore should attempt to build SISs that facilitate the easy production and usage of data. The barriers for retrieving and processing interesting SIS-data have to be reduced as much as possible, so that the probability that retrieved information is used will be maximized.

c. Although schools differ regarding their policy-making capacity, they in general are not considered to be very forceful policy-developers and evaluators. Since intensive computer-assisted policy-making and evaluation touches the whole school organization, it requires fundamental organizational development in many schools. Such development processes should bring schools to a level of organizational functioning that enables them to:
   - decide which SIS-information they need;
   - retrieve (part of) the information they need from a SIS;
   - interpret the data obtained in such a way that it can be used quickly for decision-making;
   - use the information for developing, implementing and evaluating school policy.

These activities demand a lot from schools and therefore very few schools master these skills. The complexity of decision-support in schools in general is underestimated. It is our mission to develop strategies for implementation and organizational development that prepare school staff for this comprehensive task.

Only if we are able to design and implement SISs that produce information that is interesting, easy to use and that matches the nature of schools, and if the value of these systems can be shown to school staff and we are successful in finding ways to equip for full system usage, only then might we change the nature of schooling in a fundamental way.

5 REFERENCES

Alkin, M.C. (1990) *Debates on Evaluation.* Sage Publications, Beverly Hills.

Cohen, M.D., March, J.G. and Olson, J.P. (1972) A garbage-can model of organizational choice. *Administrative Science Quarterly,* **17**, 1-25.

Goodlad, J.I. (1975) *The dynamics of educational change: toward responsive schools.* McGraw-Hill, New York.

Leighwood, K.A. and Montgomery, D.J. (1982) The role of the elementary school principal in program improvement. *Review of Educational Research,* **52**, 309-339.

Marx, E.C.H. (1975) *De organisatie van scholengemeenschappen in onderwijskundige optiek.* [The organization of comprehensive schools from an educational point of view]. Wolters-Noordhoff, Groningen.

McPherson, R.B., Crowson, R. and Pitner, N.J. (1986) *Managing uncertainty: administrative theory and practice in education.* C.E. Merril Publishing Company, Columbus.

Mintzberg, H. (1989) *Mintzberg on management.* Free Press, New York.

Riehl, C., Pallas, G. and Natriello, G. (1992) *More responsive high schools student information and problem-solving.* Paper presented at AERA conference, San-Francisco.

Simon, H.A. (1993) Decision making: rational, nonrational, and irrational. *Educational Administration Quarterly,* **29**, 392-411.

Sproull, L.S. (1981) Managing education programs: a micro-behavioral analysis. *Human Organization,* **40**, 113-122.

Sproull, L.S. and Zubrow, D. (1981) Performance information in school systems: perspectives from organization theory. *Educational Administration Quarterly,* **17**, 61-79.

Visscher, A.J. (1991) School administrative computing: a framework for analysis. *Journal of Research on Computing in Education*, **24**, 1-19.

Visscher, A.J. (1992) *Design and evaluation of a computer-assisted management information system for secondary schools* (Ph.D. dissertation). University of Twente, Enschede.

Visscher, A.J. (1995) Computer-assisted school administration and management: where are we and where should we go?, in *Information Technology in Educational Management* (ed. B.Z. Barta, M. Telem and Y. Gev), Chapman and Hall, London.

Weick, K.E. (1982) *Administering education in loosely coupled schools.* Phi Delta Kappan, 673-676.

Wild, P., Scivier, J.E. and Richardson, S.J. (1992) Evaluating information technology-supported local management of schools: the User Acceptability Audit, *Educational Management and Administration*, **20(1)**, 41-48.

Wild, P., Scivier, J. and Richardson, S. (1992) An Evaluation of a LEA's Secondary Schools IT system for LMS Support. *Education Management and Administration,* **20(4)**, 40-48.

6 BIOGRAPHY

A. J. Visscher received his Ph.D. at The University of Twente for his dissertation entitled "Design and Evaluation of a Computer-Assisted Management Information System for Secondary Schools". He has been working as an Assistant Professor in the Faculty of Educational Science and Technology since 1983. In collaboration with others he designed an integrated school information system (SIS) for secondary schools and evaluated its impact over a period of three years. He is the editor of two special issues of scientific journals on computerised SISs and has published numerous articles on this topic.

PART THREE

Organisational Culture

9

Information systems effectiveness and organisational culture: an underlying model for ITEM evaluation

C.D. O'Mahony
Department of Computing and Technology
Australian Catholic University
e-mail: C.O'Mahony@castle.acu.edu.au

Abstract

How to determine the effectiveness of an organisation's information systems is the subject of continued debate in the IS community. Difficulties surround such issues as agreement on evaluation criteria, agreement on quantitative and qualitative methods, and the politicising of the evaluation process. In this paper, the author relates the nature of school information systems to mainstream information systems research. The literature surrounding Information Technology in Educational Management (ITEM) is reviewed, and an underlying model for school IS evaluation is presented. Using previous results as a basis, the author proposes a strategy for investigating the link between a school's culture and its IS emphases.

Keywords

Educational management, administration, evaluation/formative, modelling

1 INTRODUCTION

Any discussion of Information Technology in Educational Management (ITEM) makes assumptions concerning broader concepts from the domain of educational administration and the domain of information systems. School effectiveness and school culture are two key concepts in the educational administration literature that require elaboration. This analysis will show that both concepts have important implications for ITEM.

'Effectiveness' refers to an organisation's ability to meet the various needs of its constituent groups. In terms of schools, these groups are perceived as Teachers, Administrators, Parents and Students (Friedman, 1994). Definitions of school effectiveness are often, however, subjective and lack clarity (Glatter, 1986). Turney et al (1992) identify three major viewpoints on school effectiveness. These are: effectiveness based on measurable student achievement outcomes; a humanist, ethnographic tradition of effectiveness in relationships; and organisational culture as a key determinant of effectiveness.

In the prevailing economic climate, demands for business-like efficiency in schools colour the debate on what constitutes school effectiveness. A number of educational researchers have compared school effectiveness factors with attributes of business excellence, in particular using studies published by Peters & Waterman (1982). In these studies, good schools are characterised by factors similar to those that characterise successful companies. These factors emphasise the importance of "people within the organisation, their values, their relationships and their perceptions, rather than on the structure or the product in terms of measurable outcomes or dollars saved" (Turney et al, 1992). Culture or value-set is seen to determine organisational excellence.

'Culture' is a recurrent theme in educational administration and school effectiveness literature. Again, this is a concept that eludes clear definition. The tone or climate of a school is often obvious, but hard to define. Turney et al (1992) suggest that there may be an executive culture, several teacher cultures and numerous student cultures in a school. They note that articulation between these is needed in order to form an overall organisational culture. Again, this theme has its parallels in management literature (Handy & Aitken, 1986; Dunphy & Stace, 1992), and a growing recognition in IS research (Romm et al, 1991; Yetton & Southon, 1994).

Key issues for research in ITEM, then, are the contribution of school information systems to overall school effectiveness, and the importance and impact of school culture on school information systems.

2 AN EVOLVING MANAGEMENT SECTOR

Empirical evidence is clear that schools are seeking to better manage their IS resource (Barta et al, 1995). Like many other organisations, schools have been keen to acquire and deploy new technologies as they develop. Attempts to categorise the development of ITEM have identified three distinct stages over the past twenty years (Visscher, 1991a; 1995). The first stage was internally driven, whereby enthusiastic teachers utilised their existing knowledge to provide local solutions in specific areas, such as timetabling (Smith & Hartley, 1983; Goodsell, 1995). A further stage was characterised by the emergence of hardware and software suppliers, offering solutions which involved the school as a passive participant. Since the mid-1980s, the emphasis has moved towards more integrated school information systems. This third stage is characterised by larger centralised projects that have attempted to deliver a total school package. Examples include OASIS in NSW (Dale & Habib, 1991), HKSAS in Hong Kong (Fung, 1991) and SIMS in England (Bird, 1991).

Visscher's stages have many parallels in mainstream IS. Evolutionary theories have abounded in the IS literature since 1974 (Gibson & Nolan, 1974; Nolan, 1979). Although the Nolan model has received mixed support, a similar evolutionary framework was proposed by Hirschheim et al (1988). In this instance, the model comprised three IS management phases, being "Delivery", "Reorientation" and "Reorganisation". The evolution from one phase to another is described as a function of time and an increasing education level among IS staff. Each phase is characterised by different priorities, management postures and business focus.

The author's work over the past two years has concentrated on collection of data from schools in England and Australia concerning existing IS management methods, and the development of techniques for school IS evaluation. One recurring problem noted by the author has been that purchases and implementations of IT have often been uncontrolled in schools, leading to technical incompatibilities and staff resentment (O'Mahony & Dampney, 1995). Like Visscher, the author has noted a trend towards more sophistication in ITEM. Among independent schools, for instance, a trend towards the employment of professional IS managers was clear (O'Mahony, 1995). Between 1990 and 1995, the number of IS managers had grown from 13 persent to 65 percent in the schools studied.

Another critical insight was the influence of a school's culture on its information systems resource. In particular, this was made manifest through different religious denominations. Using the author's evaluation instrument, Catholic schools rated their information systems as less successful than their non-Catholic counterparts. Individual differences between school cultures are easily perceived. Myths and shared values are made manifest through such devices as mottos and mission or vision statements. What is not easy to perceive is why and how culture influences school IS management. The reasons for this influence lie in the area of organisational culture, and beg further investigation.

3 PERSPECTIVES ON IS EVALUATION

As schools make greater investments in their IS/IT portfolios, the evaluation of ITEM is becoming a major concern. The literature in educational administration and educational computing has little to offer in terms of evaluation tools (Telem, 1993). Visscher's review of approaches to computer assisted school administration led to the conclusion that "None of the countries has studied in a systematic way the quality of the available information systems. This is a universal problem; in fact, very little empirical data on system quality are available. ... This is regrettable since insight into variables that determine system quality can help to create better systems." (Visscher, 1991b)

The literature in IS research and practice is no closer in offering a solution. Hirschheim & Smithson (1987) noted that "Although the information systems literature appears to be in widespread agreement regarding the need to evaluate the product and process of system development, the vehicle for undertaking such an evaluation is far from clear." More contemporary writers demonstrate that the area of IS evaluation is the subject of healthy debate. Bunker et al (1991) noted that "Definitions of the measurement of IS success in organisations is still the subject of fierce debate." Similarly Fitzgerald (1991) pointed out that "A review of relevant literature shows that ... very little research into ways of measuring the effectiveness of information systems strategic planning (ISSP) is reported."

Methods for IS evaluation fall on a broad spectrum from hard, quantitative techniques to soft, qualitative techniques. Quantitative approaches include measurement of IS in terms of return on investment (Weill, 1991; Willcocks, 1994). Work by DeLone & McLean (1992) suggests on the other hand that IS success is much more difficult to quantify. Hirschheim & Smithson (1987) assert that a pragmatic approach to IS evaluation is important. They point out that, although evaluation instruments should indeed be valid and reliable, they should also have practical application, and should provide a means for genuine information systems improvement. Practicality, they declare, is more important than theoretical elegance. In addition to methodological concerns, they and other researchers have noted that in many cases the evaluation exercise becomes a political exercise, thus sabotaging any potential benefits to be gained (Sauer, 1993).

The thriving debate on IS evaluation agrees with research in educational administration at least in this respect - that "effectiveness is one of the most pervasive yet least delineated organisational constructs relevant to all participants in organisational life" (Goodman & Pennings, 1977). In DeLone & McLean's terms, the dependent variable remains elusive.

4 AN UNDERLYING MODEL

Friedman (1994) has suggested that school information systems can strategically affect four key groups. These groups are Administrators, Teachers, Students and Parents. Such ITEM activities as student registration, fees collection, assessment reporting and timetabling require the participation of at least some of these four groups. The use of IT to facilitate these activities requires appropriate consideration of multiple constituent needs. Effective school IS must meet the requirements of all four groups.. Using this insight as a basis, the author proposes the PACT (Parents, Administrators, Children and Teachers) construct as an overall model for school effectiveness (Figure 1).

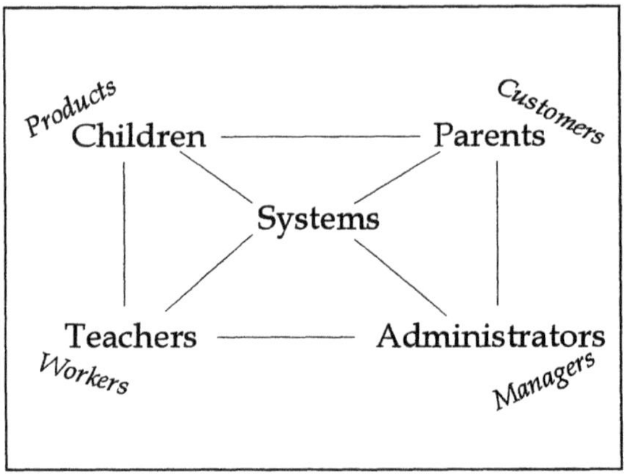

Figure 1 O'Mahony's PACT Model.

The PACT model highlights a number of relationships and dynamics within a school. The teaching/learning relationship, for instance, is readily recognised in the model, which encompasses both curriculum and administrative IT. Teachers and children make use of a variety of educational technologies to enhance the learning experience. Relationships between administrators and the other school groups are supported by a wide range of information systems. Management reporting systems, timetable generators and payroll packages all support information flow between administrators and teachers. Parents interact with the school through such functions as assessment reporting, pupil registration and invoicing, all of which can be supported by ITEM.

In a very real sense, the PACT model describes the communication of information throughout a school. This conforms with the body of opinion that positions information flow within the organisational communications domain (Bordow & More, 1991; McGrath et al, 1995). As seen in Figure 1, the PACT model can be easily generalised to represent other organisations, whereby the Administrators represent Managers, Teachers represent Workers, Parents represent Customers, and Children represent Products.

As in other organisations, interactions between different constituent groups in schools can be fraught with problems. In particular, they are prone to the classic clash between practitioners and bureaucrats. This clash has been conclusively argued in work by Yetton & Southon (1994). Using Scott-Morton's MIT'90s framework, Yetton & Southon (1994) described IS dissatisfaction in terms of conflicts between hospital clinicians and hospital administrators. In the extreme, these two groups may be opposed in their strategy, structure, processes and technology.

The case for schools is much the same, with conflicts between teachers and administrators being identified in previous work by the author (O'Mahony, 1995). The PACT model can thus be viewed in dichotomy, with teachers and children in the qualitative, pastoral, effective camp, and administrators and parents in the quantitative, pragmatic, efficient camp of the school. In reality, the school community is not so clearly polarised, but an imbalance between these two viewpoints can lead to a mismatch in school IS management.

Enid Mumford has highlighted the need for an integrated approach to IS management. She states "one of the most important principles of socio-technical design ... that if a technical system is created at the expense of a social system, the results obtained will be sub-optimal." (Mumford, 1994). This principle translates well to the PACT model: school information systems which do not support all four (PACT) groups adequately are sub-optimal. In schools, the optimal balance must be found between the quantitative and qualitative dichotomy, between efficiency and effectiveness, between "PA" and "CT".

The author has referred previously to the notion of organisational culture as a key determinant of effectiveness (Turney et al, 1992). Recent IS research also supports this claim (Romm et al, 1991; Galliers & Baker, 1995). The PACT model suggests that a school's culture is a function of the four key groups: Parents, Administrators, Children and Teachers. Differing cultures influence the design, development and deployment of school IS. The 'Optimisation Framework' (Figure 2) represents the dynamics of differing school cultures on information systems emphases. In this figure, the "PA" groups are shown on the "Administration IT" axis, and the "CT" groups are shown on the "Curriculum IT" axis.

Contrary to Yetton & Southon (1994), it is the author's contention that efficiency and effectiveness are not diametrically opposed. Rather than being at opposing poles of the same axis, they in fact represent two orthogonal axes. Thus the key to optimising IS in schools is in balancing the cultural dynamics between Parent/Administrator ('efficient') groups and Child/Teacher ('effective') groups. The ideal situation for a school is represented in the top right quadrant, where group satisfaction for both curriculum and administrative IT is high. In this case, ITEM is optimal, being both effective and efficient.

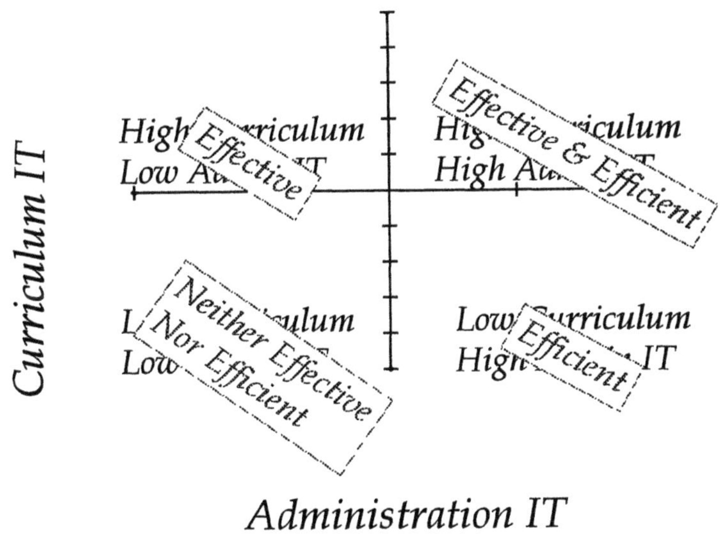

Figure 2 Optimising school information system.

Initial support for this framework has already been achieved through case studies conducted by the author in England and Australia during 1994/5. These case studies have identified different organisational cultures prevalent in schools, and positioned their IS emphases accordingly on the author's optimisation grid. In both England and Australia, comparisons were made between State-run schools and independent schools with different religious affiliations. The general evolutionary trend is from the bottom left quadrant to the top right quadrant. Complete balance between the two axes was rare, however, with schools distributed towards either the effective or efficient quadrants. Details of these preliminary case studies are available from the author.

5 APPLYING THE PACT MODEL

The author's PACT model is currently undergoing further validation through a large research project involving both NSW State schools and Catholic Systemic schools. The first phase of the project involves a survey of 120 schools. The survey instrument comprises a six page questionnaire, developed from the author's previous pilot studies, and in collaboration with experts from both the information systems and educational administration domains. After mapping results to the author's Optimisation Framework, the second phase will involve in-depth case studies of specific school archetypes.

It is anticipated that results from the research project will relate closely to conclusions and implications in the existing IS and ITEM literature. Firstly, it is expected that survey responses will demonstrate evolutionary trends among schools using ITEM. Evolutionary models have abounded in IS literature since Nolan (Gibson & Nolan, 1974; Nolan, 1979). Other examples of evolutionary models include Hirschheim et al (1988) and Visscher (1991a). Although the validity and generalisability of evolutionary models is often criticised in the literature, they persist and enjoy ongoing popularity.

Secondly, it is expected that results of the case study phase will support the growing awareness that organisational culture is an independent variable which is crucial to IS optimality. This recognition has arisen from practical research in public hospital systems (Yetton & Southon, 1994) and tertiary educational institutions (Jordan, 1994), and theoretical work by DeLone & McLean (1992).

The implications of the author's PACT model have a strong bearing on planning for schools of the future. From a reactive standpoint, ITEM developers need to consider carefully the impact of organisational culture on IS/IT developments. Conversely, ITEM developers need to consider carefully the impact of their developments on existing organisational culture. From a proactive standpoint, ITEM development can be used as an agent of change, enabling schools to progress from a position of low optimality to a position of high optimality, achieving both efficiency and effectiveness in their ITEM infrastructure. In a global climate of economic rationalism which seeks to do more with less, such strategies are particularly pertinent.

6 CONCLUSION

The evaluation of information systems in small organisations is an area of research that is still 'pre-scientific' (McGrath et al, 1995). This paper has discussed school IS evaluation in the broader context of IS research. Key issues identified are the importance of organisational culture to IS evaluations, and the inadequacy of quantitative models in assessing IS optimality.

To this end, the author has proposed the PACT model which describes the influence of constituent groups on school information systems, and an Optimisation Framework which enables analysis of the link between differing school cultures and their relative IS emphases, and particularly promotes a balance between efficiency and effectiveness cultures. The framework has already received anecdotal support, which the author aims to verify through further survey and case studies.

In this way, it is intended to expand our understanding of the principles which direct effective management of information systems in schools, which will lead to improved design, development and deployment of ITEM in the future.

7 REFERENCES

Barta, B.Z., Telem, M. and Gev, Y. (Eds) (1995) *Information technology in educational management.* Chapman & Hall, London.

Bird, P. (1991) Computer assisted school administration in England. *Journal of Research in Computing in Education,* **24(1)**, 20-40.

Bordow, A., and More, E. (1991) *Managing organisational communication.* Longman, Sydney.

Bunker, D.J., Dean, R.G., Edmundson, R.H. (1991) The management of the information systems function. *ISOP* 1991, Wollongong, 161-181.

Dale, D., and Habib, A (1991) Administrative computing in the Australian educational system. *Journal of Research on Computing in Education,* **24(1)**, 120-145.

DeLone, W.H., and McLean, E.R. (1992) Information systems success: the quest for the dependent variable. *Information Systems Research,* **3(1)**, 60-95.

Dunphy, D. and Stace D. (1992) *Under new management: Australian organisations in transition.* McGraw-Hill, Sydney.

Fitzgerald, E. (1991) Effectiveness measures for IS strategic planning. *ISOP*, Wollongong, 387-404.

Friedman, E.A. (1994) A management perspective on effective technology integration: top ten questions for school administrators. *T H E Journal,* **22(4)**, 89-90.

Fung, A.C.W. (1991) Computer assisted school administration in Hong Kong. *Journal of Research on Computing in Education,* **24(1)**, 41-61.

Galliers, R.D. and Baker, B.S.H. (1995) An approach to business process re-engineering: the contribution of socio-technical and soft OR concepts. *INFOR,* **33(4)**, 263-278.

Gibson, C. and Nolan, R.L. (1974) Managing the four stages of EDP growth. *Harvard Business Review,* **52(1)**, 76-88.

Glatter, R. (1986) The management of school improvement, in *Understanding school management,* Open University Press, Milton Keynes.

Goodman, P.S. and Pennings, J.M. (1977) *New perspectives on organisational effectiveness.* Jossey-Bass, san Francisco.

Goodsell, R. (1995) *An investigation into timetabling in schools.* Unpublished M. Comp. thesis, Macquarie University, Australia.

Handy, C. and Aitken, R. (1986) *Understanding schools as organisations.* Penguin, Harmondsworth.

Hirschheim, R., Earl, M., Feeny, D. and Lockett, M. (1988) An exploration into the management of the information systems function: key issues and an evolutionary model, in *Proceedings on the Joint International Symposium on Information Systems*, Sydney.

Hirschheim, R. and Smithson, S. (1987) Information systems evaluation: myth and reality, in *Information analysis: selected readings* (ed. R.D. Galliers), Addison-Wesley, Wokingham, UK.

Jordan, E. (1994) Information strategy and organisation structure. *Information Systems Journal,* **4**, 253-270.

McGrath, G.M., Dampney, C.N.G. and More, E. (1995) MP/L1: an automated model of organisational power and its application as a conflict prediction aid in information

systems strategy implementation, in *The 11th conference on artificial intelligence for applications*. IEEE Computer Society Press, California, 56-64.
Mumford, E. (1994) New treatments or old remedies: is business process re-engineering really socio-technical design?. *Journal of Strategic Information Systems*, **3(4)**.
Nolan, R.L. (1979) Managing the crises in data processing. *Harvard Business Review*, **57(2)**, 115-126.
O'Mahony, C.D. (1995) *Improving school information systems management: the quest for quality*. Australian Catholic University, Sydney.
O'Mahony, C.D. and Dampney, C.N.G. (1995) Trends in the management of school information systems, in *Proceedings: 6th Australasian Conference on Information Systems*. Curtin University, Perth, WA, 613-631.
Peters, T.J. and Waterman, R.H. (1982) *In search of excellence: lessons from America's best-run companies*. Harper & Row, New York.
Romm, T., Pliskin, N. and Weber, Y. (1991) Identifying organisational culture clash in MIS implementations: when is it worth the effort?. *Information Management*, **21(2)**, 99-109.
Sauer, C. (1993) *Why information systems fail: a case study approach*. Alfred Waller, Henley-on-Thames.
Smith, J. and Hartley, B. (1983) *Microcomputers for school management*. Nepean C.A.E., Sydney.
Telem, M. (1993) Information technology: a missing link in educational research. *Journal of Research on Computing in Education*, **26(1)**, 123-142.
Turney, C., Hatton, N., Laws, K., Sinclair, K. and Smith, D. (1992) *The school manager*. Allen and Unwin, North Sydney.
Visscher, A.J. (1991a) School administrative computing: a framework for analysis. *Journal of Research on Computing in Education*, **24(1)**, 1-19.
Visscher, A.J. (1991b) Computer assisted school administration and management: the state of the art in seven nations. *Journal of Research on Computing in Education*, **24(1)**, 146-167.
Visscher, A.J. (1995) A fundamental methodology for designing management information systems for schools. *Journal of Research on Computing in Education*, **28(1)**, 231-249.
Weill, P. (1991) The information technology payoff: implications for investment appraisal. *Australian Accounting Review*, **1(1)**, 2-11.
Willcocks, L. (1994) *Information management: the evaluation of information systems investments*. Chapman and Hall, London.
Yetton, P. and Southon, G. (1994) *The impact of strategic conflict on Information technology: a case study of a public teaching hospital*. Australian Graduate School of Management, Kensington, NSW.

8 BIOGRAPHY

Christopher O'Mahony is an Associate Lecturer in the Department of Computing and Technology at the Australian Catholic University. As well as holding academic qualifications in Information Systems, he has many years experience in business, particularly the finance industry. He has a growing reputation in the use of qualitative methods for information systems research. Results of his research have been presented at the Fourth and Fifth Australasian Conferences on Information Systems, and at the Second European Conference on IT Evaluation.

10

The impact of organizational culture on the success of information technology projects

M.G. Reyes
Management Engineering Department, Ateneo de Manila University
Loyola Heights, Quezon City, Philippines
Phone: (632)-9244601ext 2762 *Fax: (632)-9244599*
e-mail: greyes@admu.edu.ph

Abstract
This paper discusses organizational culture and presents a model for managing cultural change in order to foster an organizational climate conducive to the successful implementation of information systems. Four key points are made in this paper: 1) organizational culture is an information-processing system composed of people and is fueled by values and beliefs, 2) there are four types of organizational cultures based on level of risk of the tasks performed and the speed of feedback, 3) essential to an organization's adaptability is a culture where planning and information management is an integral part of the organization's processes, 4) building this planning culture involves the use of existing change forces based on the type of culture prevalent in the organization.

Keywords
Educational management, culture, information technology, organizations

1 INTRODUCTION

The system of values prevalent in any society not only influences the way organizations are structured but the way organizations use technology. Values and structures within an organization, as articulated in and supported by the organization's culture, can either limit or encourage technological innovation. For an information system to produce the envisioned benefits, the system has to fit into the organizational culture for it to be acceptable and useful. On the other hand, introducing new technology molds a new set of organizational values and drives changes in organizational structure. With the emergence of decision support systems, for example, the power to make crucial business decisions filters down the ranks to the lower levels of the traditional organizational heirarchy, thus eliminating the need for middle management. The changes in the value system that technology projects require for success, and the changes these projects will bring, calls for an awareness of the significance and impact of culture on the deployment of technology in organizations. While change must be managed during the whole systems development lifecycle, the challenge lies in managing the change upfront, before information technology is introduced.

This paper discusses the elements of organizational culture that will create a climate conducive to technological change and innovation. This will be done by first presenting the concept of organizational culture: what it is and why it is important. The next section will discuss a method aimed at fostering an organizational culture that can assimilate change. Central to the change management process is the information systems project manager who has a great degree of influence on the organization's culture.

2 ORGANIZATIONAL CULTURE AND TECHNOLOGY

The successful planning and implementation of new systems development projects rely, in no small way, on the development of a shared vision and the articulation of a shared culture that recognizes the importance of change. Alter (1988) stated that the US government is lagging 5 to 10 years behind the private sector in the adoption of IS technologies. He recognized that one obstacle had to do with a lack of leadership, coordinated planning, and integration. The solution, he states, is a more effective leadership that is based on a clear line of command, and that promotes a climate throughout the state government that favors information innovation and gets management involved.

According to research conducted through the Massachussetts Institute of Technology's Management in the 1990's Program, it is the inadequate management of organizational change that emerges as the major reason organizations do not achieve the full benefits of information technology (IT). As IT and business processes both spiral upward in complexity, the need to change the organizational structure and culture becomes more pronounced. This is so because IT moves the locus of knowledge, and its concomitant power, within the organization; IT changes the time frame within which decisions are made and processes are completed; and IT creates new organizational structures. As change is needed, resistance and other change management issues have to be addressed. But even with a commitment to manage change, companies are likely to find that people's inability to change, not technology, is the limiting factor in transforming organizations (Benjamin and Blunt, 1992).

Definitions of organizational culture

Organizational culture can be defined as "a system of beliefs or set of values that [is] transmitted, carried out, and upheld by the entire physical, psychological and social milieu of an organization" (Louis, 1980). It can also be described as a series of "cultural networks" which are composed of various "media" used to collect, interpret, share, store, and directly apply information about the organization's values or beliefs. Each cultural network uses the cultural media in its own unique way, for example, an "old boy" network of long-time workers who act as informal "historians" by telling stories about "how things were when this place first got started." (Deal and Kennedy, 1982). Cultural media can be classified into four types that embody or convey what an organization stands for: 1) heroes, 2) rites and rituals, 3) myths and legends, and 4) physical settings and work technologies.

A more formal framework describing organizational culture defines it as an information-processing system that is organic, not mechanized, because it has a purpose, it is fueled by values, and it is composed of people. This is so because information has no "value" or "meaning" unless and until people ascribe value or meaning to it. The organizational culture interacts with its external environment both at an input point (resources flowing into the organization) and at an output point (services, products delivered). This shows that an organization's culture is dependent upon its external environment for resources and for purpose. The culture has a feedback loop through which the organization is informed of the degree to which the organization is meeting external expectations (Harman and McClure, 1985). Thus, the organization's culture embodies all the elements necessary for the organization, and for the people who are the organization, to succeed in the organization's particular social and industry environments. Beliefs and values are the core of the culture because they are the reasons for the organization's existence.

Cultural Types and Subcultures

Deal and Kennedy (1982) have identified two factors that create cultural types: (1) the degree of risk associated with the tasks the organization must perform in order to succeed in its environment, and (2) the speed with which the organization learns whether or not its strategies and actions were successful. Figure 1 shows four cultural types based on the levels of these two factors.

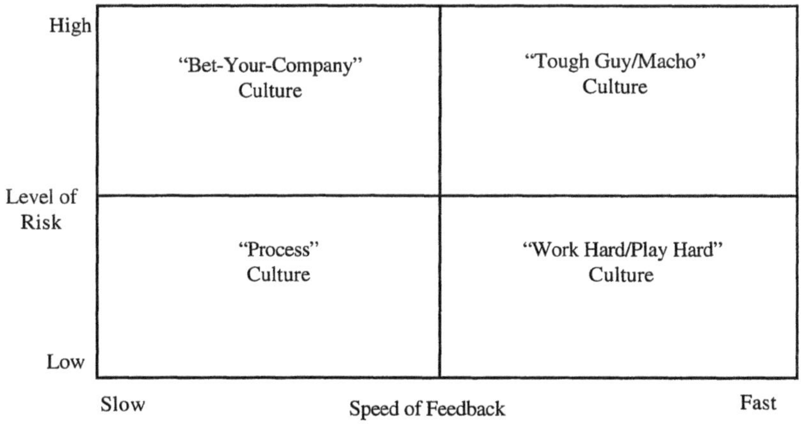

Figure 1 Cultural types (based on Deal, T. and Kennedy, A. (1982) Corporate Cultures. Addison-Wesley, Reading, MA).

As can be seen, given risk-levels and speed of feedback, it is the availability of information and the need for information which produces different types of organizational cultures and sub-cultures.

The Culture in Educational Institutions

It can be argued that since the benefits of one's education cannot be immediately realized, educational institutions are organizations with predominantly low feedback; schools cannot immediately gauge the success of their actions or strategies, unlike organizations in advertising or manufacturing.

The planning and administrative functions within educational institutions are generally high-risk functions; poor planning and inadequate administrative practices will inevitably result in the poor delivery of educational services.

The Importance of a Culture

With a higher level of risk comes a high degree of uncertainty towards a project. With a longer period of feedback comes a greater degree of ambiguity of the purpose of a project. Organizational culture is important because it is through this that employees cope with uncertainty and ambiguity. Organizations that excel at their business and have learned to deal with risk and ambiguity have one common trait: information is widely available to employees at all levels of the organization, and information sharing is actively encouraged and rewarded (Peters and Waterman, 1982). With the information sharing comes the maintenance and development of that system of beliefs that push an organization forward. This kind of successful culture is called a 'planning culture'.

A planning culture

A planning culture is defined as:

> "a widely shared belief or philosophy, which is expressed in an organization's culture, that planning and information management are an integral part of the organization's essential tasks and, when conducted effectively, promote better organizational performance by engendering and enhancing organization members' personal commitment to excellence and continuous improvement" (Harman and McClure, 1985).

It is with this planning culture that favorable organizational attitudes may be developed towards adaptiveness, flexibility, and innovation. Coordination of effort across functional boundaries is one way to ensure the success of information systems. Integrating the information systems function into the business essentially means building a planning culture that recognizes information management as integral to the business. One way to achieve this is for the CEO to create the planning and control mechanisms within which his managers do their planning and controlling, particularly with regard to IS.

3 ORGANIZATIONAL CHANGE

Building a planning culture

Harman and McClure proposed a generic three-phased plan for building a planning culture. The plan depicts the creation of a planning culture as a continuous process with a feedback loop from the third phase back to the first phase.

The first phase involves envisioning a planning culture within the organization and this requires top management or project managers to display their values and beliefs by making sure that they are consistent in what they say and do. Here the manager seeks to distribute a sense of responsibility for the organization by concentrating upon the development, as opposed to the evaluation, of employees. This is called the ethic of creation. Once the managers begin to exemplify this ethic of creation, the second phase can begin.

The second phase involves creating a blueprint for change. This is done by identifying existing change forces within the organization, an effort that will enable management to deal with resistance to change by powering the change effort with change processes already underway within the organization. This way the change will be perceived as a natural response to pressing or widely felt needs with which the organization must cope (Moss, 1983). Certain change forces are characteristic of the predominant cultural type exhibited by the organization. Cultures which exist within a high-risk environment rely more on planned types of change forces, such as strategic decisions, as compared to low-risk cultures. These cultures actively promote change, while low risk cultures are more "reactive" by nature. The cultures created by slower feedback cycles and lower environmental risk tend to have gradual departures from tradition as the key force for change. See Table 1.

Table 1 Forces for Change for Different Cultural Types (Harman and McClure, 1983)

Type of Culture or Subculture	*Level of Environmental Risk*	*Most Likely Pre-existing Force for Change*	*Type of Change Force*
Tough Guy/Macho	High	Individual Prime Movers Strategic Decisions Crisis/Galvanizing Event	Planned Planned Natural
Work Hard/Play Hard	Low	Gradual Departures from Tradition	Natural
Bet-Your-Company	High	Strategic Decisions Action Vehicles	Planned Planned
Process	Low	Gradual Departure from Tradition Action Vehicles	Natural Planned

The third phase in the cultural change process is a transition phase wherein the change that has been initiated begins to form sturdier foundations. Encouraging modification of procedures to reflect new values promotes greater participation in and acceptance of the change, and shows that management is consistent in both word and deed. Monitoring the effect on the organization's bottom line is needed to ensure that the change is positive, shown in effects such as reduced turnover or increased employee productivity. Communication in this phase is critical in order to avoid hostility and resentment.

Harman and McClure also propose certain change tactics for each of the different change forces. See Table 2.

Table 2 Change tactics for different cultural forces

Forces for change within culture	*Corresponding Change Tactic(s)*
Action vehicles	• Use transition rituals such as celebration or award dinners • Provide transition training such as using problem-solving simulations to spur creativity and innovation • Build tangible symbols of the new directions, such as changing the configuration of the offices, simplifying internal review forms, introducing new technology

Individual prime movers	• Position a hero in the change process, such as in giving recognition to successful project directors • Bring in outside experts
Strategic decisions	• Insist on building security during transition, such as in involving people in planning committees, searching for seed money to support projects
Crisis or galvanizing event	• Insist on security by bringing in successful outsiders • Call on heroes
Gradual departures from tradition	• Use transitional rituals such as developing new procedures • Provide transition training such as training employees in new procedures • Build new symbols such as producing new procedures manuals

Those responsible for overseeing a new project should also prove adept at overseeing the cultural change process because before they initiate a project this process must take place. Managing change is important because employees my revert to former attitudes and modes of behaviour. This can happen if the employees perceive the change process as creating uncertainty, upheaval, and unnecessary hardship. For those in charge of projects, time and patience is required of them especially during project start-up when they simultaneously have to get the project running and have it integrated into the culture.

4 CONCLUSION

Organizational culture has been described as an “organic” network composed of “heroes,” rites and rituals, “myths and legends,” and physical settings and work technologies. It is through this network that the values and beliefs of the organization are expressed. Since organizational culture is the means through which the organization copes with risk and ambiguity, the nature of this culture can either promote or hinder the successful deployment of IT in an organization. Often, the power and benefit of an information system is not limited by technology but by people’s inability to change. The more ambiguous and risky an IS project is, the less likely it is to be accepted and successful. Organizations that have successfully dealt with ambiguity and risk have created a culture where planning and information management are processes considered critical to and an integral part of the business. To create such a culture, top management must begin by envisioning this end. Change management starts by recognizing and using existing culture change forces already underway in an organization to channel and focus the change effort.

5 REFERENCES

Alter, A. (1988) The art of the state. *CIO*, **2(2)**, 28-39.

Benjamin, R. and Blunt, J. (1992) Critical IT issues: the next ten years. *Sloan Management Revie*, Summer 1992, 16-17.

Deal, T. and Kennedy, A. (1982) *Corporate cultures.* Addison-Wesley, Reading MA.

Harman, K. and McClure, C. (1985) *Strategic planning for sponsored projects administration.* Greenwood Press, Connecticut.

Louis, M. (1980) Organizations as culture-bearing milieux, in *Organizational Symbolism* (eds. L. Pondy et al.), University of Chicago Press, Chicago.

Moss, K. (1983) *The change masters.* Simon and Shuster, New York.

Peters, T. and Waterman, R. (1982) *In search of excellence: lessons from America's best run companies.* Warner Books, New York.

6 BIOGRAPHY

Gina Reyes teaches systems analysis and design at the Ateneo de Manila University. She has undergraduate degrees in management science and in computer science. She holds a masters degree in Information Systems from Golden Gate University in San Francisco. At present, she is working on various administrative information systems projects in the Ateneo.

PART FOUR

Evaluation & Implementation

11

Implementation of the School Administration and Management System: a Hong Kong experience

B.C.H. Ip Tsang and S.Y.F. Lee
23/F, Wu Chung House, Wanchai, Hong Kong
Fax: (852)-25758952

Abstract

In September 1993, the Hong Kong Government allocated a sum of HK$570 million (US$73 million) for the implementation of a five-year Information Systems Strategic Plan in the Education Department. About forty percent of the sum is for the School Administration and Management System (SAMS) project. This paper aims at sharing the experience of implementing that project in Hong Kong schools. Extensive user participation and carefully planned implementation tasks are the key elements in the SAMS project. The paper describes the mode and the extent of user participation and the major implementatation tasks required. Management issues arising from the implementation of SAMS are highlighted and the way forward in the management of the project is proposed.

Keywords

Educational management, government, information technology

1 INTRODUCTION

In 1990 the Hong Kong Government Public Sector Reform Study Team recommended that the Education Department (ED) should obtain expert help to identify the information needs of the Schools Education Programme and develop appropriate management information systems. A consultancy study was then conducted and a five-year Information Systems Strategic Plan (ISSP) was proposed. The ISSP covered two parts: Corporate Systems for the ED and SAMS for the schools.

In September 1993 the Hong Kong Government allocated a sum of HK $570 million (US$73 million) for the implementation of the ISSP in the ED within a five-year period, about 40 percent of which was for the SAMS project. The SAMS project aims to provide an integrated computerised system to schools for supporting the major management and administrative processes, and for transmitting electronically information on students, teachers and schools between schools and ED. The SAMS consists of twelve core applications and four supporting applications.

The SAMS project adopts an in-house development approach in which the Information Technology Services Department (ITSD) of the Hong Kong Government acts as the developer. Two major methodologies have been used for the project management and system development. They are the methodology of Projects In Controlled Environment (PRINCE) for the project management and the Structured System Analysis and Design Methodology (SSADM) for the development of applications.

The SAMS project is characterised by the following features:

1. *Linkage with ED*: Schools and ED communicate frequently with each other, through circulars, letters, surveys or forms. Under the ISSP, there is a standardisation of data definitions across the ED Corporate Systems and SAMS. Coupled with the provision of a dial-up telephone line, communication between both parties through electronic media is enabled.

1. *Bilingual system design supporting both Chinese and English languages*: The Official Language Ordinance of Hong Kong provides that the official languages in Hong Kong are English and Chinese. In practice, for undertaking the administrative tasks, Hong Kong secondary schools usually use both languages while primary schools use Chinese language predominantly. To meet the schools' needs, the SAMS is a bilingual system with the options of Chinese and English screen display. In view of the limited Chinese character set available from Microsoft Chinese Windows, the ED has co-ordinated the creation of an extended Chinese character set with an additional 2,700 Chinese characters.

1. *Centrally-developed tailor-made system for 1300 schools*: The target users of the SAMS are 1300 schools of various types. The design of the SAMS therefore emphasizes its flexibility to suit the basic needs of the diverse school types (e.g., curriculum, financial modes, number of administrative units made up by different sessions or heads, assessment systems, student information requirements).

1. *Pilot roll out and application enhancement*: Piloting is adopted for testing the users' receptiveness to the system and for identifying areas for fine-tuning. In SAMS version 1.0 ten schools of different nature were selected as pilot schools. The lead time for the actual rollout after the piloting was two months, which however proved to be inadequate for any crucial fine-tuning to be made. Based on that experience, in the subsequent rollout, the piloting period has been extended. Concerning the application enhancement, there are various channels through which users may give suggestions on the design and functionality of SAMS for consideration in the future version of SAMS that are released on a half-yearly basis.

2. *Local Area Network (LAN) with Graphical User Interface (GUI)* : Regarding the system configuration of the SAMS, in each primary and secondary school, a group of microcomputers will be installed and linked together to form a local area network (LAN) in the school building. The LAN consists of one to two file servers connected to five to nine workstations depending on the total number of operating classes of the school. Together with SAMS, standard software packages on word processing, spreadsheet and database management are provided. Windows NT Server 3.5 is used as the network operating system. The system is developed under a Windows environment with Graphical User Interface (GUI), allowing users to communicate with SAMS by using a mouse.

3. *Provision of End-user Computing tool*: At the time of the selection of the development tool, FoxPro could fulfill the requirement of running under Windows. It had the required GUI; was capable of efficient database management, and was considered the most appropriate tool for users at the time. Furthermore, FoxPro for DOS had already been in use in schools at the time when the SAMS project was initiated. As the users had already been trained in the use of the FoxPro, they have little difficulty in moving to FoxPro for Windows. The same software is also taught in the secondary school curriculum and is very popular among school teachers, which helps pave the way for the development of end-user computing in SAMS schools.

4. *Keep abreast of the latest technology*: The Hong Kong Government has been providing both hardware and software enhancement to this centrally developed system. The equipment supplies contracts are periodically renewed to ensure that the project can benefit from the latest technology. For example, the workstations currently provided to schools are a 80486 DX4 100 Mhz system instead of the 80486 33 Mhz system provided in the early stage. Additional hardware such as the LaserJet 4 Plus printers and Chinese writing pads are further provided on top of the standard configuration. Besides, implications of deploying new software to schools are always studied and new releases of software are supplied if needed. Currently the impact of using Chinese Windows 95 in SAMS is being explored.

2 QUESTIONS TO BE ANSWERED

In the following sections, we would like to share our experience in the implementation of SAMS in the public sector schools in Hong Kong by answering the three questions stated below:

(a) What are the essential tasks involved in the development and execution of this centrally developed school management information system?
(b) What are the implementation issues to be addressed and how to manage the issues?
(c) What is the way forward for this system?

3 ANSWERS TO QUESTIONS STATED

In providing answers for question (a) above, the modes of user participation and other major tasks will be analysed; for question (b), the various issues will be identified and the method of management analysed; for the last question, a plan for the on-going development of the System will be proposed.

3.1 User Participation

Throughout the development of the SAMS, user involvement is extensive - on both regular and need basis.

Teacher Secondment - Under the scheme of teacher secondment, teachers with school administration and IT skills are seconded to work full-time in the ED on a one-year tenure. Since the commencement of this secondment system in September 1994, about 30 heads and teachers from different types of schools have worked jointly with the ED staff in the SAMS project team. As the nature and requirements of the 1300 target schools are diverse, it is neither cost-effective nor operationally feasible to interview all schools to collate their requirements. Being the end-users of the SAMS, the seconded teachers give comments and suggestions during all stages of system development and project implementation. They also collate requirements from the co-workers in schools, assist in the design of test plans, provide test data and conduct user acceptance tests.

Advisors - There is an advisor system, through which heads, teachers or school clerks are performing an advisory role in specifying user requirements during the feasibility studies, system analysis and design and implementation stages. The advisors play an important role in advising on the priorities set for those diverse requirements. Since the kick-off of the SAMS project, about 20 heads, teachers and clerks have been serving as part-time advisors to the SAMS project.

System Implementation Co-ordinators - There are also experienced SAMS teacher users serving as part-time system implementation co-ordinators. They perform the dual roles of suggesting the appropriate functions to be included in SAMS and serving as the regional co-ordinator to offer on-site advice and support to schools in the neighbourhood. At present, there are about 20 teachers serving in this capacity.

ED Officers - Working alongside the above users are the ED officers who have both teaching and school administration experience. They perform the role of middlemen between the developer (i.e. ITSD) and the end-users. To ensure that the schools' diverse needs are identified, screened, prioritised and properly addressed in the applications, these officers co-ordinate activities like school visits, workshops, check-point meetings, application walkthroughs with the participation of a good representation of schools with different characteristics.

Others - Participants in the above meetings are school representatives from major sponsors, school councils and all types of schools. The number of participants for each meeting ranges from about 5 to 60. In almost all meetings and various school visits, the ITSD developers are also present to acquire first-hand information from the school users, which facilitates the subsequent information exchange and discussion among ITSD developers and the ED officers. Since the inauguration of the SAMS project in September 1993, over 120 meetings have been organised with the participation of more than 3000 person-sessions from about 20 percent of the 1300 target schools.

3.2 Other major tasks

Before the actual operation of the SAMS in schools, the ED identifies resources, plans and co-ordinates a series of tasks. Although all the tasks are relatively simple, the aggregate amount of work, due to the number of schools involved and the pledges to complete all installation tasks for a single school within a short period of time, has made the administrative and co-ordination work very difficult. The major tasks involved are described below:

1. *Site preparation*: Schools have to identify suitable sites for the installation of the networked system. After the relevant authority's approval of the network requirement reports, the contractor carries out the site works, including installation of power points, signal cabling and minor builders' works. Delivery, installation and acceptance of hardware and software then follow. Detailed planning, close supervision, frequent communication and better coordination are the keys to the successful installation of the LANs in schools.

1. *Data conversion and system uploading*: Schools have to convert existing data, in either manual or electronic forms, into the data format of the SAMS. In choosing the methodology for data conversion, the use of optical mark reader or optical character recognition has been ruled out as the former method requires a lot of transcription work for teachers while the latter needs much skill in writing and effort in fixing errors. Conversion can now be done by using a conversion program or filling in coding sheets for data preparation service arranged by the ED.

1. *Training*: School staff attend training courses on basic IT (covering operating system, spreadsheet, Chinese word processing and database management), SAMS applications (ranging from one to two days for each application) and the related courses like 'management of change' for heads and 'LAN administration' for system administrators. Other courses or seminars with special themes are also organised on a need basis.

1. *Outside professional services*: To meet the pledge of completing the implementation of SAMS in all 1300 schools within a five-year period, and to minimise impacts on schools resulting from the initial implementation of the SAMS, the ED has been adopting two methods of service acquisition. First, there are some services contracted to outside service providers. The contract services include those for site preparation works, compilation of SAMS procedure manual and training kits, data input tasks and on-site SAMS uploading. Second, allowances are given to teachers who help to perform in-house basic IT training, data conversion and related SAMS implementation tasks.

3.3 Identification and management of issues arising from SAMS implementation

With the implementation of the SAMS, there are some related issues that require the ED's close monitoring. In the following paragraphs, the issues are identified and the methods of management are also outlined.

3.3.1 *Core functions in SAMS not satisfying individual needs of schools*

In spite of the efforts made to address the requirements of different types of schools, there are comments from schools suggesting that the core functions provided cannot meet their specific needs. Taking the assessment system as an example, though there is a mechanism built in SAMS for applying different algorithms in mark calculation, among the 1300 target schools, there are some cases that the SAMS cannot handle. In fact, the SAMS has been developed with the objective of providing the core functions essential to assist schools in performing the daily administrative and management tasks. At the beginning of the system studies, it had been noted that with schools' varied characteristics and diverse needs, SAMS may not fully meet the individual requirements of each and every school. For addressing this issue, two lines of action have been adopted. First, with user feedback, SAMS is constantly enhanced aiming at enriching and improving the functions. For example, in SAMS version 1.4, released about one and a half years after version 1.0, there are several new functions. The functions provide facilities for the processing of multiple school levels and sessions, different subject groups, special purpose classes and educational programmes. Such inclusions increase the flexibility and functionality provided in the various applications like assessment and reporting. Second, facilities are available to extract data from the SAMS database for further manipulation and processing. An end-user development tool, Microsoft FoxPro 2.5b for Windows at present, is provided to schools for developing tailored add-on programmes. Authorised users with programming background can access the databases in read only mode. Data dictionary is also prepared for users. In addition, since the commencement of the SAMS rollout in September 1994, an individual Section has been set up in ED with the mission to promote and co-ordinate add-on programme development by planning, supporting and offering training relating to end-user computing.

3.3.2 *Users' reservation of switching from existing computer systems to SAMS*

In some schools, especially the secondary ones, some systems are already in use, assisting in the administrative tasks. The systems may have been in service for a while and are proved to be functionally effective. The need to switch to another system of SAMS surely causes a certain amount of resistance. In this regard, most schools are adopting an open attitude. In actual fact, the SAMS does have the merit of being a centralised system; teachers familiar with SAMS can carry this knowledge and experience with them when they change from one school to another. As SAMS becomes a common tool among schools, the loss of 'technical hands' is no longer a threat to the smooth school administration. For addressing this concern direct, enhancements are being made to the coming version of SAMS in which 'crossing bridges' will be provided to allow the import of data generated from other computer systems. Data imported to SAMS should be in the pre-defined data format. In this approach, the flexibility for schools in using existing systems for the processing of certain functions not provided under the existing scope of SAMS increases tremendously.

3.3.3 *Varied computer literacy and users' resistance to change*

In some schools, teachers are not ready to use computers to assist in their daily work as it is not their normal practice. To help eliminate their resistance to the use of computers, different types of training in improving their computer literacy are organised. In addition to training in SAMS applications, basic IT training courses are also organised. Training modes are varied in order that more teachers can grasp the required skills. For example, school-based training is planned in which teachers of the same school, mostly computer teachers, may perform the role of trainer giving lessons outside school hours to all teachers of the same school. This reduces the disturbance to the normal lessons and increases the incentives of teachers to attend training session in a familiar environment.

Furthermore, the ED is providing an active supportive service to all schools in using SAMS. Help desks are operated by means of hot-lines, bulletin board services, fax, etc. On-site service is provided and appointment can be made in which officers can stand-by serving schools using the SAMS in performing time-critical tasks like report card printing. Experienced SAMS users are also recruited to serve as part-time system implementation co-ordinators offering on-site coaching to schools with difficulties in using SAMS. Besides, Saturday workshops and talks on special themes are regularly organised to resolve the schools' problems in using SAMS.

3.4 The way forward

Unlike those development tools for workstations or a mainframe platform, the tools for the PC platform of SAMS are cheaper, easier to manage and have more options. Coupled with the good computer literacy among the teachers who have knowledge of the school's daily business, a significant number of users, especially those from secondary schools, have been developing add-on programmes using the SAMS data. The Add-on Programme Development Section of the ED has been set up to formulate strategies on End-User Computing (EUC) and to plan and conduct activities relating to the nurturing of EUC culture among school users. In addition, regional resources centres are planned to be set up for organizing EUC activities including training, development of add-on programmes and trying out of new development tools. Moreover, the regional resource centres provide the meeting ground for school users to share their experience and to provide peer-to-peer support services. In the long run, with the germination of the EUC culture, it is hoped that the school users who know their business needs well and have the ability to develop add-on programmes, will supplement the SAMS to cater for the needs of individual users.

4 CONCLUSION

The development and implementation of the SAMS project are due for completion by 1998. The completion of the project does not signify an end to the ED's information system strategy in schools. Instead, in order to keep pace with the new requirements arising from changes in educational policies and the trend of information technology, the SAMS will expand and evolve, with enhancement and maintenance of the core functions on the one hand, and the development of end-user computing activities on the other. It is our vision that the SAMS acts as the backbone of the Hong Kong school administrative and management system, and concurrently, that the users continue to develop add-on programmes to this centralised system, making it more useful and beneficial to users.

5 BIOGRAPHIES

Mrs Betty Ip is the Senior Education Officer (Administration) of the Education Department of Hong Kong. She obtained a Bachelor of Science Degree in 1976 and a Master of Education Degree in 1985, both from the University of Hong Kong. She has worked on the application of information technology in education administration and management for fifteen years. In the past three years, she has been responsible for the overall administration of the School Administration and Management System Project.

Mr Steve Lee is the Senior Education Officer (Administration) of the Add-on Programme Development Section of the Education Department of Hong Kong, responsible for the promotion and development of End-user Computing for the Information System Strategy Project. He obtained a Bachelor of Science degree in 1977 and a Master in Business Administration in 1992, both from the Chinese University of Hong Kong. In 1995, he obtained a Master of Science degree in Information Systems from the George Mason University. He has been working as an education administrator for thirteen years of which seven years have been in the information system for education management field.

12

An operational model for the implementation of computerised school information systems

C.J.P. Nolan, D.A. Ayres and D.H. McKinnon
Massey University, Palmerston North, New Zealand
Phone: (64)-6-3504577 Fax: (64)-6-3505619
e-mail: P.Nolan@massey.ac.nz

Abstract
The paper presents an operational model for the implementation of computerised school information systems and it conceptualises implementation as complex, interrelated with other processes and problematic. In order to explain implementation, viewed in this way, the model links Levels of Use from the Concerns Based Adoption Model (CBAM) devised by Hall, Wallace & Dossett (1973) with generic change processes shown by research to be constitutive of educational change and innovation in educational institutions. Discussion suggests ways by which practitioners and researchers, alike, might employ the Model to better manage the implementation of computerised systems and better understand the factors and forces affecting implementation.

Keywords
Educational management, administration, implementation, information technology

1 INTRODUCTION

In this paper, we develop an operational model for the implementation of computerised school information systems. The model provides strategies for both managing and researching the complexity, inter-relatedness, and problematic nature of implementation. It uses concepts from both educational change theory (Fullan, 1991; Fullan, 1993; McKinnon, Nolan, Openshaw & Soler, 1991; Ruddick, 1991; Adams & Chen, 1981; Hall, Wallace, & Dosset, 1973) and computer assisted school administration (CASA) research (e.g. Visscher, 1996; Visscher, 1991; Visscher and Spuck, 1991).

Change theory contributes an understanding of the innovative (and thereby potentially problematic) character of computerised information systems (Nolan, Ayres, Dunn and McKinnon, 1996). When first introduced to schools, computerised systems typically challenge individuals to modify, perhaps even abandon, tried and seemingly-true ways of doing things and replace them with alternative and new methods, behaviours and ways of thinking.

Furthermore, change theory (Fullan, 1991) by identifying implementation as one of three stages in the change process, along with adoption and utilisation, is consistent with the theoretical model (Visscher, 1991) most commonly used to conduct CASA research. The Model was designed to analyse the development, use and impact of computerised administration systems. In a recently updated version (hereafter called the Visscher Model), Visscher (1996) identifies features of the implementation process as a key variable which directly affects the magnitude and manner in which information systems are utilised and, in turn, the extent of their impact.

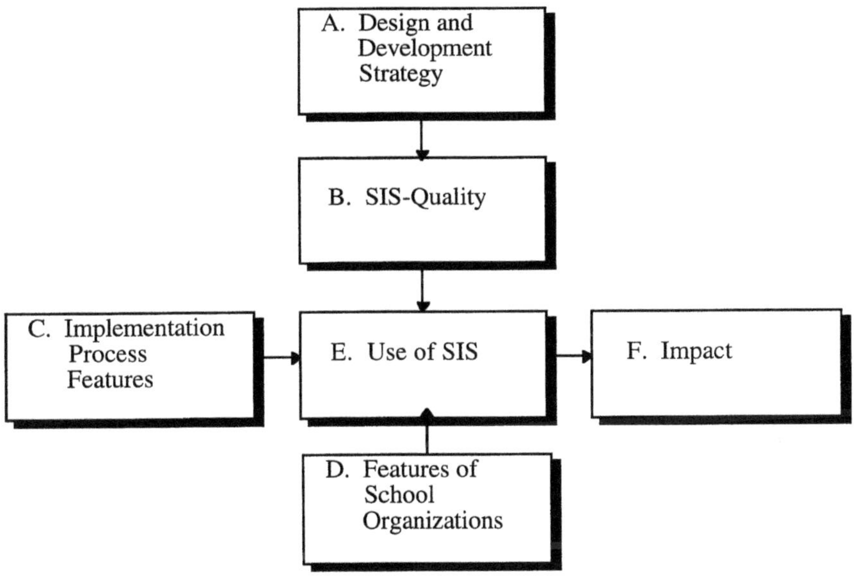

Figure 1 Visscher's (1996) Model of the Development, Use and Impact of Computerised School Information Systems (SISs).

In the Model, Blocks A, C, and E identify the computer system-related processes which impact on computer assisted school administration (CASA), namely, system development, implementation and use.

Within CASA, implementation of changes (e.g., acquisition of a new application or replacement of the existing computer platform) is strategic in the sense that it lies at the interface between the intentions of developers and the ways that information systems are actually used. If this is the case, then effective implementation strategies appear to be a key factor influencing the extent to which such systems may enhance school administration and management and impact positively upon the content and delivery of school education.

To date, the Visscher Model has been successfully used as a framework within which to examine "top-down" approaches to computerised school information system development and adoption (Visscher and Spuck, 1991). Our purpose, here, is to extend its application to capture the dynamics of development and adoption when a "bottom-up" approach is employed. Such an approach predominates in New Zealand.

New Zealand schools (Nolan and Ayres, 1996), must elect to use computerised information systems because the Government has maintained a policy of non-involvement. The predominant system, MUSAC (Massey University School Administration by Computer), has been designed and developed by a self-funded

University research and development centre, using a "bottom-up" approach which consisted of: (i) initial system development for a small group of schools; (ii) further development of the system for all schools; and (iii) the ongoing development of the system based on feedback from users (see Nolan and Ayres, 1996). This stands in contrast with a "top-down" approach which typifies computerised information system development, implementation and use in countries where schools are mandated by government to adopt computer assisted school administration.

It is in the nature of "top-down" approaches to simplify the three change processes of system development, implementation and use into a linear sequence to be worked through in a step-wise progression. In reality, the processes are inherently complex and inter-related (Nolan, Ayres, Dunn & McKinnon, 1996). A "bottom-up" approach explicitly acknowledges the complexity and inter-relatedness by identifying interactions between the processes of development, implementation and use as essential. For example, with the MUSAC system in New Zealand (see Nolan and Ayres, 1996), the relationship between development and use is reflected in the constant flow of information and ideas between users and developers. This, in turn, results in the developers constantly changing the configuration and capabilities of the system in response to user suggestions.

New Zealand research (Nolan et al, 1996) has shown that schools were able to deal with both the complexity and the inter-related aspects of change when they employed an adaptive yet systematic methodology. Use of the methodology, in its turn, provided empirical support for the model of implementation and its conceptualisation that is the main topic of this paper.

2 THE IMPLEMENTATION MODEL

The Implementation Model presented here takes Levels of Use from the Concerns Based Adoption Model (CBAM) (Hall, Wallace & Dossett, 1973) and links them with the three generic processes of innovation adoption, implementation and utilisation now commonly identified in the literature (Fullan, 1991; McKinnon, Nolan, Openshaw & Soler, 1991; Ruddick, 1991; Adams & Chen, 1981) as constitutive of change in educational institutions.

CBAM was developed and applied in the 1970s and 1980s (Hall et al, 1973; McKinnon & Nolan, 1989) specifically to assist researchers and practitioners to analyse and manage educational change through innovation. The model specifies a hierarchy of eight "Levels of Use" (see Figure 2). The levels depict behaviours which individuals exhibit over time in relation to the innovation and they provide an indication of the progress of the innovation, itself.

Figure 2 shows how the eight Levels of Use correspond with the three change processes, (i.e., adoption, implementation and utilisation), and indicates a degree of overlap. The overlap occurs because orientation can occur in both the adoption and implementation stages of the change process, and mechanical use can occur in both the implementation and utilisation stages. Furthermore, while it is possible to make analytical distinctions between adoption, implementation and utilisation, they stand in a relationship of interdependency. That is to say, the practicality of change taking place at several levels simultaneously, e.g., institutional, group and individual, means that the boundaries between the three processes are, in reality, blurred.

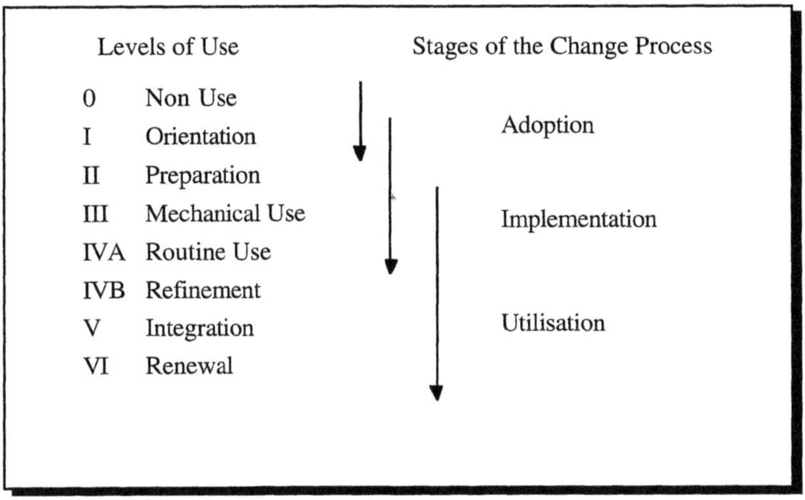

Figure 2 Implementation Model for Computerised School Information Systems.

2.1 Adoption

Typically, innovation adoption includes development of awareness that a situation needs to be addressed, and orientation activities which predispose decision-makers to take a particular course of action (Hall et al., 1973). Together, awareness and orientation lay the foundation for implementation.

Developing awareness involves key personnel recognising that a computerised information system may actually be needed. The reasons may range from systemic pressures from a higher authority (e.g. the Ministry of Education in New Zealand) through community pressures to internal school reasons.

In the adoption stage, orientation involves key personnel seeking knowledge and ideas which will inform their decisions. For instance, it is likely that they will wish to know about such matters as tasks the computerised system will perform, the kinds of outcomes that might be expected, the levels of funding and support that might be required to both acquire and implement the system, and the relative merits and shortcomings of competing systems.

2.2 Implementation

It is often the case that the decision to adopt a computerised information system is made by administrators or other people in authority. This may not always be the case, though, as some schools may use inclusive decision-making strategies. Depending upon the strategies that a school actually uses to reach the decision to adopt, varying numbers of personnel will have been through orientation when implementation begins.

Furthermore, the manner in which adoption is carried out may either support or impede implementation and thus affect the eventual utilisation of the new system. This is suggested by the inclusion of Features of Schools as Organisations in Block D of the Visscher Model.

The specification of implementation in Figure 2 as covering orientation, preparation and mechanical Levels of Use, captures the essentially introductory character of implementation activity. While key decision-makers in the adoption stage may have successfully oriented themselves towards the innovation, those personnel who are starting at the level of non-use will require orientation in order to accept the innovation and perceive it as valuable to them and their institution (McKinnon et al, 1991). It is in this respect, that implementation of a computerised school information system (innovation) may be problematic.

The preparation Level of Use engages personnel in the activities of setting up the system for practical use. Typically, this level of use includes acquisition and installation of the system, the determination of locations (e.g. where to place the file server and remote networked terminals), the assignment of staff roles and responsibilities, and the initiation of staff training.

Mechanical use, the final implementation step, involves staff members learning to use the system. Implementation ends when everyone who the school identifies as needing to use the system (or a part of it), has mastered the program(s) and is using it to carry out day-to-day tasks.

2.3 Utilisation

In the Visscher Model, utilisation is represented in Block E, Use of SIS. Figure 2 shows that utilisation is characterised by the remaining four Levels of Use in CBAM. These are: routine use where "attention shifts from the management of computerisation to the management of information" (Visscher, 1991:3), and the execution, by computer, of day to day administrative and clerical activities; refinement where the school may modify the system, or parts of it, to suit their own specific needs and requirements; integration where school staff understand ways by which computerised administration can, and does, support not just specific and school-wide management decisions but also learning and teaching; and renewal where the users evaluate the quality of use of the innovation and examine new developments with a view to setting new goals.

Once integrated into a school's day-to-day administrative and operating procedures, the quality of use is evaluated in terms of impact outcomes as signified by Block F, Impact, in the Visscher Model. To the extent that the evaluations are favourable, a school may decide to expand the existing system by introducing a new component, i.e., initiate a new implementation stage. In this way, implementation can be seen to be typically on-going and incremental as schools progressively adopt new components of a system.

3 DISCUSSION

At the point of writing, only limited case study research (Nolan, Ayres, Dunn & McKinnon, 1996) has been conducted using the Implementation Model presented here. The research indicated, however, that the Model and the operational definitions derived from it, provided a framework within which: (i) researchers can study and document the form and direction that schools might take to implement computerised information systems; and (ii) the schools, themselves, might implement a computerised system, and evaluate their implementation endeavours.

A seemingly successful implementation strategy commonly employed involves the following four steps:

1. document the existing situation through an administrative review and/or needs analysis to identify actual needs and possible directions;
2. do collaborative problem solving to analyse the results and determine goals, priorities and the resources and support required, based on the results;

3. key staff who will drive the innovation, formulate a detailed implementation plan including staff training and support to develop the necessary confidence and competencies; and
4. carry out regular, well-structured staff training and support on an as-needs basis, thereby enabling staff to learn and master specific programs by using them to complete real management and administration tasks.

While all the steps were necessary, the fourth is vital. Schools known to have implemented computerised systems effectively (i.e. they had progressed to a stage of routine and integrated use) commonly employ the services of an external support agency to help them take the fourth step and frequently the others as well. Somewhat ironically, many agencies, in their turn, have come to understand that their aims and objectives must include: (i) helping schools to increasingly take responsibility for meeting their own learning needs; and (ii) empowering schools to implement and use their computerised administration systems relatively unaided.

The steps, above, correspond with the awareness, orientation, preparation and mechanical use activities identified in the Implementation Model. Its initial use in chronicalling the way schools progress through the steps of implementation suggest both a strategy that schools might adopt and a set of propositions that researchers might test in future research on the implementation of computerised school information systems.

The new conceptualisation stands somewhat in contrast with the way that implementation is viewed in the Visscher Model which conceptualises school information systems as complex products of a finite design and development process. Consequently, implementation is also conceptualised as a process with a definite beginning and end, contained within one block of the Model.

While the conceptualisation of implementation presented here fits within the Visscher (1996) framework, the research conducted to date, and experience, show that the complexity of change means that implementation activities are on-going and incremental and they interact with factors in all the other blocks of the Model rather than being contained just within one block, i.e., Block C, Implementation Process Features.

Thus, implementation must be viewed as on-going, incremental, and interactive, rather than as a finite process. For instance, specific features of the school as an organisation (Block D) interact with implementation in ways that can either impede or support it. For example, in a recent secondary school case study (Nolan et al, 1996) a team approach, involving collaboration between teachers and administrative staff across organisational levels and departmental boundaries, demonstrated how a positive school climate can support implementation. In this case, staff took ownership of, and became committed to, the process. Collaboration and team work fostered staff perceptions that their work, using the system, was of real value to the school. This, in its turn, elevated the status of staff by recognising them as individuals with skills and expertise important to the team and the school.

At another level, the interaction of implementation with design and development strategies (Block A) can lead to better and simpler ways to manage school information. In New Zealand, where a "bottom-up" approach to system development and design predominates, developers constantly refine the system used by most schools by inviting users to suggest improvements. This results in system quality (Block B) constantly being enhanced by the injection of ideas from actual users. Through this interaction, implementation is also enhanced by the sense of involvement that users have in the design of the system (Block A in the Visscher Model). In this way, the system has been made more "user-friendly" since its initial inception and it produces output which the end-users perceive as valuable (Block F, Impact).

If the existing Visscher Model were further developed to include the conceptualisation of implementation presented here then its scope might be expanded to include a wider range of school information systems and educational systems. If this were to happen, its explanatory power and capability to enhance practice would also be enhanced. In this way, two seemingly desirable consequences may more easily eventuate. Firstly, practitioners (support agencies, teachers and school administrators) might be better placed to more effectively adopt and implement computerised information systems and use them more effectively to achieve desirable administration, management and educational outcomes. Secondly, researchers might be better placed to unravel the complexity and problematic aspects which have made adoption, implementation and utilisation of computerised systems such a difficult exercise in the past and continue to do so.

4 REFERENCES

Adams, R.S. & Chen, D. (1981) *The process of educational innovation: an international perspective.* Kogan Page, London.

Fullan, M. (1991) *The new meaning of educational change.* Columbia University, Teachers College Press, NY.

Fullan, M. (1993) *Change forces: probing the depth of educational reform.* Falmer Press, London.

Hall, G.E., Wallace, R.C. & Dosset, W.A. (1973) A *developmental conceptualisation of the adoption process with educational institutions.* The University of Texas, Austin.

McKinnon, D.H. & Nolan, C.J.P. (1989) Using computers in education: a concerns-based approach to professional development for teachers. *The Australian Journal of Educational Technology,* **5(2)**, 113-131.

McKinnon, D.H., Nolan, C.J.P., Openshaw, R. and Soler, J. (1991) New Zealand curriculum innovation in historical and political context: the Freyberg integrated studies project and parallel projects of the 1940s. *Journal of Curriculum Studies,* **23(2)**, 155-175.

Nolan, C.J.P. & Ayres, D.A. (1996) Developing a "good" information for schools: the New Zealand experience. Forthcoming in *International Journal of Educational Research*, **25(4)**.

Nolan, C.J.P., Ayres, D.A. Dunn, S. & McKinnon, D.H. (1996) Implementing computerised school information systems: case studies from New Zealand. Forthcoming in *International Journal of Educational Research*, **25(4)**.

Ruddick, J. (1991) *Innovation and change.* Milton Keynes: Open University Press.

Visscher, A.J. (1991) School administrative computing: a framework for analysis. *Journal of Research on Computing in Education*, **24(1)**, 1-19.

Visscher, A.J. (1996) Information technology in educational management as an emerging discipline. Forthcoming in *International Journal of Educational Research*, **25(4)**.

Visscher, A.J. and Spuck, D.W. (1991) Computer assisted school administration and management: the state of the art in seven nations. *Journal of Research on Computing in Education*, **24(1)**, 146-168.

5 BIOGRAPHIES

Pat Nolan is a Professor in the Massey University Department of Educational Psychology and Director of the Massey University Educational Research and Development Centre. His professional and research interests include curriculum development and design, education with computers, experiential education, educational administration and management and school development.

Debbie Ayres is lecturer in the Massey University Department of Educational Psychology. Her professional and research interests include curriculum development and design, educational administration and management with computers and early childhood education.

David McKinnon is a senior lecturer in teacher education at Charles Sturt University, Mitchell, Australia. His professional and research interests include professional development for teachers, education with computers and science education.

13

Administration, management and IT in education

I.D. Selwood and H. Drenoyianni
School of Education, The University of Birmingham
Edgbaston, Birmingham, B15 2TT, UK
Phone: (44)-121-4144851 Fax: (44)-121-4144865
e-mail: I.D.Selwood@Bham.AC.UK

Abstract
This paper examines how computerised Management Information Systems (MISs) can support the information and decisional needs of educational managers. Furthermore, the capabilities of such information systems will de described and discussed together with the benefits of using Information Technology (IT) in managing educational organisations. Section three of the paper describes a small scale piece of research that examined senior educational managers' perceptions and usage of IT in Educational Management (ITEM), and suggests some reasons for the lack of usage of IT to support management decision making.

Keywords
Educational management, information technology, administration, management

1 INTRODUCTION

Visscher (1995) in his paper entitled 'Computer Assisted School Administration and Management: Where are we and where should we go?' outlined four stages of the development of Computer Assisted School Administration (CASA). Whilst it is difficult to disagree with his first two stages, 'initiation' and 'expansion', he claims: "the third stage 'integration' can be 'characterised by 'integrated modules' and 'the production of management information'" (Visscher, 1995); and that the fourth stage, 'stabilisation', can be characterised by computer assistance reaching its full potential and the focus shifting to systems maintenance and refinement. These final two stages are somewhat open to debate. It is possible that systems, even though they may comprise 'integrated modules', may not be flexible enough to provide information for management decisions (Mitchell and Wild, 1993). Other considerations such as: lack of appropriate training for senior educational managers; and constant revision of systems due to technological change, may also inhibit progress. In the UK it would appear that the third stage of the evolution of CASA is basically that i.e. the use of computers to aid school administration, and that the fourth stage is the development of the use of ITEM (Information Technology in Educational Management) i.e. the use of computerised MISs (Management Information Systems) to support Educational Managers.

It is perhaps, sensible for the purpose of this paper to distinguish between administration and management. Administration can be thought of as the tasks associated with the day to day running of an organisation that ensure that the organisation performs smoothly and efficiently to achieve its pre-determined goals. Management, however, is concerned with analysing information, making decisions, defining strategies, tactics, and goals for the organisation and ensuring that an organisation works towards these goals in an efficient and effective manner (Fidler and Bowles, 1989). Goals and strategies will need periodic re-appraisal to ensure that they remain appropriate.

2 COMPUTER-BASED MANAGEMENT INFORMATION SYSTEMS

In the UK, the Education Reform Act (ERA) (House of Commons, 1988) required that headteachers and governing bodies in every school should embrace a role similar to that of managers in commercial companies. According to the DES, they (governing bodies) should 'formulate a management plan for the school' and 'secure its implementation with the collective support of the school's staff' (DES, 1988). They should be concerned with managing the budget, the curriculum, human resources, premises, property and learning resources. Particularly, they should make decisions and be responsible for the impact and implications of their decisions on the running of the school. As experience in commercial and industrial organisations has shown, 'effective decisions must be based on a steady flow of quality, up-to-date information' (Thierauf, 1987). Educational managers need also to consider the value and the nature of information needed for decision making and strategic planning activities, and decide upon "the form and extent of their management information system" (Strain, 1990).

Computer-based management information systems have been used for some time in commerce for storing, processing and transforming data to information that is valuable for supporting managers in their duties. Moreover, the Coopers and Lybrand report (1988) for local management of schools, a key feature of the ERA, had identified the need for computerised management information systems. It is therefore apparent that educational managers are expected to take advantage of the computers' potential, to store and process rapidly and accurately vast amounts of data, by using MISs to augment their managerial and administrative responsibilities.

The question raised here concerns the nature of a computerised MIS and how educational managers can benefit from using them. Definitions of MISs are multiple and varied. Several authors (Hicks, 1993; Thierauf, 1987) agree that a number of information systems, such as Decision Support Systems or Executive Information Systems, fall under the umbrella of Management Information Systems, while others (Bank and Williams, 1987; Carter and Burger, 1994) consider them as significantly different systems designed for a specific purpose. A lengthy discussion concerning the technicalities of such distinctions is inappropriate here. A good useful working definition coming from the former category of writers, which concentrates on the general use of MISs, is probably appropriate. Accordingly a computer-based MIS is "an integrated user-machine system for providing information to support operations, management, and decision-making functions in an organisation" (Davis and Olson, 1985)

The above statement infers that there is an interactive relationship between the user and the computer, a dialogue, in which both are engaged in "different but complementary roles" (Levacic, 1995). Further it stresses the need to support "management and decision making functions." Computers can help educational managers to access large amounts of data in a timely and accurate manner but it is the managers who actually find relations, interpret and give meaning to the data. However, having stated this, it is clear that computers can connect and combine data but only if they are instructed to do so - the design of the MIS is therefore crucial to the sort of query it can answer, and the type of decisions it can support. This capability of computers to associate data, when they are instructed to do so, can be seen through a description of the components used in the database approach to information processing on which the structures of most MISs are based. According to Hicks (1993), one component of the database environment is the user. The users - educational managers and staff in a school, for example - communicate with the database through a number of application programmes by inputting, differentiating, cutting out and manipulating data for pupils, teachers, premises and generally everything about a school. The application programmes used, can be general, such as word-processors or spreadsheets, or specific, i.e., concerned with budgeting, planning school development, managing the curriculum, managing staff development, school appraisal, pupil records, premises, learning resources, accounts, payroll or attendance.

The database approach as applied in most MISs' structures has the major advantage of arming managers who use such systems with a major 'weapon' against their demanding managerial responsibilities: information based on a thorough, broad and coherent collection of data. All the data contained in the specific application programmes of the system for administrative purposes can be accessed and managed in an integrated way. This is particularly important for educational managers. For example, it should enable educational managers to bring together data about pupils, parents, teachers, attendance and timetable to investigate truancy by analysing data, seeking trends and patterns, hypothesising on possible reasons and forming appropriate policies. This policies, once implemented can then be analysed in a similar manner. This sort of analysis can support educational managers in understanding and gaining insights into particular educational setting's structures and operations. "Decision-making in educational institutions involves a complex process that requires the structuring of a broad range of alternatives and the analysis of numerous policy variables." (Cameron Fisher et al., 1990)

Since MISs, as a consequence of their structures, can be responsive to the above requirements, their use can support educational managers in making decision, more easily and efficiently. To be more specific, people who are most responsible for managing a particular school, like managers in commercial organisations (Hicks, 1993), make decisions of different types and at different levels, by following certain stages in order to find solutions.

The management process is primarily concerned with decision making. Whenever for example, headteachers and governing bodies in a school form a vision of where the school is going, establish aims and objectives, prioritise them and develop a plan for the accomplishment of these objectives, they are involved in strategic decision making. Whenever, they are making decisions concerned with the implementation of the school's development plan (e.g. appoint or dismiss teaching or other staff), their decisions may be considered as tactical. Finally, whenever they have to carry out clear and specific tasks (e.g. ordering supplies) they are making operational decisions.

A well designed and implemented MIS should be capable of supporting all types of decision making, no matter the level. Consequently MISs should assist educational managers in planning, organising, controlling, reviewing, monitoring and evaluating procedures. In particular, they should be able to supply managers with precise and consistent information for the identification of problems, the analysis of the problem to its smaller and controllable parts, the identification of alternative solutions to it, the examination and evaluation of each solution's feasibility and the prediction of their implications. In other words, MISs should help educational managers to give answers to questions like (Telem, 1990): (1) 'What has happened?' (e.g., In which areas of the curriculum do students fail to achieve high grades?) (2) 'Why did it happen?' (e.g. What are the possible causes of certain groups of students' under-achievement?) (3) 'What would happen if....?' (e.g. What would happen if we changed the methods of assessing pupils? What would happen to the budget if we changed the card index library system to a computerised system?). It should be possible with an MIS to produce reports: required by statute, about the school's general operation; for discovering and analysing particular problems; and producing highly specific reports responsive to varied needs and requests. MISs should also improve the presentation of information and data. All of these reports and presentations could be supported by graphics. It is self evident that MISs should also be capable of performing rapid statistical and mathematical analysis, this is not only particularly essential in financial and budgetary planning, but also in many of the previously mentioned applications. With the addition of local area networks and electronic mail facilities MISs should also improve communication amongst not only users in the school, but also between the school and the LEA, public examination boards, educational suppliers, and other schools, etc.

There are significant benefits in using MISs in educational management, but educational managers can only profit from them if they are aware of, and take advantage of the capabilities outlined above.

3 MANAGEMENT INFORMATION SYSTEMS - USE IN SCHOOLS?

3.1 Background

During 1995 a series of two day residential conferences were run for senior educational managers, headteachers and deputy headteachers, entitled 'Making SIMS[1] Work for You'. The objectives of the conference were wide, but included the objective of raising awareness of the management uses of IT. An independent, follow-up evaluation of the conferences was carried out by the authors of this paper, in early 1996. As a part of this evaluation survey the perceptions of senior educational managers regarding the use of ITEM, their previous training in educational management and their actual uses of ITEM, were investigated. The following sections report on this part of the survey.

3.2 Methodology and Objectives

A postal survey of the conference delegates was undertaken in January 1996. The prime purpose of the research was to try to evaluate the lasting effectiveness of the series of conferences, which took place between February and June 1995. Whilst the particular results concerning the conferences are interesting they are beyond the general scope of this paper. The second part of the questionnaire concerned perceptions and uses of IT in educational management in general (and SIMS in particular) and had the following objectives:

- To ascertain whether the respondents felt that the conference had helped them to use SIMS for management purposes;
- To find out if the respondents had ever attended a management training course, and details of these courses;
- To ascertain if the respondents felt that their current SIMS systems could be used as a management tool;
- To investigate what modules in SIMS were being used for management purposes.

---

[1] SIMS (Schools Information Management System) - The market leader in proprietary software for educational administration and management in the UK (Selwood, 1995).

3.3 Questionnaire Design

The part of the questionnaire with which we are concerned used a variety of question types. Some questions were open ended, others closed, and others expected a ranking. To ensure that all respondents were aware of the distinction being sought between 'educational administration' and 'educational management' their attention was drawn to an appendix to the questionnaire that contained definitions of the two terms.

3.4 Results

The response rate for a postal questionnaire was quite good, 70 percent. This consisted of 29 (74% of the possible respondents) primary schools, 1 (50%) middle, and 8 (61%) secondary. The ratio of 29:1:8 also corresponds well to the proportions of the types of school in the geographical area covered by the survey. The numbers are low, but we do feel they are a good representative sample. Moreover, all had chosen to attend a conference and all had been using SIMS for at least 2 years, some much longer.

In response to the question "Do you feel the conference helped you to use SIMS for management purposes?" the majority responded positively, but, 16 percent felt the conference had not helped. However, it should be noted, in relation to a later question concerning whether the respondents felt their current SIMS system "could be used as a management tool", these 16 percent also expressed a negative view.

When asked about their attendance on management training courses, all the headteachers (26) responded that they had attended management training courses. The types of course attended varied greatly, from M.Ed courses (2), through diploma courses (4), to a half day course (1). Several respondents did comment that their courses had contained no IT component. Of the other respondents (12), who were not headteachers, only one had attended a management course.

The responses to a series of questions concerning the use of SIMS as a management tool were in general positive. However, a significant percentage (18%) felt their current SIMS system could not be used as a management tool. Of these, 57 percent said that this was due to SIMS not being suitable, and 86 percent said that there was lack of management understanding of how to use SIMS as a management tool. An additional three respondents also noted lack of management's understanding of the use of SIMS as a management tool as a problem, giving 24 percent of total respondents noting this.

The respondents were asked if their school used SIMS for management purposes. Almost 60 percent (57% of primary, 62% secondary, and the middle school did not) claimed their schools did use SIMS for management purposes - 42 percent claimed their school did not use SIMS for management purposes or did not respond to the question. Of the respondents who claimed their schools did use SIMS for management purposes - all cited the financial management module (LRM) - used for budget planning, with 32 percent giving this is as the only example. Other modules cited as being used for management purposes included 'Attendance' 45 percent, 'Midas' (Management Information Data Access System) 14 percent (though several schools noted they did not have this module yet) and 'Exams' (14%) (though this module is only used in secondary schools). Several other modules 'STAR', 'Personnel', and 'Assessment' were also listed by several respondents. The elaboration given, of how their schools used these modules, could however have been interpreted as purely an administrative function.

3.5 Discussion

The survey only covered a small number of schools, and thus one can not read too much into the results. It would appear that the only major widespread educational management decision making processes that utilise IT are concerned with finances. However, it is apparent that many schools are still not using SIMS for management purposes - informing decision making. The reasons for this may be:

- As Mitchell and Wild (1993) suggested, the system may not be flexible enough to provide information for management decisions;
- SIMS are in the process of re-writing all their modules to work under Microsoft® Windows™ and thus the constant updating of modules, and modules that do not integrate because some run under DOS and some under Windows, has slowed progress in this area;
- The training offered to senior managers is inappropriate. In evaluating the conference a significant number (26%) offered the unsolicited opinion that the conference was far better than all the others they had attended on ITEM. The reason for this assertion was given as the conference was not a "'hands-on' press this key to do this course," which they felt was fine for clerical staff, but not for managers;
- The lack of management training of those who are not heads and some of the heads may well act as a block to using IT for management purposes.

4 CONCLUSION

Visscher's (1995) view concerning the developmental stages of CASA, does appear in the UK's case to need some slight modification to include a stage where IT is used widely for administration, but management usage is limited. Having examined the nature and use of MISs in section two of this paper it is apparent that there is a need for MISs in school to assist educational managers in planning, organising, controlling, reviewing, monitoring and evaluating the operation of their schools. However, for significant benefits to accrue, not only do educational MISs need to be well designed and implemented but educational managers must be aware, and take advantage of, the capabilities of their systems. It is also clear from the small survey that SIMS is not being used for management purposes, and some suggestions for this are made above. Developments that may lead to greater use of SIMS, in particular, and MISs in general, to support educational management are the production of new SIMS modules concerned with planning; increased competition from other suppliers; and the introduction of 'Headlamp'. 'Headlamp' (The Headteachers' Leadership and Management Programme) is a new national scheme in the UK to improve the quality of school management; unfortunately there is no mention of IT or MISs anywhere in the nationally specified course outline. (Teacher Training Agency, 1995).

5 REFERENCES

Bank, A. and Williams, C.R. (1987) The coming of instructional information systems, in *Information Systems and School Improvement: Inventing the Future* (eds. A. Bank and C.R. Williams), Teacher College Press, New York.

Cameron Fisher, J., Semrau, P. and Turban, E. (1990) Decision support systems in elementary and secondary educational administration. *School Organisation*, **10(1)**, 91-105.

Carter, D.S.G. and Burger, M. (1994) Curriculum management, instructional leadership and new information technology. *School Organisation*, **14(2)**, 153-168.

Coopers and Lybrand (1988) *Local management of schools.* A Report for the Department of Education and Science. DES, London.

Davis, G.B. and Olson, M. H. (1985) *Management information systems*. McGraw-Hill, New York.

DES (1988) *DES Circular No. 7/88. Education Reform Act: management of schools.* DES, London.

Fidler, B. and Bowles, G. (Eds.) (1989) *Effective local management of schools.* Longmans in Association with British Educational Management and Administration Society, London.

Hicks, J.O. (1993) *Management information systems: a user perspective (3rd ed.).* West Publishing Company, St. Paul.

House of Commons (1988) *Education Reform Act 1988: Chapter 40.* HMSO, London.

Levacic, R. (1995) *Local management of schools: analysis and practice.* Open University Press, Buckingham.

Mitchell, S. and Wild, P. (1993) A task analysis of a computerised system to support administration in schools. *Educational Administration and Management*, **21(1)**, 53-61.

Selwood, I. (1995) The development of ITEM in England and Wales, in *Information Technology in Educational Management.* (eds. B.Z. Barta, M. Telem, and Y. Gev), Chapman & Hall, London.

Strain, M. (1990) Resource management in schools: some conceptual and practical considerations, in *Local Management of Schools: Some Practical Issues.* (eds. E. Cave, and C. Wilkinson), Routledge, London.

Teacher Training Agency (1995) *HEADLAMP - an initiative to support newly appointed headteachers.* TTA, London.

Telem, M. (1990) DSS in educational organisations. *Computers in Education*, **14(1)**, 61-69.

Thierauf, J. R. (1987) *Effective Management Information Systems (2nd ed.).* Merrill, Ohio.

Visscher. A J. (1995) Computer assisted school administration and management: where are we and where should we go?, in *Information Technology in Educational Management* (eds. B.Z. Barta, M. Telem, and Y. Gev), Chapman & Hall, London.

6 BIOGRAPHIES

Ian Selwood has been involved in IT in Education since the early seventies. Firstly as a teacher introducing computers into classrooms and teaching computer studies, then as an advisory teacher for computing and IT. In addition to writing textbooks for Computer Studies he has had papers published on a variety of topics concerned with IT in Education. Appointed as a lecturer in Information Technology in Education at the University of Birmingham in 1987, he is concerned with both the initial training of teachers and their further professional development. He has been involved in research and teaching about the use of IT in administration and management since 1988.

Helen Drenoyianni obtained her BEd at the University of Athens-Greece (1992) and she is currently a student at the University of Birmingham, registered for the degree of MEd with a sponsorship from the Greek State Scholarship Foundation.

14

Evaluation of ITEM for proactive development

P. Wild
Department of Education, Loughborough University
Loughborough, UK
Phone: (44)-1509-222768 Fax: (44)-1509-223912
e-mail: p.wild@lboro.ac.uk

A.C.W. Fung
Department of Education Studies, Hong Kong Baptist University
Kowloon Tong, Kowloon, Hong Kong
Phone: (852)-23395679 Fax: (852)-23397894
e-mail: alexfung@hkbu.edu.hk

Abstract

Evaluation will be the key to effective and efficient implementation and use of information technology in education management. As hardware, software and the needs of users develop and change, such evaluation will need to be both proactive and dynamic in that it must continually inform how the systems need to be modified to allow the potential to be fully realised. Dynamic evaluation can then be used to inform the system design, training, support and documentation to ensure end-user acceptance of the systems and provide administration support and information relevant to enhanced decision making processes. Findings from a preliminary study in early 1995 of the Hong Kong School Administration and Management System (SAMS) will be used to illustrate the problems which can occur without carefully planned and contextualised evaluation.

Keywords

Management information sytems, schools, evaluation, user-acceptability

1 INTRODUCTION

Institutional organisations are dynamic. This has been particularly the case for education in many countries in recent years as many governments have implemented new education policies over short time scales. Such changes have occurred in parallel with information technology advances which have brought computerised information systems into the scope and affordability of schools. However, most, if not all, commercial information systems which have been developed for schools have fundamental problems as perceived by users. Any conversation with system managers and users inevitably revolve around the inability of the software to do what the user wants in a way that they want it. "It will not print out particular lists", "it will not allow additional fields", "no additional relational modules can be added to meet the needs of the autonomous institutions" are but a small sample of the many reported shortcomings. Much of this is due to innate inflexibility of the software from the early design process resulting from a 'we know what you want' approach rather than really analysing what was needed and what the new information technologies could offer. In addition, the lack of any properly constituted and planned post-implementation evaluation of the systems, either objective or subjective, has meant that such problems have continued into later versions of the same packages.

In their paper titled 'A two-dimensional approach to systems development', Henson & Hughes (1991) discuss the weakness and waste of resources in the traditional linear SDLC (System Development Life Cycle) approach to the five phases of problem definition, analysis, design, production, and implementation. These writers have suggested the need to have foresight, i.e. anticipation of the impact of the current phase on a later one in the SDLC. Their two-dimensional model of SDLC provides for "the expression of an alternative approach that accommodates the integration of phases. .... emphasizes the inherent, direct relationships between phases that the traditional approach ignores" (Henson & Hughes, 1991, pp. 43). This need for the integration of phases has also been referred to as "the intertwining of specification and implementation" by Swartout & Balzer (1982).

The evaluation methodologies considered in this paper do not include an analysis of the impact of ITEM systems on the fundamental working of the institutions. This is not to ignore the importance of such studies when the investment is so large. However, the evaluation of the system that is implemented as a result of the investment in a proactive and cyclical way will help to ensure that the design and use are the best possible for the level of investment, with a greatly improved chance that the investment gives value for money in terms of positive effects on the management and success of the schools.

Wild (1995) highlights the importance of user participation for successful school information systems (SISs) development and implementation. A major reason for many failures in SISs is the lack of formative evaluation which could feedback valuable information during the innovation process. The UAA (User Acceptance Audit) recommended by Wild as an evaluation tool is not only a summative instrument to be applied at the end of the implementation process but incorporates formative evaluation throughout the whole SIS-development and implementation process. Information and feedback collected with the UAA would provide timely feedback both to the SIS-users and developers for necessary adaptations and modifications. The UAA thus formalises the evaluation process for both objective and subjective measures of system functionality and usability. Resulting from a preliminary study of the Hong Kong SAMS, a possible cyclical model of evaluation (Figure 1) has been proposed which could impinge on, and enhance, many aspects of the implementation and is a further development of the initial application of the UAA in the education context in the UK (Wild et al, 1992). Various issues of user concern have been identified through initial focused questions and discussion which can be used to develop a more structured analysis process in schools already using the systems (phase 1). Results from this would then be used to review the issues and feedback the results to the relevant point in the development chain. It is likely that such an analysis would identify both barriers and promoters of the system being developed and implemented. Barriers can then be removed and promoters can be used to encourage increased acceptance of the system. The same evaluation process would then be used for the next phase of implementations, hopefully with less barriers and more promoters being identified.

Identify issues for users →	Phase 1 .... 2 ....3 etc →	Review each issue
Hardware	*for each issue carry*	*Feed back results to*
Software	*out an issue specific*	*designers, programmers,*
Training	*UAA*	*trainers, support team etc*
Installation		
Implementation		
Data input/transfer		
Report specifications		
Printing		
Support systems		
Feedback systems		

Figure 1 A cyclical User Acceptance Evaluation.

There has been some debate in the evaluation methodology literature about the validity of using 'user satisfaction' as a measure of system success as opposed to more objective measures (see for example Hirschheim and Smithson 1987). However, recently reported research into whether direct user satisfaction is valid as a surrogate measure of information system effectiveness has been carried out by Gatian (1994). She worked from the hypothesis that if an effective system is defined as one that adds value, any measure of system effectiveness should reflect some positive change in user behaviour such as improved productivity, fewer errors and/or better decision making. Extensive questionnaire and statistical analysis focused on direct and indirect users of a college and university information system at thirty nine campuses. The direct users were those who controlled the systems and indirect users were the academic department heads. Conclusions of this extensive research certainly suggest that user satisfaction is an important ingredient for system effectiveness. In another study (Iivari & Ervasti, 1994) the major research question is whether user information satisfaction can be used as a surrogate measure of information system effectiveness through indirect user satisfaction. Again there is extensive research based on twenty one different application information systems in a public organisation and the results suggest that user information satisfaction may, within the well defined limits of the research, have some applicability as a predictor of information system effectiveness and as an indicator of implementability. Such research is adding further credibility to the use of the UAA as an holistic evaluation methodology which could be applied in the education sector ideally as a support to the full process of design and implementation for new systems, but at least as an identifier of barriers to system success and effectiveness at the stage many countries are now at; trying to improve present systems introduced reactively and piecemeal without proper analysis of needs. The small scale pilot projects in the UK also suggest that, through careful contextualisation, the UAA can provide a degree of objectivity to such evaluations (Wild et al, 1992).

2 THE PRELIMINARY STUDY OF SAMS

At this stage in our development of thinking about evaluation methodology, it has been useful to start to apply some of the ideas to a real system. In the crucial issue of user involvement and participation, the SAMS case has revealed two interesting questions: (1) who is the genuine user? and (2) is the involvement genuine, i.e. does the genuine user have a real say?

SAMS stands for 'School Administration & Management System' which is a project started in 1993 by the Hong Kong government. The project aims at providing a standard

SIS for all public-sector primary and secondary schools (about 1,300) in five years time. In the SAMS project, the Education Department of Hong Kong (ED) is technically supported by the Information Technology Services Department (ITSD) of the Hong Kong government. As a policy, ITSD oversees all IT services in Hong Kong government departments and its roles in SAMS thus include the 'expert in control' on the one hand, and the 'service provider' on the other.

Although SAMS is a project to develop an administration and management system for school use, ITSD consider the ED as their client department and user, and not the schools. Although there is a group of user-representatives from schools, formed under the ED to advise on the system development of SAMS, no such member is found on the Project Board. System requirements are therefore not directly collected from nor negotiated with schools by ITSD, but instead through ED. The 'user set', using King and Cleland's (1987) term, is thus differently interpreted by ITSD and by the schools, which consider themselves naturally as the primary users. This omission of 'stakeholder analysis' (Lyytinen, 1987) could be a major factor impeding the future implementation of SAMS in schools.

The second important question, of whether user-involvement is genuine or not, has no easy answer. In the SAMS case, although ED is the sponsor of the project, government policy of ITSD taking both roles of 'expert' and 'service provider' simultaneously has apparently given rise to conflicts of interests. ITSD considers suggestions and requirements from the ED and the user-representatives group but is not required to act on them. Much time and effort were spent on negotiations, yet interviews with the user-representatives indicate strong dissatisfaction with the system functionality finally produced and the support provided during supply and implementation. The answers to questions on specific implementation issues showed that the direct and indirect users were already identifying problems with the system which would have been identified earlier by more careful analysis and formal evaluation:

- The screen input format for pupil data is slow - the Deputy Head quoting 6 minutes per pupil.
- The subject by subject input was slow and did not match the user environment.
- The school is happier with its own system, used for 18 months prior to SAMS.
- The same pupil address has to be entered 3 times.
- The printer was being run through a dedicated computer print server to try to speed up printing - this computer was therefore removed from other uses.
- The school was not happy with the fixed format reports provided with the system.
- The Deputy Head rang the area SAMS support co-ordinator who appeared not to know the system well enough to help.
- The school had the feeling that they had been given the system and "left to get on with it".
- They used their own printer as the one supplied for the system was too slow, especially for Chinese character printing.
- The special data conversion program supplied for entering initial data to be installed into SAMS was very slow and so the school IT co-ordinator had written his own in Access to produce the data in the required format.

In addition some problems were identified which are associated with the bi-lingual nature of the system:

- The system is slow when using Chinese characters.

- There had been insufficient training on the inputting with Chinese characters.

Methodology is therefore one thing, how the methodology is being applied in terms of end-users is another.

3 THE METHODOLOGY OF SAMS: PRINCE AND SSADM

The PRINCE (Project In a Controlled Environment) methodology has been developed by the Central Computer and Telecommunications Agency (CCTA, 1990) in the United Kingdom as a structured set of procedures designed specifically for managing projects in IS/IT environments. ITSD has adopted PRINCE as the framework within which the SAMS project can be specified, designed and implemented.

PRINCE in essence is a project management and control method with at least two key stages, namely project planning and then implementation of the plan. Each PRINCE stage has five components: Organization, Plans, Controls, Products, and Activities. Following this method, the SAMS project has a 3-tier organization structure with a Project Board (with executive, senior user, and senior technical membership), a Project Management (with a project manager and stage managers), and a Project Assurance Team (with business assurance co-ordinator, user assurance co-ordinator, and technical assurance co-ordinator membership). Plans, and controls based on these plans, are the responsibilities of the respective organization levels:

For the Project Board -- Project Resource Plan & Project Technical Plan;
For the Project & Stage Managers -- Stage Resource Plans & Stage Technical Plans;
For the Stage Teams -- Detailed Resource Plans & Detailed Technical Plans;
For the Individual -- Individual Work Plan.

Provision is made for an Exception Plan only when a deviation from the plans in terms of cost or elapsed time has exceeded, or will exceed tolerances previously defined by the Project Board.

Without going into details, it is fair to say that PRINCE in SAMS is a methodology intended for quality assurance of the object system production and implementation, with strong user involvement. Participation of users in information systems development is quite well accepted nowadays as one of the most critical factors in implementation success (Mumford & Weir, 1979; Ives & Olson, 1984; Jarvenpaa & Ives, 1991). For instance, ETHICS is a method that specially advocates user participation throughout the systems design stage to produce a socio-technical system (Mumford & Weir, 1979; Mumford, 1983). JAD (Joint Application Design) similarly stresses user-involvement in the systems development process (Wood & Silver, 1989; Kettelhut, 1993). Furthermore, as King & Cleland (1987) have suggested, there is considerable evidence that the lack of involvement of users in different phases of systems development has been a significant factor contributing to the failure of many MIS to perform as expected.

SSADM (structured system analysis and design methodology), according to CCTA (1990), is "a structured set of procedural, technical and documentation standards, designed specifically for analyzing business needs and undertaking software development. It consists of a two-part framework covering business requirements analysis and design - which is sectioned into stages. Taken together these stages provide a complete set of techniques for data modelling, requirements analysis and software design." (pp.17)

ITSD adopted SSADM in May 1988 and it has become a mandatory standard for all systems development by ITSD since November 1991 (ITSD, 1994), and thus SAMS should accordingly be developed with the SSADM methodology. According to the documentation on SSADM (ITSD, 1994), the 'System Development Life Cycle'

(SDLC) of a project development process is divided into the different phases of Project Initiation, Feasibility Study (FS), Systems Analysis & Design (SA&D), Implementation, and Post Implementation Review. The Project Initiation phase defines the area of study, business objectives for the proposed project and the resources available for it. The FS phase marks the beginning of SSADM, which is followed by the SA&D phase (including systems analysis and logical system design stages) and the physical design stage of the Implementation phase. At this end-point of the SSADM application, the major final outcomes are the program specifications and a database or file specification. Subsequently, the four stages in Implementation (program development, system integration & testing, user acceptance test, and system installation & production) are carried out, with the final Post Implementation Review phase concluding the SDLC.

The SSADM structure is thus:

1. Feasibility Study Module (Stage 0: Feasibility)
2. Requirements Analysis Module (Stage 1: Investigation of Current Environment; Stage 2: Business System Options)
3. Requirements Specification Module (Stage 3: Definition of Requirements)
4. Logical System Specification Module (Stage 4: Technical System Options;
   Stage 5: Logical Design)
5. Physical Design Module (Stage 6: Physical Design)

SSADM should thus be the essential part in the SDLC attending to the systems analysis and design aspects of the 'SAMS' system.

In the SAMS case, the Feasibility Study was not done by ITSD but by an external consultancy that carried out the Information Systems Strategy Study (ISSS) for the ED. Government funding was then secured by the ED, with the support of ITSD. The ISSS report subsequently became the blue-print on which negotiations between ED and ITSD were based. Insufficient time and effort, as far as the authors can see, was spent on Systems Analysis and Design. This is evidenced by the fact that ITSD did not spend enough time with schools directly for their requirements analysis. User-representatives and the ED provided the major inputs for this aspect of the SSADM. Davis (1987) has pointed out that "asking users for information requirements may not yield a complete correct set" (pp. 237) but the consequence of asking indirectly has been indicated by the preliminary study. Furthermore, from the products of Modules 3 and 4, one can easily judge that the information systems development perspective is 'datalogical' and not 'infological' (Methlie, 1987). The datalogical perspective takes the information requirements as given by the existing data flows in the organization and the objective of the systems development task is to improve efficiency. On the other hand, the infological perspective looks for an effective information system for the organization that can help support managerial decision-making. Although SAMS is a system named to provide administrative and managerial support for schools, only a datalogical approach has been taken. The information requirements as given by the existing data flows in schools are taken for granted and the objective of the systems development task is to improve efficiency by computerizing manual procedures and data files. There is no trace of the infological approach aiming to develop an effective SIS for the school organization that would support managerial decision-making.

Theoretically, SSADM should be quite comprehensive and detailed in its standards, and should have a number of benefits as proclaimed in the SSADM User Notes (ITSD, 1994). In the SAMS case, these *intended benefits* are considered, in the list below, and observable performance gaps as identified in the preliminary study are noted within square brackets under each item:

1. *assure system quality*
   'The high quality of a project is achieved by viewing the system from three independent viewpoints: Function, Data, and Event which will cross-check one another to minimize omissions and other possible errors.'
   [User-representatives and ED staff did not have access to the technical documents developed from the three viewpoints. Such documentation, in any case, could be too technical and complex for lay users. Moreover, quite a number of bugs were identified during the User-Acceptance-Test for the four SAMS modules released to ten pilot schools. Schools also have complaints about the slow speeds in printing out.]

2. *better project planning and control*
   'A checklist for products and a structural framework of procedures can assist planning in terms of minimizing redundant work and providing more accurate estimation of resources requirement.'
   [Users found that some data input was needed in triplicate, and printing was slow, with printer specifications not matching the required task. It has also been noted that there was a division of labour among more than ten programmers in producing the different applications in SAMS. Individual programmers might not be fully communicated about what their colleagues were doing.]
3. *increase productivity*
   'Developers do not have to figure out the documentation format and contents from scratch, these are provided in SSADM, as a result much time can be saved.'
   [This is assuming that all members in the development team including teacher-representatives are fully conversant with SSADM, which is a matter of doubt.]

4. *meet user requirements*
   'Users will be involved from the earliest stage of the project. Throughout the structure of SSADM, users have opportunities to raise their requirements, walk through and review the deliverables and select the Business System Option. The common language between the users and developers means better communication and hence user requirements can be met more precisely.'
   [Much has been said already in this paper on user involvement. The only point to raise here is that users do not generally have a sufficient command of the language in SSADM, even after training for one or two days as in SAMS, to enhance communication with the developers. Moreover, when users were flooded with thick documents of Function Requirements (deliverables), sometimes quite technically written, they often did not know what they really had to agree with. It was only when prototypes in SAMS were available that the users could appreciate whether their requirements were met or not.]

5. *avoid reliance on a few key persons*
   'With the use of a standard and consistent approach, the system development process can be followed easily even by new staff.'
   [No information is available for any comment to be made.]

6. *increase adaptability*
   'With a complete specification of a software logical design independent of hardware-specific solutions, the implementation options are kept open for as long as practicable. This can have considerable advantages in large, long duration projects which may be able to take advantage of technological or marketing developments which do not exist at the outset.'
   [One system limitation which contradicts this was that the programmers had removed the windowing facility inherent in modern software, leaving a linear DOS type system using only full screen windows. Only time can tell since the SAMS project is only in

its early implementation. One point to note is that the programming language had been decided to be FoxPro for Windows very early on, even before the Logical Design stage.]

7. *reduce maintenance cost*
'Problems can be identified earlier. With fewer omissions from the start, the sound design reduces the chance of logical errors; and there would be less maintenance due to deviation from expectation. It would be easier to implement any changes in data or process even though it has to be performed by a team of new staff because of the adequate and standardized documentation.'
[Since SSADM is a subset within the SDLC, to be concluded before implementation of the product system in user organizations, early identification of problems in design and production is expected. Apparently there were still many problems waiting to be solved when four SAMS modules had already been installed in about 300 schools; and the roll-out plan was due to reach many more by the end of 1996. The user acceptance 'test' used between ED and ITSD is not clearly defined and differs widely from the more formal UAA which is really required to identify problems and match systems to user expectations. In addition, training can be focussed to overcome identified mismatches.]

4 CONCLUSION

The lack of a formal and cyclical evaluation strategy has so far limited the effectiveness of the SAMS implementation. The only formal evaluation, the Post-Implementation Review, will occur too late to identify the problems and user acceptability issues which will already have discouraged many teachers, caused much extra work and infused a lack of confidence in the system as a whole. Our findings show that 'local' school experts are already spending time producing their own data transfer programs and reporting functions, which could have been developed centrally if there had been more emphasis on early analysis of real user needs. The speed of implementation has denied the opportunity for a formal and proactive evaluation of the type proposed in figure 1 to be carried out at the early stages before users find problems. Results from such an evaluation would have overcome many of the identified problems and, at the same time, identified the requirements and content of training courses and better informed design and implementation teams which might have overcome many of the real and perceived problems. Barriers and promoters could then have been dealt with in an organised and structured way so that new users would have felt more confident from the start that the system would help in the administration and management of the school. At the time of the preliminary study, many felt that they wanted to wait "until SAMS was as good as their own" but that striving for a standardised system was a worthy aim.

Preliminary results in the study of SAMS reinforce earlier findings in the UK that a more formal evaluation tool needs to be developed in the context of information systems in the school environment. Such a tool would form a basis for a systematic study from an early stage of development so that schools more quickly and easily gain from the implementation of ITEM. Wide communication of evaluations would help to ensure that new systems learn from the mistakes of earlier systems, which does not seem to be the case at present.

5 REFERENCES

CCTA (1990) *PRINCE overview: the PRINCE project management method.* Her Majesty's Stationery Office, London.

Davis, G.B. (1987) Strategies for information requirements determination, in *Information analysis: selected readings* (ed. R. Galliers), Addison-Wesley Publishers, Sydney.

Gatian, A.W. (1994) Is user satisfaction a valid measure of systems effectiveness. *Information and Management*, **26(3)**, 119-131.

Henson, K.L. and Hughes, C.T. (1991) A two-dimensional approach to systems development. *Systems Development*, **8(1)**, 35-43.

Hirschheim, R. and Smithson, S. (1987) Information systems evaluation: myth and reality, in *Information analysis: Selected readings* (ed. R. Galliers), Addison-Wesley Publishers, Sydney.

ITSD (1994) *SSADM: end user notes*. Information Technology Services Department, Hong Kong Government, Hong Kong.

Iivari, J. and Ervasti, I. (1994) User information satisfaction: IS implementability and effectiveness. *Information and Management*, **27(4)**, 205-220.

Ives, B. & Olson, M.H. (1984) User involvement and MIS success: a review of research. *Management Science*, **30**, 586-608.

Jarvenpaa, S.L. and Ives, B. (1991) Executive involvement and participation in the management of information technology. *MIS Quarterly*, **15(2)**, 229-42.

Kettelhut, M.C. (1993) JAD methodology and group dynamics. *Information Systems Management*, **10(1)**, 46-53.

King, W.R. and Cleland, D.I. (1987) The design of management information systems: an information system analysis approach, in *Information analysis: selected readings* (ed. R. Galliers), Addison-Wesley Publishers, Sydney.

Lyytinen, K. (1987) A taxonomic perspective of information systems development: theoretical constructs and recommendations, in *Critical Issues in Information Systems Research*, (eds. R.J. Boland Jr. and R.A. Hirschheim), John Wiley & Sons, New York.

Methlie, L.B. (1987) Systems requirements analysis - methods and models, in *Information analysis: selected readings* (ed. R. Galliers), Addison-Wesley Publishers, Sydney.

Mumford, E. (1983) *Designing human systems*. Manchester Business School, Manchester.

Mumford, E. and Weir, M. (1979) *Computer systems in work design - the ETHICS method*. Wiley, New York,

Swartout, W. and Balzer, R. (1982) On the inevitable intertwining of specification and implementation. *Communications of the ACMI*, **25(7)**, 438-440.

Wild, P. (1995) The use of task analysis and user acceptability audits in implementing information technology systems in schools, in *Information technology in educational management* (eds. B. Barta, M. Telem and Y. Gev), Chapman and Hall, London.

Wild, P., Scivier, J. and Richardson, S. (1992) An evaluation of a LEA's secondary schools IT system for LMS Support. *Education Management and* Administration, **20(4)**, 40-48.

Wood, J. and Silver, D. (1989) *Joint application design*. Wiley Press, New York.

6 BIOGRAPHIES

Phil Wild gained his Ph.D. in 1976 in the area of cosmic ray astronomy but then immediately moved into the education field, gaining his PGCE before becoming a science and IT teacher and advisor for 10 years. He then moved to Loughborough University as Science Tutor and IT coordinator before becoming Head of the Department of Education. His main area of research and writing is in IT in the school curriculum and school management. His publications include papers on the evaluation of ITEM, the work of IT advisory teachers and the use of datalogging in school science lessons.

Alex C.W. Fung received a B.Sc. in 1970 from the University of Hong Kong and Cert. Ed., Adv. Dip. Ed. and M. Ed. in subsequent years from the same university. He received his Ph.D. in educational management and administration in 1992 from London University Institute of Education. He was a secondary school principal in Hong Kong for more than twenty years before he joined the Department of Education Studies of the Hong Kong Baptist University as senior lecturer in 1994. He is currently Associate Professor and also Director of the SAMS Training and Research Unit at the University. His research is focussed on IT in education management, teacher support systems and managing change and school improvement.

PART FIVE

Systems Development

15

Distributed ITEM for the future: moving towards client-server systems

Bill Davey
Department of Business Computing, RMIT University, Australia
124 LaTrobe Street, Melbourne, Victoria, Australia 3000
Phone: (613)-96605975 Fax: (613)-96605850
e-mail: Billd@RMIT.edu.au

Arthur Tatnall
Department of Business Information Systems, Victoria University of Technology, Melbourne, Australia
e-mail: arthur@cougar.vut.edu.au

Abstract

The pressures on ITEM systems include legacy systems being distributed among a diverse database. This diversity includes different hardware and software platforms in a variety of geographical situations. Client-server technologies offer a solution for the integration of information hardware and software sources into a system wide information resource. This paper relates experience of client-server technologies in the general literature, both positive and negative, to the needs of ITEM developers.

Keywords

Client-server, information technology, educational management

1 INTRODUCTION

Educational institutions typically have developed a number of information and communication systems that have been developed in isolation for specific purposes. Educational management is seeing the need for information from these sources to be gathered so as to aid in informed decision making. This scenario is typical of those that have been effectively solved using client-server technologies. Client-server architecture and applications can solve distributed data source problems, but introduce difficulties of their own. The ITEM developer can gain from knowledge of problems that have arisen in other domains before choosing a client-server solution.

2 THE RISE OF CLIENT-SERVER COMPUTING

There have been negative reports in the computing press of some particular client-server implementations. These point out the disappointment of expectations raised by theoretical gains to be made from downsizing and distributing through client-server architectures. These reports seem to have made little impact on the move toward client-server (CS) when measured in terms of expenditure and number of new applications.

There are two trends that point out the importance of client-server architectures and the need for more training in the area:

- the rapid increase in products from solution developers, and
- the extent to which the growth in the use of client-server technologies in applications is not being met by trained graduates.

As evidence that industry is moving towards client-server, Marc Myers (1995) reports that "IBM is currently pouring 75 percent of its development efforts into client-server related projects." Myers also reports on a survey showing a rapid increase in other vendor products in the area. Julia King (1995), reports on a survey of 400 IS executives carried out by Deloitte Touche of New York. This showed that "50 percent of IS executives who expected benefits from client-server tools actually realised them. On average the IS budget is 16 percent higher in the companies where 25 percent of applications run on advanced client-server architectures. In 1994 43 percent of all applications ran under client-server compared with 27 percent in 1993." This type of result shows that client-server technology is expanding despite not meeting the expected cost and time savings. In fact the rapid expansion of CS caused the Deloitte survey to find "finding experienced people to design client-server systems remains a problem" and "last year 79 percent of IS managers had difficulty recruiting technical architects and distributed database experts." Clearly there is an established trend towards CS technologies in the general IS field. The reason for this trend and the gap between perceived benefits and practice is a little more difficult to explain.

3 WHAT IS CLIENT-SERVER COMPUTING

Client-server computing is based on the notion that some functions are best handled on a local basis while others are better done centrally. It is thus a blend of the central, timesharing approach, with distributed processing which emphasises local use. Client-server computing involves the use of a mixture of pcs and mainframes, typically connected by a wide area network. Application processing is shared between the pc clients and one or more servers. To make full use of client-server computing, application software must be designed specifically to run in such an environment.

Unfortunately there are many views of what constitutes client-server. A definition provided by Jeff Schulman (1993) of the US based consultancy Gartner Group says that "client-server is the splitting of an application into tasks that are performed on separate computers, one of which is a programmable workstation." A similar popular definition is "a client-server architecture is one where the application is split up into a back end, running on a powerful server that stores, retrieves and processes data, and a front end, running on a local client workstation that handles user interaction." Tatnall and Davey's (1994a) definition introduces the idea of a two tier client-server architecture. Of course we now have three tier architecture involving a "middle" step or tier. Robertson-Dunn (1993) also provides a more technical definition of client-server computing "A model of computing in which a system is partitioned into modules where commands and responses pass between modules such that one module acts as a request agent (the client) and another acts as the service provider (the server). The server keeps no requester specific information or states. This means that each command is complete and is not dependant on previous or future commands. It is possible for a server to also act as a client by requesting services of another server."

4 CLIENT-SERVER TOOLS FOR ITEM

The literature points to five important areas in which client-server architecture may be a useful concept in defining better ITEM systems:

- designing client applications;
- designing client interfaces;
- designing server applications;
- communicating from client to server;
- the concept of integrated information systems.

In Victoria, Australia a number of attempts have been made to integrate available ITEM applications at the school level. The attempts make use of the data transfer abilities of Visual Basic to incorporate information sources from across the school. As a client-server tool, VB has the advantage of being very widespread in the community, lying second in installed base to all environments. The tool is excellent for designing user interfaces and third party components make access to almost all data sources relatively easy. In addition to VB there are many tools. These include Delphi, Visual Age, SQL Windows, and Personal Oracle. All these tools are available to classical ITEM developers, both in terms of cost and learning curve.

Problems have emerged with the use of client-server tools in the local situation. These are typical of first tries in client-server technology and the limitations are those of two tier client-server systems. A three tier system incorporating a business services layer would overcome these and all the tools mentioned above allow the production of three tier systems.

4.1 Problems with client-server ITEM systems

Three tier systems provide answers to these problems. The addition of an extra tier allows us to develop systems where the user interface, business rules (such as who can view certain data, who can update and data validations) and the original data capture applications can be separated in a similar manner to object oriented systems. Products like R/3 by SAP and TP monitors like CICS and Tuxedo have allowed three tier systems, but have been too complex and expensive for traditional school based ITEM systems. The new enterprise edition of VB allows true three tier development.

5 CLIENT-SERVER EXAMPLES IN ITEM

In a typical school in Victoria, data will exist in the schools administrative package which is provided centrally and runs under the Dataflex product. This package provides student academic records, personal details, and some transaction processing ability for financial transactions of the school. The package was originally designed to provide some reporting to the school but emphasised a standardised administrative system throughout schools that enabled easy access to school data from the central government department. Much of the data on the system was useful to school administrators but was unavailable to them in any form relevant to decision making. Each school also had a wealth of additional data: library systems, student reporting, and local, teacher designed systems to do anything from timetables to sporting teams. The data redundancy of and integrity problems produced by this plethora of independent systems have not been addresses in the past due to the enormity of replacing all systems with a monolithic solution. Client-server approaches to this scenario would see a set of possibilities:

- meeting strategic planning objectives;
- meeting tactical aims;
- providing feedback on strategic measures such as attendances, performance, budgets, staff development, environmental management;
- operational control such as staffing, resource allocation;
- removing redundancy problems such as lost students;
- removing integrity problems such as exhaustive checks;
- providing information in a relevant format;
- improving communication through centralised retrieval;
- improving productivity by removing redundancy.

These possibilities have recently been addressed by a VB front end supplied to schools that provides some DSS support using the centralised database package.

Research (Tatnall and Davey 1994a) has shown that most information systems are produced to handle transaction processing. These systems can be improved to provide support for higher level management decision making. In the Victorian system an interface to the classical transaction processing system provides summary data. This can be tailored to the mission statements and their measures for each school.

Research by Davey and Tatnall (1994b) has shown that good Graphical User Interface front- end writing tools are available to the classical ITEM developer both at system and school levels. This research points to a number of conceptual problems that arise in the move to client-server but hints that these difficulties can be overcome.

6 CONCLUSION

The amount of data in an ITEM system far exceeds that which is used for educational decision making. This is often because of the diverse nature of the databases and physical distribution of the data throughout the educational system. Client-server technologies have matured, and tools are available, to such an extent that client-server solutions are available in most ITEM situations. These tools provide a mechanism for moving from disparate sources of data to an integrated information system. The lessons of the introduction of client-server systems in the broader IT world show us that client-server systems have a start up cost which is only offset by the quality of the information available from the system.

Experiences in Australian schools have shown that a client-server approach can produce an integrated information system. The wide variety of data sources and hardware in the Australian system has not proved an insurmountable problem when using modern client-server tools: However the ITEM designer must be aware of the potential weaknesses of the two tier approach.

7 REFERENCES

Davey, B. & Tatnall, A. (1994a) Problem solving and management information systems, in *Reflections on problem based learning*, Sydney, Australian PBL Network.

Davey, B. & Tatnall, A. (1994b) *Introducing object environments: cognitive difficulties.* SIGRET'94, Dunedin.

King, J. (1995) IS undeterred by the complexities of client/server. *Computerworld,* **29(17)**, 8.

Myers, M. (1995) Examining IBMs client/server blueprint for the future. *Network World,* **12(11)**, 16-19.

Roberston-Dunn, B. (1993) Cautionary tale of client-server. *Informatics,* October 1993.

Schulman, J. (1993) Quoted by G. Philipson, In search of client-server. *Informatics,* August 1993.

Tatnall, A. & Davey, B. (1994c) *Information systems: design and implementation.* Data Publishing, Melbourne.

Tatnall, A. & Davey, B. (1995) *A guide to Visual Basic.* Data Publishing, Melbourne.

8 BIOGRAPHIES

Bill Davey is a Senior Lecturer in Business Computing from RMIT, one of Australia's largest Universities. He is interested in management education, particularly the implications of client-server technologies to executive information systems. Bill lectures in systems implementation, client-server systems, end user computing and various computer languages.

Arthur Tatnall is a currently Senior Lecturer in Information Systems at Victoria University of Technology, Melbourne, Australia. Before moving to tertiary education, Arthur spent a number of years as a secondary school teacher and administrator, then a consultant and systems analyst with the Victorian State Computer Education Centre. He has written a number of school and university texts on Computer Science and Information Systems. His research interests centre around the areas of computing curriculum and management information systems in schools and business.

16

Developing information systems for schools of the future

C.L. Fulmer
Northern Illinois University
Leadership and Educational Policy Studies, 201 Gabel Hall
DeKalb, Illinois, USA
Phone: 815-748-3615
e-mail: p60clf1@wpo.cso.niu.edu

F.P. Frank
Georgia State University
Educational Policy Studies, University Plaza
Atlanta, Georgia, USA
Phone: 404-651-1199
e-mail: ffrank@gsu.edu

Abstract
This article explores the lack of interface between educators and information systems and highlights the inclusion of teaching and learning variables as key to developing information systems which touch core needs of educators and inform teaching and learning processes. The assumption that more and better training will close the gap between educational need and information system adoption is questioned. The authors argue that information systems will be more readily adopted by educators if systems make teaching and learning variables more central. A model for developing this new generation of information systems is presented.

Keywords
Professional development, educational management, information technology

1 INTRODUCTION

Educational information systems have evolved over the last forty years from business management models which are effective for inventory control, personnel management, cost analysis, and audit. Extant educational information systems have reflected these strengths but have tended to be far less effective at depicting the conditions of teaching and learning. Recent information systems serve the purpose of evaluating programs, personnel, or for generating data for accreditation purposes. They have not provided quality data for analyzing and intervening in processes of teaching and learning. We explore some reasons why information systems are not being used more extensively in school settings, and why educational leaders have not taken a leadership role in this area in an attempt to reframe arguments for retraining educational leaders. If one holds that an educational leader is a person who has the capacity to assign resources to system needs, he or she is a key person to the invention and application of information systems in the schools. To date, however, educational leaders have not been heavily invested in information systems development. This article outlines the uses of information systems in schools and offers explanation for the lack of interface between educators and information systems.

2 USES OF COMPUTERS AND INFORMATION SYSTEMS

A review of the literature provided the following list of uses of information systems for administrative purposes in schools: student records (Barbour, 1987; Crawford, 1985; Haugo, 1981; Naron & Estes, 1985; Ogletree & Haskins, 1983; Walters, 1987), staff/personnel records (Bosch, 1988; Crawford, 1987; McIsaac, 1984; Spuck & Atkinson, 1983), financial management such as budget preparation and financial reports (McIsaac, 1984; Pogrow, 1985; Rolley, 1986), inventory and property records (Crawford, 1987; Haugo, 1981; Pogrow, 1985; Vogt, 1988), student scheduling (Crawford, 1987; McIsaac, 1984; Pogrow, 1985), grade reporting and analysis (Marcum, 1987; McIsaac, 1984; Pogrow, 1985) attendance reporting (Barbour 1987; Haugo, 1981; Spuck & Atkinson, 1983; Vogt, 1988), media center/library records (Bosch, 1988; Crawford, 1985; McIsaac, 1984; Spuck & Bozeman, 1988), student transportation (Bosch, 1988; Crawford, 1987; Naron & Estes, 1985; Walters, 1987), test scoring and records (Barbour, 1987; Naron & Estes, 1985; Ogletree & Haskins, 1983), athletic records (Crawford, 1987; Haugo, 1981), student discipline records (Lindelow, 1984), special education/IEP records (Bosch, 1988; Crawford, 1987), instructional management/computer-managed instruction (Spuck & Bozeman, 1988; Taylor, Cole, Hemenway & Hillman, 1989; Wagner, 1985), computer-scored examinations (McKenzie, 1984), computer-assisted examination (Brown, 1984; McIsaac, 1984); accessing information from data banks (Crawford, 1985), student guidance (Crawford 1985), energy management (Lindelow, 1984; Pogrow, 1985), and food service operations (Crawford, 1987).

Two studies (Mikulcik, 1993; Tiede, 1992) provide evidence of actual use of information technology by principals. The principals studied were high-end users who would be most likely to apply those systems to pedagogically related decision making. The researchers found that actual use does not measure up to the promise of information system applications. According to Mikulcik (1993) and Tiede (1992), principals claimed that they were self-trained through trial and error, or took computer workshops or computer classes at vendor sites. Their formal preparation programs did little to provide them with the requisite computer skills. Computer integrated course work was absent from their preparation programs. Each researcher investigated principals' computer usage for system tasks (record keeping, correspondence and communications, monitoring student progress, and other building management) and found that principals used the computer in order of preference: correspondence, communications, student progress/classroom grades, test data, and discipline records. Mikulcik (1993) and Tiede (1992) recommended that actual computer usage would increase when principals received further training.

3 THE ISSUE OF ADMINISTRATOR TRAINING

Typically, administrator training in IT (Fulmer, 1990) has been handled in three ways: (a) require students to provide evidence of computer skills before admitting them to the programs, (b) require students to take a computer competencies course, or (c) require preparation programs to develop computer integrated curricula through which students can acquire computer competencies (Frank, Fulmer, & Mackett, 1991; UCEA, 1993a, 1993b). While it would be hard to argue against more or better computer training for administrators, it is our position that the training failure is, in part, the outcome of lack of perceived usefulness of information systems. Put most simply, those who see a tool as being central to success will be highly motivated to master the use of the tool. We argue that the lack of perceived usefulness of information systems is rooted in the comparative absence of information systems which focus on the dynamics of teaching and learning in the classroom. Put another way, educational leaders and teachers who are not very skilled at conceptualizing or using information systems do not perceive a fit between information systems and their everyday needs and are disinclined to invest energy in learning. In Roger's (1983) stages of acquiring an innovation, the most critical juncture in the process is when people decide to adopt the innovation. As teaching and learning are honored in information systems, the training issue will disappear or be reshaped as educators become serious adopters.

4 RECONCEPTUALIZING THE PROBLEM

We assert that an alternative to training educators to use systems that do not meet their core needs is to help them generate and use a system that does. Such a system will offer educators meaningful use of information system technology and fundamentally alter the way people are trained to use it.

4.1 Etic/Emic origins of information systems

We are using the paired phrase emic-etic to denote an approach to information system development. From the ethnographic tradition, frameworks constructed from inside an organization are termed *emic* and frameworks constructed from outside that organization and juxtaposed on that environment are termed *etic*. Educational information systems based on traditional management thinking would tend to be etic systems and educational information systems based on processes of teaching and learning would tend to be emic systems. Most systems in education were adapted from management thinking because we have more often been interested in evaluation of people and programs. Further, the complexity of inventing new teaching and learning focused information systems has been daunting. As an example, educators themselves have tended to value more highly and therefore invest more time in normed measures; normed measures have dominated even the emically generated systems (Lemann, 1995a, 1995b).

4.2 The importance of variables about teaching and learning

In the interest of illustrating this point we show in Figure 1 a hypothesized evolution of the applications of three kinds of information systems over the last forty-five years. The projection points are based on our experience in the field and illustrate our sense of how this technology has evolved. We assert that management data has had the highest priority and the highest application. As a result, its potential for affecting decision making in educational organizations has been most fully explored. This is also true of normed achievement data which has been almost equally explored. In both of these cases, norms, operational procedures, and supporting technology have slowly but surely evolved to support decision making. In the case of both management data and normed achievement data, analyzing data for purposes of decision making were similar to those being used in business and other social enterprises. Persons with linear mind sets pursued with all good intention the etic frameworks they brought to their understanding of the educational enterprise. In these cases, information system developers exploited with great success the potential of information technology to inform their work.

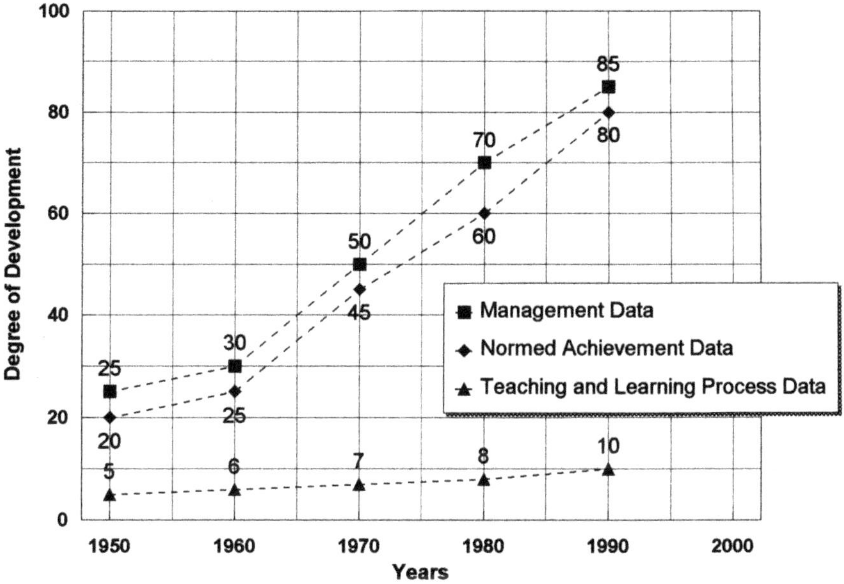

Figure 1 Hypothesized developmental gains on three dimensions on information systems applications in education.

Evolution of the teaching and learning process data into a viable information system required starting from a more primitive beginning. In fact, there was essentially no parallel usage in business, and therefore there was nothing for educators to borrow. A focus on teaching and learning variables has been comparatively absent during the last forty years of evolution of information technology.

4.3 Georgia's state wide student information system

For purposes of illustrating the comparative absence of teaching and learning data in information systems we refer to a system currently in use in the state of Georgia for monitoring data in K-12 educational systems. The state-wide student information system recently established by statute contains 421 variables centered on each child in the system. These data elements are collected around three broad categories. Of the 421 variables, 137 are devoted to the child's surroundings outside the school building such as school system where student resides, English proficiency, bus route, parent/guardian name, and emergency phone. The next major category is composed of 134 variables which deal with the conditions and surrounds of the child's in-school experience such as advisor code, bus route mileage, reason for summer school, course grade received and parent-teacher conferences. The next major bank of 150 variables are scores on normed and criterion referenced achievement tests such as math, writing, Iowa Test of Basic Skills, Grade level tests of achievement and proficiency, and American Collegiate Test. Of the 421 variables only 8 could be classified as teaching and learning variables such as perceptual orientation. We believe that these systems are insufficient rather than wrong minded.

5 CLOSING THE GAP

As these three types of information systems (management data, normative achievement data, and teaching and learning process data) are integrated, the relationship between variable banks will be explored. This will accelerate development and produce integrated information systems. Ironically, this emphasis on emically created variable systems is also part of the latest developments in information systems in business (Frank, Mackett, & Abrams, 1988; Fulmer, 1995). Schuler and Namioka (1993) give examples from around the world of developmental systems in industry using the world of the end user/worker/practitioner as a source for analyzing production problems. This is a significant development in management thinking about information technology in the work place. Similarly, Newberg (1995) has held that the greatest gains in achievement variance are produced by a system where teachers provide continual support. The core of the method he describes for the support is in the rich knowledge that teachers bring to the understanding of the teaching and learning experience of each child over time. In Newberg's model, normed achievement scores are but a thoughtful counterpoint to the more significant work of teachers involved directly with children.

An integrated system should link up a range of data that at its lowest level starts with the learning processes of individual children in classrooms and expands child by child, group by group, school by school, district by district to aggregated data required for state, national, or international analysis. This type of system must have multiple ports of input and output and multiple levels of analysis (Fulmer, 1995). This task is within reach. The hardware capacity and the potential for software development exist. Knowledge of teaching and learning processes and sound pedagogy are well documented. The power of information systems are evident for impacting systems, educational or otherwise. The remaining problem is that developmentally, the worlds of educators and the realities of existing information systems are immature and not well integrated.

6 CREATING THE INTERFACE

In our view, the educational information systems of the future will be developed from data gathered in the following activities. First, a vision of teaching/learning driven educational information systems must be developed through a dialogue with the following participants: teachers, administrators, state, national, and international organizational representatives, and developers of existing educational information systems. Diversity of knowledge and technical expertise are needed in this effort. Second, an audit should be conducted in the following areas: existing information systems, existing data management strategies of teachers, data currently required at various organizational levels, kinds of data required at all instructional levels, and types of data required at all instructional levels. Current formation systems have valuable structures that need not be reinvented. However, an analysis of extant systems would yield both common and missing components. Discovering all the kinds of data required by age level and subject matter as well as the types of data (narrative, biographical, journal, and anecdotal data) are indispensable for building a useful information system. The third step would be that technological and data analysis experts would deal with interface problems. Data already in the system have to be compatible with new data coming into the system. Microcomputer and mainframe compatibility is a must. Interfacing with the practitioner/end user is also a must. The fourth step would be to implement the newly created system in several school districts or educational organizations. The purpose would be to test the usefulness of the system and to initiate cycles of revision. To do so, such a system must model both linear dynamism and temporal immediacy. Linear dynamism is the capacity of a linear system to evolve at the hands of the end user. Temporal immediacy refers to the capacity of a system to provide timely answers for users in educational settings. Day to day educational decisions can not wait for quarterly and yearly data reports. The system must be manipulable from multiple levels, starting at the classroom level. The final step would be to fine tune the system's responsiveness to the ongoing needs of education organizations over several years. Care should be taken that an emically generated system not be inflexible and mimic an etic system.

7 PROPOSED ACTION PLAN

The following is an action plan that school district partners could follow to develop the information systems described above.

1. Audit existing educational information systems, variable taxonomies and data analysis protocols being used throughout the United States and elsewhere (Israel, New Zealand, Australia and Canada have invested in this work). Elements in the audit will be variables collected, data record layout, data analysis procedures, software used, confidentiality, units of analysis, sampling, access time delay before data are available for classroom or building use, accuracy of data, compatibility of data sets, display screens, size or comprehensiveness of data sets.
2. Form a cadre of five interested school districts to provide access to their information systems and whose personnel will provide input and clinical settings. Work groups will be formed (e.g. classroom teachers, counselors, principals, special education teachers) in schools of each system. District partners would participate in the development of information systems and provide a setting for BETA testing of new systems.

3. In each participating school, a staff development trainer should work with a project researcher to define needs and indicators of meeting those needs. Qualitative research methodology is used to document the process and give further clarification.
4. Data obtained from all project researchers and staff development trainers should be used by the researchers to create models of analysis that will help teachers and administrators begin to decode achievement and behavior patterns at the individual student level. Analysis protocols can also be generated at the classroom, grade, and school levels.
5. Researchers should work with teachers and administrators to explore ways to plot teaching and learning patterns over time. Protocols for the analysis of multi-year data should be generated to show the long term patterns of individual student growth and behavior. Long-term analysis offers a way to look at teacher effectiveness and pedagogy over time.
6. Functional data collection instruments will be assembled in an encyclopedia for the use of all educators participating in the development of the system. This encyclopedia would continue to expand with continued work on the system.
7. Researchers and educators will continue to further revise and update the information system.

8 CONCLUSION

In sum, more or better training for administrators is not a complete answer to the problem of the lack of interface between educators and information systems. While the literature contains many references to the uses of information systems in educational organizations, research findings report the actual use of information systems by even high-end users falls far short of data analysis for decision making. We have argued in this paper that the problem of lack of use of information systems can not be attributed solely to poor training, but rather that the systems are not meeting a core need. We view this problem as developmental in nature. A process that includes the needs of educators engaged in processes of teaching and learning in the design of information systems, will insure the increased use of information systems. Educators and information systems experts who are able to integrate the realities of educational learning environments and the capacities of information systems will construct responsive information systems and participate in their natural evolution.

9 REFERENCES

Barbour, A. (1987) Office romance: why administrators are hooked on technology. *Electronic Learning*, **6(7)**, 18-23.

Bosch, K.A. (1988) A microcomputer literacy training model for school administrators. *Journal of Research on Computing in Education*, **20**, 331-8.

Brown, D.T. (1984) Automated assessment systems in school and clinical psychology: present status and future directions. *School Psychology Review*, **13**, 455-460.

Crawford, C.W. (1985) Administrative uses of microcomputers, Part I: needs evaluation. *NASSP Bulletin*, **69(480)**, 70-3.

Crawford, C.W. (1987) Administrative uses of microcomputers. *The Practitioner*, **13(3)**, 1-12.

Frank, F., Fulmer, C. and Mackett, M. (1991) An open challenge to the field of educational administration to mainline information technology: a town meeting to bring together technophobes, techno-indifferents, and technophiles. A town meeting conducted at the annual meeting of the University Council for Educational Administration, Baltimore, Maryland.

Frank, F., Mackett, M. and Abrams, P. (1988) Microcomputers-based information systems and management of student achievement: A description of a working model. *Journal of Information Resources Management*, **1(2)**, 37-55.

Fulmer, C.L. (1995) Maximizing the potential of information technology for management: Strategies for interfacing the technical core of education, in *Information Technology in Educational Management* (eds. B. Z. Barta et al.), Chapman and Hall, London.

Fulmer, C.L. (1990) *The integration of micro-computer applications in educational administration curricula.* An unpublished dissertation, The Penn State University, University Park, Pennsylvania.

Haugo, J.E. (1981) Management applications of the microcomputer: Promises and pitfalls. *ADES Journal*, **14**, 182-8.

Lemann, N. (1995a) The structure of success in America. *The Atlantic Monthly*, August 1995, 41-60.

Lemann, N. (1995b) The great sorting. *The Atlantic Monthly*, September 1995, 84-100.

Lindelow, J. (1984) *Microcomputers in the school office: primer for administrators.* Management Digest Series No. 30, Eugene. (ERIC Document Reproduction Service No. ED 248 571).

Marcum, D. (1987) Putting your school on line: Problems and benefits. *NASSP Bulletin*, **71(495)**, 110-2.

McIsaac, D.M. (1984) Managing school information systems (second of a three part series). *AEDS Journal*, **23**, 20-21.

McKenzie, G.D. (1984) Using microcomputers to increase productivity in academia. *Journal of Geographical Education*, **32**, 171-175.

Mikulcik, P.J. (1993) *A study of selected junior high/middle school principals use of computers for administrative purposes.* An unpublished doctoral dissertation, Northern Illinois University, DeKalb, Illinois.

Naron, N.K. and Estes, N. (1985) *Technology in the schools: Trends and policies.* A paper presented at the Annual Meeting of the American Education Research Association, Chicago. (Eric Document Reproduction Service No. ED 262-775).

Newberg, N.A. (1995) Clusters: Organizational patterns for caring. *Phi Delta Kappan*, **76(9)**, 713-7.

Ogletree, E.J. and Haskins, T.C. (1983) *A survey of microcomputer use in Illinois schools.* National Institute of Education, Washington, DC. (ERIC Document Reproduction Service No. ED 252 189.

Pogrow, S. (1985) Administrative uses of computers: what is the ideal system? *NASSP Bulletin,* **69(485)** , 45-50.

Rogers, E. (1983) Diffusion of innovation (3rd ed.). Free Press, New York.

Rolley, M. (1986) *Administrative uses of computers in elementary schools.* Paper presented at the annual meeting of the National Catholic Education Association, Anaheim, CA. (ERIC Document Reproduction Service No. ED 268 661)

Schuler, D. and Namioka, A. (1993) *Participatory design: principles and practices.* Lawrence Elbaum Associates, Hillsdale, NJ.

Spuck, D.W. and Atkinson, G. (1983) Administrative uses of the microcomputer. *AEDS Journal*, **17(1-2)**, 83-90.

Spuck, D.W. and Bozeman, W.C. (1988) Training school administrators in computer use. *Journal of Research on Computing in Education*, **21(2)**, 229-236.

Taylor, B.L., Cole, D.W., Hemenway, M.W. and Hillman, G.L. (1989) Computer use in curriculum development and curriculum management. *Educational Technology,* **29(4)**, 49-51.

Tiede, L.J. (1992) *A study of selected elementary school principals' use of computers for administrative purposes*. An unpublished doctoral dissertation, Northern Illinois University, DeKalb, Illinois.
UCEA (1993a) Update: UCEA computer simulation project. *UCEA Review,* **34(1)**, 14.
UCEA (1993b) UCEA IESLP project takes off. *UCEA Review,* **34(4)**, 1.
Vogt, J. (1988) *The amount of principal and secretarial use of microcomputers in elementary schools and principals' perceptions of the actual and ideal importance of selected administrative tasks*. Unpublished doctoral dissertation, Northern Illinois University, DeKalb, Illinois.
Walters, D.L. (1987) *PC's and the principalship*. Paper presented at the annual meeting of the University Council for Educational Administration, Charlottesville, VA. (ERIC Document Reproduction Service No. ED 293 193).
Wagner, W. (1985) Computer-managed instruction: how teachers and principals can improve learning. *NASSP Bulletin,* **69(478)**, 22-27.

10 BIOGRAPHIES

Professor Fulmer earned her Ph. D. in Educational Administration at The Pennsylvania State University, University Park, Pennsylvania, USA. Currently, she is an Associate Professor in the Department of Leadership and Educational Policy Studies at Northern Illinois University and serves as the Faculty Chair for the Educational Administration and School Business Management program. Connie's research has focused on redefining teaching and learning environments to include pedagogical-based processes and the integration of technology into educational administration curricula.

Professor Frank earned his Ph. D. in Education Administration at the State University of New York at Buffalo, New York, USA. Currently, he is Professor in the Faculty of Educational Leadership and Chair of the Department of Educational Policy Studies at Georgia State University, Atlanta, Georgia, USA. Fred's research has focused on the development of school based information systems and data analyses for informing teaching and learning environments.

17

TESS: an interactive support system for school timetabling

W.Y. Ng
Department of Information Engineering, The Chinese University of Hong Kong, Shatin, N.T., Hong Kong
e-mail: wyng@ie.cuhk.edu.hk

Abstract
A timetabling package called TESS, which stands for Timetabling Expert Support System, has been developed for use in Hong Kong schools. It is representative of the decision support system (DSS), being highly interactive and supportive of different practices of expert timetablers. Its distinctive feature is a suite of seemingly simple tools. Being simple, they behave in manners transparent to the user, who is then ready to command them at will to solve his/her particular timetabling problem.

Keywords
Educational management, interactive, tools, algorithms

1 INTRODUCTION

It is a humbling experience for researchers, especially those who are theoretically inclined, to observe how seemingly intractable problems are solved in practice by the naked mind. School timetabling, an instance of a scheduling problem, is a typical case. Consider Hong Kong where there are over one thousand schools. That translates to over one thousand NP-hard problems solved per year, each with an average of 1000+ lessons, a variety of resource constraints, as well as many conflicting goals for educational and administrative purposes. Typically, a team of one to four teachers spends a few days to produce an acceptable timetable. Apart from a minority of schools, many do so without direct computer assistance. However, the majority have developed ad hoc habits and tactics to facilitate their work.

We may draw a few observations from this. First, whatever the problem of school timetabling may be, it is NOT that feasible solutions cannot be found soon enough. Rather it is the toil of the timetabling process which demands much concentration and hard work from the team. Secondly, stable ad hoc habits and tactics are the mark of an experienced practitioner. Such habits and tactics vary widely, being strongly influenced by the particular school situation such as different degrees of resource scarcity and the relative importance of the many goals and constraints.

To computerize timetabling has been a professed goal of many researchers in operational research (OR) for some thirty years (de Werra, 1985). The classical OR methodology is often applied; namely, a problem model is first derived, working assumptions are then made to adapt it to a tractable form, finally a standard or tailored algorithm is found, and shown to solve the problem with reasonable performance. However, such results mostly remain academic, and few have been implemented for practical use. In fact, school timetabling to date remains largely a handicraft.

There are in fact many useful timetabling packages available (Chahal and de Werra, 1989; de Gans, 1981). The typical package allows the user to describe a school timetabling problem in the form of a particular model deemed amenable to the powerful scheduling algorithm implemented. However none have been in popular use due to many reasons. Some of the reasons are economical: the benefit is not worth the costs of computerization which remained high for schools until recent years. Others are technical, which we shall discuss in more detail later. At this point, it suffices to say, the core problem is that their being powerful in a sophisticated way has made them overly difficult to use.

We are going to describe yet another timetabling package, TESS (CUHK, 1995), which stands for Timetabling Expert Support System. We intend TESS to distinguish itself by properly acknowledging the user as a timetabling expert with particular habits and tactics. TESS assumes the role of a supportive assistant who works (1) to release the expert of the chore of managing the many data and constraints; (2) to compile statistics and comparisons to assist in making better informed decisions; and (3) to carry out iterative and repetitive tasks in a supervised manner. TESS is by no means intended for automation. Its success shall be as an intelligent secretary, who enables its master to concentrate on higher objectives. In school timetabling, that means the quality of class schedules, resource usage, resolution of conflicting goals, etc. Such higher objectives are often compromised when the expert is burdened under the toil of constructing the timetable manually.

We elaborate in the next section our system goals, and in section three the system design and functionality. By then it shall be apparent to the reader that the utility of TESS comes from the synergy of simple but specialized tools integrated in a highly interactive and controllable environment. Section four reports on developing TESS as the Timetabling Application of SAMS (CUHK, 1995; ED, 1995), the School Administration and Management System developed by The Education Department for the 1000+ schools in Hong Kong. TESS was used for the first time in summer 1995 and we shall recount some feedback from the first time users. The final section concludes the paper with lessons learnt and the outlook for future development.

2 SYSTEM GOALS AND APPROACH

2.1 Problem Definition

As previously remarked, the problem with school timetabling is not that feasible solutions cannot be found soon enough. Frankly speaking, the solution is often feasible not with respect to the initially specified set of requirements, goals and constraints, but only with respect to the set compromised to some extent. For instance, some teachers may not have their free periods as requested and some classes may have too many English lessons on one day. However, such compromise is the rule rather than the exception. There being no accurate feasibility test, the set of requirements, goals and constraints have to be continually manipulated at the same time as the timetable is being constructed.

The toil of the timetabling process is however a grave problem. The team suffer heavy cognitive load during those few days, and consequently they are often ready, probably too ready, to compromise when facing time clashes. The quality of the constructed timetable suffers as a result. As the team is continually drawn to "low-level" tasks related to feasibility, many higher objectives are not given their due attention.

Last but not least, timetabling is more than fitting lessons into time slots. Data preparation takes up a significant portion of the overall time and effort spent. Collected data have to be maintained; class curriculum, staff deployment and lesson accommodation have to be planned; and timetables and various summary reports have to be compiled afterwards.

Many timetable packages have their focus on the design of powerful sophisticated algorithms that minimize the number of kick-outs. With little useful results from the OR community, many developers resort to designing heuristics, some of which emulate what the experienced practitioner does. We contend that such an approach is not effective for the following reasons. First, it is not addressing the true problem of timetabling. Second, it often structures the timetabling so much that the experienced practitioner finds his worthy habits and tactics difficult to apply. Third, it tends to create new problems which sometimes more than offset any time saved from automation. The new problems come from (1) the difficulty of using sophisticated algorithms and (2) the kick-out dilemma - the well-known fact that the fewer the kick-outs, the more difficult they are to handle (Johnson 1980). (The reasoning goes like this: The fewer the kick-outs, the more "powerful" the algorithm must be. Therefore the kick-outs must be more difficult to handle as even the more powerful algorithm does not manage them.)

2.2 System Goals

Naturally, we formulate the system goals in relation to the problem definition above.

First, the system shall enable the user to construct the timetable manually if he so wishes, with comparable and hopefully greater ease than he barehanded. The timetable content may be directly manipulated while moves feasible and infeasible are made visible and logically controlled.

Second, the user should be in control all the time - initiating, configuring, interrupting and backtracking command executions at will; and well informed to be alert to and act upon problems, choices and opportunities early.

Third, the system shall assist the user in handling time clashes - preempting them as much as possible, and finding resolving moves should any arise.

The kick-out dilemma mentioned is a result of time clashes not resolved early enough. Some time clashes are due to incompatible requirements whose resolution necessitates the user's deliberation, which may not be taken care of by any algorithm. Our system instead aims to empower the user to detect and resolve clashes "on the spot".

Fourth, the system shall provide comprehensive "spreadsheet" like support for data maintenance as well as timetable planning.

On the whole, the system shall be a supportive assistant who complements the human user throughout the timetabling process. The user shall be released of the chore of low-level tasks, but remains in good control, free to exercise his/her own habits and tactics and attend to higher objectives more effectively.

3 SYSTEM DESIGN AND FUNCTIONALITY

3.1 System Design

An event-driven graphical user interface (GUI) which supports direct manipulation of visually rendered timetable entities is almost mandatory for our stated goals. TESS was implemented as a Microsoft Windows application with a WIMP interface.

Timetable data comprise a rich collection of related entities, including classes, teachers, accommodation, subjects, time slots, requirements, constraints, groups, etc. which warrant careful data modelling. We decided to build TESS as a database application. A database schema was designed to capture the rich semantics of the timetable data. System functions were then built on top of the database management system. Care was taken to ensure that the TESS schema is sufficiently generic for the wide variety of Hong Kong schools.

TESS transactions involve potentially compute-intensive search procedures and the quality of the GUI is critical to its success. Performance and programming flexibility are crucial. Therefore, unlike most database applications implemented on top of 4GL systems like FoxPro or DBase, TESS uses an embedded database engine so as to remain a proper Windows application and avoid the compromise on performance and programming flexibility.

On system functions, we follow the "toolbox" approach (Kernighan and Plauger, 1976) which is appropriate for systems intended for users who are expert in their domain. The toolbox approach calls for the design of a collection of software tools, each of which is highly specialized for a simple task that the user understands well. (That implies we shall not implement any single "blackbox-does-it-all" algorithm.) The system is more transparent as a result and its behaviour more predictable. We also make an effort to make tools more controllable by allowing the user to configure and interrupt tool actions.

3.2 System Functionality

Functionality design is guided by a task model of the timetabling process (Sprague and Watson, 1993) which comprises three stages distinguished by where attention is focused: (1) a relatively conflict-free stage characterized by sparsely filled timetables and high lesson insertion rates; (2) a conflict avoidance stage when conscious effort is spent to preempt time clashes; and (3) a conflict resolution stage when clashes arise that have to be resolved.

Furthermore the tools are designed with the following principles in mind: (1) usability - useful and easy to use; (2) control - with behaviour easy to understand and control and with minimal invisible side effects; (3) flexibility - with minimal constraints on the way they may be used; and (4) power - incorporating powerful algorithms; and in that order. That means, for instance, complex heuristic rules which could have improved the insertion rate, and may be considered powerful, are NOT used due to poor control (being difficult to understand) and potentially adverse usability (being prone to the kick-out dilemma).

Data Model and Management

We focus the description on data management during the core stage when unscheduled lessons are being inserted into time slot.

TESS displays the timetable of a class, a teacher or a location (classroom, special rooms, playground etc.) in a window which shows time slots as being empty, blocked, or occupied by scheduled lessons. A timetable window also responds to mouse actions for inserting or removing lessons.

A lesson in TESS is either simple or a composite lesson block (CLB). A simple lesson is a record with five attributes, namely, class, teacher, location, duration and scheduled-time attributes. A lesson with its scheduled-time attribute being null-valued is unscheduled, and is scheduled otherwise. A CLB is a collection of simple lessons of the same duration that are constrained to have identical scheduled-time attributes. CLB models either explicit concurrence constraints, or implicit ones like split classes and combined classes.

A browser window provides a flexible interface for retrieving and filtering unscheduled lessons by attributes. While scheduled lessons appear as icons in time slots of their respective timetables, unscheduled lessons are list items with all attributes displayed within the browser window when retrieved. Scheduled lessons may also be click-dragged from one time slot to another.

Prioritizing Unscheduled Lessons
A most powerful tool of TESS is the priority function. TESS computes for each unscheduled lesson a numerical measure that estimates the chance of not being able to find a feasible time slot for it. Retrieved unscheduled lessons may then be sorted to put "difficult" lessons on top. The user is encouraged to exercise the "difficult-lessons-first" heuristic which is most effective for conflict preemption.

The priority function is unique in that we believe it probably outperforms any experienced user in early detection of imminent conflicts.

This tool is placed in the browser window, and the unscheduled lessons may also be sorted by their attributes. Using the retrieval functions and the sorting functions together effects very flexible manipulation of even a large number of unscheduled lessons.

Scheduling Unscheduled Lessons
By means of the retrieval and sorting functions, the user may select and order unscheduled lessons at will in the browser window for subsequent scheduling. TESS provides two FIND functions for finding time slots for a given unscheduled lessons, namely, FIND-FEASIBLE and FIND-BEST. FIND-FEASIBLE finds the time slots for which all entities involved, namely class(es), teacher(s) and location(s) for the unscheduled lesson, are available. FIND-BEST selects the "best" among the feasible, whose usage results in a most even distribution of scheduled lessons in the timetables of the entities involved. It is another known rule that the more evenly distributed the available time slots, or equivalently the scheduled lessons, are for a timetable, the less likely shall clashes arise. FIND-BEST is intended for preempting clashes.

An AUTO-PUT function is available which performs FIND-BEST for the current list of selected unscheduled lessons in the browser window. However, as lessons are inserted by AUTO-PUT, the priority function values may change. The user may set a count of insertions for updating the values of remaining unscheduled lessons. He may choose a small count for more effective execution of the "difficult-lessons-first" heuristic, and a large count for more speedy execution of AUTO-PUT.

For user control, AUTO-PUT may also be interrupted any time by a mouse click. It also halts at any unscheduled lesson for which no "best" slots are found, whence the user may analyze the clash, resolve it himself, or call up the conflict resolver to help. (We could have let AUTO-PUT attempt to move some scheduled lessons to make way for it but we do not. Movement of lessons already scheduled will render the system less predictable, and may even undo deliberate choices the user previously made. This is another case of the concern for usability and control being over that of power.)

Resolving Clashes
TESS incorporates a conflict resolver to assist the user in finding feasible resolving moves (FRMs) when no "best" slots are found for an unscheduled lesson (Lam, 1993). An FRM is a sequence of displacement of some scheduled lessons that creates a feasible slot for the unscheduled lesson.

There are many ways to construct a conflict resolver in terms of its behaviour and the algorithm used. We again aim for one that is simple and with good utility.

First, the TESS resolver is designed to be called from a timetable window of a particular class, teacher or location, and finds FRMs that involves only scheduled lessons therein. A useful consequence is that FRMs found may be visualized in the same window for easy analysis and comparison.

Second, the user may specify whether the FRMs may or may not pass over some soft constraints, namely, maximum teaching load per day for teachers and balanced subject distribution for classes.

Third the user may also specify the maximum "depth" of search, or equivalent, the maximum length of FRMs returned.

Fourth, scheduled lessons may be toggled so that only FRMs that do not involve them will be returned.

The TESS resolver uses a brute-force breadth-first search to look for FRMs one by one. The user may also specify the number of FRMs returned. The resolver terminates when one of the following happens: (1) the specified number of FRMs is found; (2) the maximum depth of search is exhausted; (3) the user interrupts. FRMs found are then displayed for the user to choose to use.

We do realize that experienced practitioners sometimes use FRMs that involve scheduled lessons not all contained in one class, teacher or location timetable. Our hope is that a proper use of TESS preempts serious clashes and FRMs found by the TESS resolver should suffice for those that do arise. In fact, some experienced TESS users manage to develop effective tactics in using the resolver in conjunction with many FIND functions that show the "degrees of freedom" of scheduled lessons and empty slots across multiple timetables. Such is possible with the toolbox approach and the event-driven user interface of the TESS environment. We also hope that useful tactics that experienced practitioners have developed in the past may also be adapted effectively to be carried out in TESS.

4 IMPLEMENTATION EXPERIENCE IN HONG KONG

TESS has been selected and subsequently developed to be the Timetabling Application of the School Administration and Management System (SAMS) for all government and aided schools funded through the Education Department in Hong Kong.

TESS was essentially a byproduct of an applied research project (Lam, 1993; Wong, 1992) developed for field use. We have essentially revamped the input and output interfaces for user-friendliness and coherence with established SAMS standards. Much design effort was also spent in developing a Planner Module for planning class curriculum, staff deployment and lesson accommodation. As this tends to be an iterative process, especially when planning for staff deployment, a spreadsheet like WYSIWYG interface is incorporated.

However, the core functions that actually construct the timetables are relatively untouched for some good reasons. First, we believe and the test users seem to agree that the core functions as they stand already provide very good utility. Second, proposed modifications at such an early stage come from sophisticated users that tend to trade usability for power. For instance, some have suggested to enhance the TESS resolver to find FRMs across multiple timetables. This however would be undesirable to less sophisticated users who are the majority of our target users in the 1000+ Hong Kong schools.

5 CONCLUSION

We have received very positive responses from our client and the first batch of school users. There are criticisms of course but most concern the I/O interface rather than the overall system approach.

As the Timetabling Application of SAMS, TESS will be further refined and progressively distributed to all schools in Hong Kong in a few years time. Being deployed at such a scale, we anticipate TESS to become a standardization vehicle de facto and encourage better sharing of expert skills in timetabling. Further, we hope TESS users shall become the new generation of school timetabling experts who develop habits and tactics no less effective than current ones while being more portable and easier to acquire.

TESS is representative of the decision support system (DSS) approach to designing systems for domain experts to handle ill-structured problems (Sprague and Watson, 1993). The DSS approach relies on a high level of interactivity and usability that is potentially costly. It is only the cost-effective PC technology available in recent years that puts a system like TESS within reach of schools. Beyond TESS, we anticipate DSSs of other kinds to assist other educational management and planning functions. The classical view sees DSS as the next step after MIS (Sprague and Watson, 1993) and it points to a natural way forward for SAMS to deliver computerized support to Hong Kong schools.

6 REFERENCES

Chahal, N. and de Werra, D. (1989) An interactive system for constructing timetables on a PC. *European Journal of Operational Research*, **40**, 32-37.

Chinese University of Hong Kong (1995) *Timetabling Expert Support System - system manual*. Unpublished manual, Hong Kong.

Education Department (1995) *School Administration and Management System*. Hong Kong Government.

de Gans, O.B. (1981) A computer timetabling system for secondary schools in the Netherlands. *European Journal of Operational Research*, **7**, 175-182.

Johnson, K. (1980) *Timetabling*, Hutchinson, London.

Kernighan, B.W. and Plauger, P.J. (1976) *Software Tools*. Addison-Wesley, Reading, Mass., USA.

Lam, H.M. (1993) *A conflict resolver for an interactive timetabling support system*. Unpublished B.Eng. Thesis, Department of Information Engineering, The Chinese University of Hong Kong, Hong Kong.

Sprague, R.H. and Watson, H.J. (1993) *Decision support systems: putting theory into practice*. Prentice Hall, Englewood Clifts, N.J., USA.

Wong, K.H. and Ng, W.Y. (1990) An interactive system for school timetabling, in *Proceedings of the International Conference on Systems Management'90*, Hong Kong, 307-313.

Wong, K.H.(1992) *A decision support system for school timetabling*. Unpublished M.Phil. Thesis, The Chinese University of Hong Kong, Hong Kong.

de Werra, D. (1985) An introduction to timetabling. *European Journal of Operational Research*, **19**, 151-162.

Yoshikawa, M., Kaneko, K., Yamanouchi, T. and Watanabe, M. (1996) A constraint-based high school scheduling system. *IEEE Expert*, **(11)**, 63-72.

7 BIOGRAPHY

Wai-Yin Ng received his B.A. in engineering in 1985 and Ph.D. in Control engineering in 1989, both from the University of Cambridge, U.K. He has been a Lecturer of Information Engineering in the Chinese University of Hong Kong since 1988. Being a professed interdisciplinary researcher, he works on and supervises R&D projects of a broad range of subjects. His current research interests include decision making, interactive systems, distributed applications, 3D image analysis, image coding, computer-aided design, optimization, control engineering, and any interesting engineering problems he appreciates enough to work on.

18

The intelligent discussion supporting system over the computer network

T. Okamoto and A. Inaba
The Graduate School of Information Systems, University of Electro-Communications, 1-5-1 Chofugaoka, Chofu, Tokyo 182 JAPAN
Phone: (81)-424 83 2161 Fax: (81)-424 81 5934
email: okamoto@ai.is.uec.ac.jp

Abstract

The purpose of this paper is to propose a technical and psychological framework of intelligent computer supported collaborative work/learning environment which we call "iDCLE" (intelligent distributed collaborative learning/working environment). To realize iDCLE, we constructed a real-time sharing communication system for collaborative work/learning on computer networks. We describe the mechanism for iDCLE in this paper, and discuss the mechanism of supporting discussion. Using our model, the discussion support system in iDCLE can identify participants' states of discussion. The system can also diagnose the process of discussion for the purpose of making progress. When advice is needed after the diagnosis, the system gives the appropriate feedback to the participants.

Keywords

Distance learning, artificial intelligence, collaborative Learning

1 INTRODUCTION

Recently, networking technology like the Internet has developed rapidly and we can communicate and discuss with others in a distributed environment. Under such a network environment, we can communicate with people in foreign countries and share various kinds of educational knowledge like new teaching methods, educational materials, curriculum contents, and evaluation methods. The educational environment is changing from a closed system to a global and open system.

With those considerations, we propose an "iDCLE" (intelligent Distributed Collaborative Learning/working Environment) where people can exchange knowledge and solve problems through effective group thinking. Many researchers on educational technology attempt to extend the field of study from a stand-alone learning environment to the group learning environment, where multiple agents interact with one another (Baker, 1994, 1995; Blandford, 1994). The concept of CSCL (Computer Supported Collaborative Learning) has attracted th terest of many researchers who wish to study a mechanism of dynamic group learning and evelop more flexible communication technology. This concept is based on the rationales of nowledge constructivism and social learning. In the case of group learning under the etworking environment, though it is necessary to provide multi-modal means of ommunication, we suppose that verbal communication is especially important (Lave and 'enger, 1991; Salomon, 1993). It is quite important for the educational system to be designed earing in mind the cognitive interaction among the participants in order to improve their ommunication skills.

New interactive technologies based on remote computing as networking and multimedia ave helped to provide the interactive communication previously lacking in distance education. ortunately, computer-mediated multimedia communication systems are starting to be ploited by the various kinds of organizations/institutes as alternative delivery environments dependent of time and distance (Okamoto, 1994).

In the study of CSCL, some researchers aim to construct a system which is equipped with a ansparent and seamless environment for supporting effective collaborative work/learning. ther researchers aim to construct a system which can monitor and coordinate appropriately e process of group work/learning using artificial intelligence technology. We used the latter proach in order to enhance group productivity and the self-monitoring ability of each rticipant.

In this study, we constructed the iDCLE framework in which the participants attain the ucational goal through interaction with one another (Okamoto, Inaba and Hasaba, 1995; aba, Hasaba and Okamoto, 1996). In collaborative learning, it is necessary to communicate ith others. Thus, how to support the discussion is one of the most important issues in search on collaborative learning. We embed the expert system which plays the role of ordinator to support discussion based on the model of transition on dialogue states in CLE.

RESEARCH OBJECTIVES

ır study has three research objectives:

- to construct a dialogue model for discussion on a computer network;
- to develop an intelligent discussion supporting system which can identify the state of discussion and help the discussion by the model described above;
- to clarify appropriate strategies for guiding the discussion based on collaborative knowledge.

THE iDCLE SYSTEM

this section, we describe the fundamental configuration of the iDCLE system. The system is nstructed on UNIX workstations connected by TCP/IP. The core of its graphical user erface (GUI) is constructed on the X11 window systems.

In iDCLE, each participant can freely choose either of two workspaces or both. One is the rsonal Work Space, which is a closed private area and cannot be accessed by other rticipants. This enables the participants to explore their individual information and to learn/work something individually as a performance support system. The participant can us several tools for problem solving in this space, e.g. a word processor, a drawing tool, and s on. Another work space is the Collaborative Work Space shared by all participants. This spac is used to exchange opinions and to solve problems collaboratively. This space has two places which are called the Communication Channel and the Clear Board.

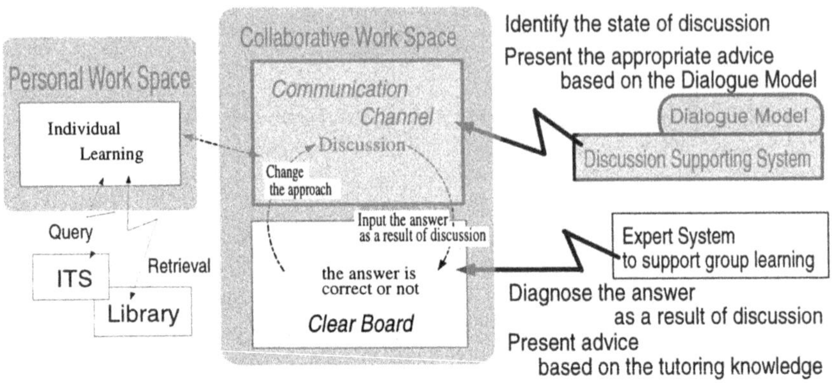

Figure 1 The Learning Environment.

Figure 1 shows the learning environment in iDCLE. The participants discuss a given tas through the Communication Channel. The discussion support system including the comput coordinator can identify the state of discussion and give the appropriate advice by tracing th dialogue model. That is, the participants present some sentences through the Communicatio Channel. The system can extract intention-information from utterance sentences by processin natural language for context understanding of conversation. Then the sequence of extracte intention is stored on working memory in a discussion support system. The discussion suppo system diagnoses a state of discussion and identifies a participant's role in a discussion proce based on the sequence of intention-information on the working memory. The system generat appropriate advice through this Communication Channel. As a result of the discussion, th participants input the answer to the Clear Board. The Clear Board is a space which enabl participants to share an application software such as an expert system. The shared expe system diagnoses whether their answers are correct or not, then gives some advice t coordinate group learning appropriately if it is necessary. When the answer is not correct, th participants may discuss again and change the answer.

4 SUPPORTING DISCUSSION

As mentioned above, the discussion on the Communication Channel is supported by t computer coordinator in iDCLE. This mechanism is described in this section.

We have constructed a discussion support system as a prototype (Okamoto, Inaba ar Hasaba, 1995). The system can diagnose four states where the system should intervene:

- the divergent state of discussion, i.e. when each participant gives his/her idea, and does n say anything related to utterances of the other participants;

- the impasse state of discussion, i.e. when a participant explains something about his/her opinion, and the other participants disagree with the explanation;
- the state in which a participant gives little utterance for a while;
- the state in which a question is not answered.

We conducted some experiments to evaluate the system's functions of coordinating the flow of discussion. As a result, it was suggested that the system should have the function to identify each participant's role in the discussion process. Therefore, we have improved the model of transition on dialogue states and the rule bases on the discussion supporting system which we call the Coordinator system.

4.1 Model of Dialogue

We propose a model of transition on dialogue states by analyzing data of protocols taken from some cognitive experiments. We classify the various kinds of information existing in participants' utterance into two categories. One is concerned with the semantics of the utterance. The information included in this category is related to both the domain knowledge and the context of discussion. Another kind of information is concerned with the participant's intention in making the utterance. Considering a method of supporting discussion, it seems inevitable that the system utilizes the intention-information included in the participants' utterance to coordinate the discussion flow. We contrived the sophisticated mechanism by which the intention-information can be separated from the contents of a given problem to propose the general purposed framework of iDCLE.

The supporting functions of our system are:

- to make users participate actively in the discussion;
- to facilitate group discussion smoothly in the desired direction (such as finding the adequate solution for a problem).

To realize the functions mentioned above, the system should have the function to identify the state of discussion. We classify the participants' intention into ten categories as shown in Table 1.

Table 1 The categories of utterance's intention

Function	*The function of starting a topic*	*The function of expressing a participant's position on other's opinion*	*Other function*
Category	Proposition 1* Proposition 2† Confirmation Question	Agreement Disagreement	Explanation Answer Supplement Others

* Proposition about a way to develop the discussion
† Proposition of next topic for the problem solving

We propose the model of transition on dialogue states bearing in mind the ten categories described in Table 1. We regard a discussion as the sequential structure of some topics. So, we have only to explore the structure of the transition on dialogue states in a topic. The model of transition on dialogue states consists of four modes: the Guide mode, the Development mode, the Confirmation mode and the Query mode. The structure of each of the four modes is shown in Figure 2.

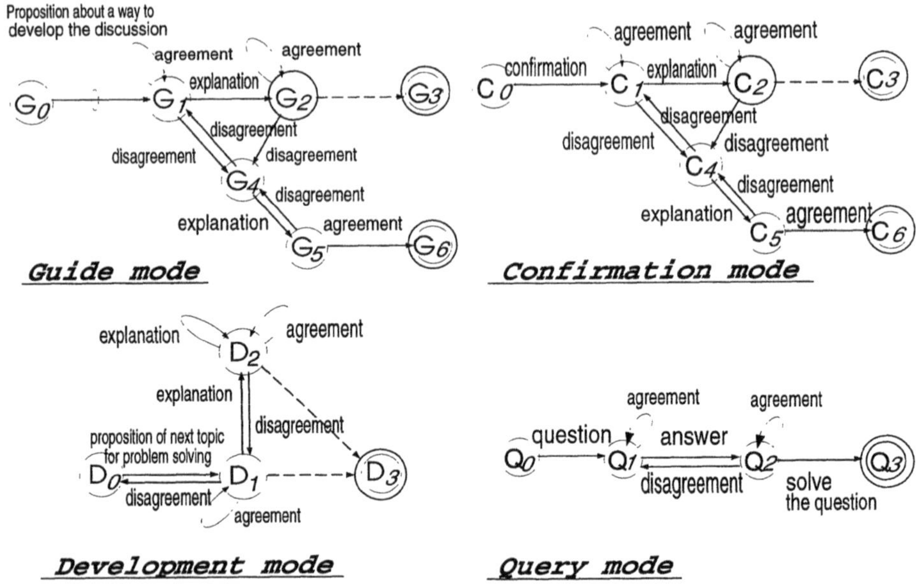

Figure 2 The model of transition on dialogue state.

Guide mode

The Guide mode means dialogue transitions related to making progress in the discussion process. The model on Guide mode works when a participant gives the intention-information of the proposition for developing discussion. The discussion moves from one state to another according to intention. For instance, when the current state is G1 and somebody gives an explanation, then the state moves from G1 to G2. As another instance, when the current state is G2 and somebody disagrees with the current proposition, then the state moves from G2 to G4. When a state transition on this mode exists and a new intention-information of a proposition is given (i.e. the dialogue focus moves to a new topic), the system checks the current state. If the current state is G1 or G2, then the state transition reaches final state G3 On the other hand, if the current state is G4 or G5, then the state transition reaches final state G6. When the current proposition is accepted by the participants, the state transition reaches G3. If the participants do not accept the current proposition, the state transition reaches G6.

Development mode

The Development mode means dialogue transitions related to finding an appropriate way for problem solving. The model on the Development mode works when a participant gives the intention-information of a proposition of next topic for problem solving. If the state is D1 or D2, and almost all participants agree with the proposition, then the state transition reaches the final state. When a state transition exists and a new proposition is given, a new state transition gets working and the old one is suspended and labeled "WAIT". This labeled state of WAIT means the state which all of the participants do not agree with the current proposition, therefore the system suspended this one.

Confirmation mode

The Confirmation mode means dialogue transitions related to specifying an idea offered by a participant. The model on the Confirmation mode works when a participant gives the intention-information for the confirmation. Similar to Guide mode, when the current confirmation is judged to be correct by the other participants, the state transition reaches C3. When the participants judge the confirmation to be incorrect, the state transition reaches C6.

Query mode

The Query mode means dialogue transitions in which a participant asks a question, and the other participants try to answer the question. The model on the Query mode works whenever the participant asks. When the state is Q2 and the participant, who asked the question, solves it, the state transition reaches the final state.

4.2 Expert System as Coordinator

Each participant can interactively communicate the intention of utterance by selecting the appropriate button in the intention-menu which has the ten categories mentioned in section 4.1. The sequence of inputted intention is stored on working memory in the Coordinator system which is the expert system to coordinate the flow of the discussion.

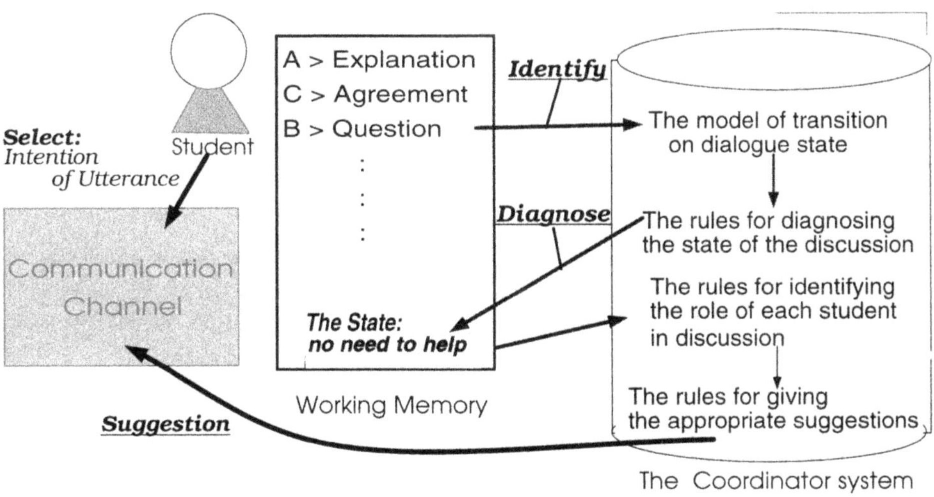

Figure 3 The Coordinator system.

We show the framework of the Coordinator system in Figure 3. The Coordinator system has four kinds of rules as follows.

Rule set-A: The rules for tracing the model of transition on dialogue states.
Rule set-B: The rules for diagnosing the state of discussion.
Rule set-C: The rules for identifying the roles of each participant in discussion.
Rule set-D: The rules for giving the appropriate advice.

These rules were extracted from the results of cognitive experiments on group learning/discussion. The system can identify the state of discussion by referring rule set-A in the production system, and diagnose when the system should intervene by referring rule set-B. The system identifies the roles of each participant in discussion(e.g. a leader in the group) by referring rule set-C. Finally the system gives appropriate advice to the participant who plays a specific role in the discussion process by referring rule set-D.

When the system decides to give the participants some advice, it tries to classify all participants' roles into the following categories:

- the participant who leads the discussion process;
- the participant who has the initiative in the current topic;
- the participant who understands the contents of discussion well;
- the participant who does not understand the contents of discussion;
- the participant who often asks;
- the participant who gives little utterance;
- the participant who gives propositions which the other participants do not accept;
- the participant who does not belong to the above categories.

Then, the system gives the appropriate advice to each participant with the role corresponding to each category standing for the state of discussion.

5 CONCLUSION

In this paper, we proposed a model of transition on dialogue states and a framework of the system which coordinates/supports group learning intelligently using the production system with four layers of rule sets. We contrived the model of transition on dialogue states which utilizes the intention-information included in participants' utterance. We have developed an intelligent discussion supporting system for iDCLE based on this framework. Our intelligent discussion supporting system, called the Coordinator system, would be able to contribute to understand and coordinate the discussion process by realizing the following functions;

- The system can recognize participants' discussion process;
- The system can diagnose some discussion states in which the system should intervene;
- The system can identify each participant's role during discussion process;
- The system can give appropriate advice for each participant's role on self-involvement in discussion.

As a task for further research, it is important to clarify more appropriate strategies for guiding discussion flow based on collaborative knowledge.

6 REFERENCES

Baker, M. (1994) A model for negotiation in teaching-learning dialogues. *Journal of Artificial Intelligence in Education*, **5(2)**, 199-254.

Baker, M. (1995) Negotiation in collaborative problem-solving dialogues, in *Dialogue and* Instruction (ed. R.J.Beun, et al.), Springer-Verlag, Berlin.

Blandford, A.E. (1994) Teaching through collaborative problem solving. *Journal of Artificial Intelligence in Education*, **5(1)**, 51-84.

Inaba, A., Hasaba, Y. and Okamoto, T. (1996) An intelligent supporting of discussion for the distributed cooperative learning environment. *The Transactions of IEICE*, **J79-A(2)**, 207-215.

Lave, J. and Wenger, E. (1991) *Situated learning*. Cambridge Univ. Press, Cambridge.

Okamoto, T. (1994) Global communication literacy, in *Proceedings of Symposium, JET/Japan Academy of Cooperation Foundation*, 20-26.

Okamoto, T., Inaba, A. and Hasaba, Y. (1995) The intelligent learning support system on the distributed cooperative environment, in *Proceedings of Artificial Intelligence in Education* **95**, 588.

Salomon, G. (Ed.) (1993) *Distributed cognitions*. Cambridge Univ. Press, Cambridge.

7 BIOGRAPHIES

Toshio Okamoto graduated in 1971 from Kyoto University of Education and completed coursework in graduate school in 1975 at Tokyo Gakugei University. He obtained Dr. of Engineering from Tokyo Institute of Technology. Presently, he is a Professor in the Information Systems Laboratory, University of Electro-Communications. He is engaged in research on AI models for intelligent CAI systems. He translated Artificial Intelligence and Intelligent CAI Systems. He is a member on the Board of CAI Society, and Japanese Society of Educational Technology. He also is a member of several committees including that of Educational Engineering, Artificial Intelligence & Knowledge Engineering in IEICE, and a member of Society of Artificial Intelligence.

Akiko Inaba graduated in 1991 and completed coursework in graduate school in 1993 at Ibaraki University in Japan. She obtained a Master's degree of education. Presently she is a doctoral student at the Graduate school of Information Systems, University of Electro-Communications. She is engaged in research on Computer Supported Collaborative Learning.

19

Benchmarking for education managers

J.D. Warwick
SIMS Education Services Ltd
Priory Business Park, Cardington, Bedford, MK44 3SG, England
Phone: (44)-1234-838080 Fax: (44)-1234-838091

Abstract

Central Governments have always collected education data to inform the formation of policies and decision making. The world wide trend of decentralising education systems is resulting in an increasing amount of source data being located in schools. In addition, decentralisation gives rise to the need for Central Government to analyse data in a manner that can provide information on the relative performance of Regional Governments or individual schools. Decentralised educational systems have a double challenge; how to collect data without placing too great a burden on schools and how to supply education leaders and managers at the school level with information that will support them in their policy formation, decision making and performance management. Drawing on experience in the United Kingdom, the paper identifies ways in which information and communication technology can meet this challenge and, using examples of recently developed software, identifies the benefits of making national information available in a format that enables schools to easily benchmark their inputs, processes and outcomes.

Keywords

Education management, evaluation/formative, future developments, government, national policies, self assessment

1 INTRODUCTION

Monitoring and evaluation are essential to good strategic management and effective managers seek to build into their organisational systems, procedures that enable them to receive relevant and accurate feedback on how the organisation is operating and what it is achieving. Central governments compile statistics to report on the functioning of the education system and to provide aggregated data for policy makers and strategic planners. In centralised educational systems most of the source data is held within the Ministry of Education. However, as in most organisations "much of the information is dispersed, inconsistent, incompatible and inaccessible" (ICL, 1992, 9). One of the key findings of a major research project on 'Management in the 1990s' conducted by the

Sloan School of Management at the Massachusetts Institute of Technology was that integration provides the main opportunities for improving business effectiveness: "Various forms of integration are at the heart of many of the necessary changes. It is not just a matter of combining databases or using a common database across all the departments of an organisation. It covers the wider issues of achieving close and effective working relationships between various parts of an organisation, for example in terms of structure, working relationships, common or inter-linked processes and shared information. Integration will be essential both within an organisation and across organisational boundaries" (op cit, 8).

The need for integration over and above the creation of similar databases is an important insight but creates difficulties in a climate, such as education, where there is a world wide trend to decentralise and delegate responsibility to front line institutions, namely schools. Such self managing organisations can set up administrative and management structures best suited to local needs. Difficulties may arise when data needs to flow between organisational boundaries. As an example, consider the issue of reporting on spending patterns. In a centralised system all financial details are likely to be held at the centre with ledger codes and cost centres set up to meet central strategic management needs. Reporting on expenditure patterns is a relatively easy task. Self governing schools in England and Wales can create their own ledger codes and cost centres with no guarantee that the same headings mean the same in each school or that similar transactions will be coded in the same way. The process of providing feedback to managers at the centre becomes difficult or costly at all levels in the system as alternative and often parallel forms of data collection need to be instigated.

2 COLLECTING EDUCATIONAL DATA IN A DELEGATED SYSTEM

Data gathering is a difficult task even when most of the data is at one level of government. In larger countries, with regional levels of Government exercising varying amounts of responsibility for policy formation and decision making, collecting data becomes even more costly because of the proliferation of disparate systems and because the data may be formatted in ways to meet local rather than central needs. When management responsibilities are delegated to the school level, the problems of data collection are considerably magnified because much of the source data will be in schools. In any system that relies on paper returns, validation has to take place at the centre and much time and energy can be taken up in entering data, chasing late returns or in querying inaccuracies.

Collecting accurate data has always been a time consuming and expensive task made worthwhile only if the resulting information has a value and leads to some action for improvement. The problem within delegated systems is that the cost of collecting data falls on schools, whilst most of the value is derived at the centre because it is the centre that determines the indicators to be used and publishes the information at a time and in a format useful to central government.

Data will always be required to flow to Central Government in order to provide feedback to strategic managers. In delegated systems, equivalent data is also required at the level of local government or school: education managers at all levels need information to enable effective policy formation and decision making. Feedback can be concerned with absolute measures, for example Ministries of Education regularly produce demographic or financial reports. Such information clearly has a role, particularly when systematically collected and reported as part of a longitudinal study in order to determine trends. The value of such information increases if schools are able to make comparisons with other, similar, institutions.

This is the principle of benchmarking which has been described as "an external focus on internal activities, functions or operations in order to achieve continuous improvement" (Liebfried & McNair, 1994, 1). Although the concept of benchmarking is not new to education, its use is certainly not widespread and is often limited to international reports comparing performance across countries. One reason for this may be the basically centralist nature of education systems, with all schools being seen to operate the same procedures. In countries where regional government or schools are involved in policy formation and strategic planning, central government will also seek to compare inputs, processes and outcomes in order to inform choice and learn from best practice. In England and Wales, for example, the Government is keen to compare the performance of different local education authorities and schools and to publicise the results. All political parties are committed to making more information available to the public and there is unlikely to be any decrease in the amount of information that is now being made available. Indeed, it is likely to increase. As an example, school inspection reports are now available on the Internet (http://www.open.gov.uk /ofsted/ofsted.htm).

Collecting data in order to publish information about the performance of individual schools requires the highest level of accuracy and validation. and the exercise has the potential for being very costly. Initial attempts, in England and Wales, to collect data from third parties, such as examination boards, caused considerable problems because schools challenged the accuracy of the published figures. Additional costs have had to be borne in order to check and negotiate the figures with schools prior to publication. Local management and self governance have been welcomed by schools in the UK; what has not been is the perceived increase in bureaucracy and collection of data with minimal tangible benefits to those supplying the data.

3 AN INFORMATION TECHNOLOGY SOLUTION

The challenge faced by decentralised educational systems is to make the whole process of providing feedback to strategic and tactical planners at all levels in the system more productive. This challenge can be broken down into two basic issues; how to collect accurate and validated data in the least inconvenient way to schools and at least cost; and how to make the resulting information available in a form that is of most value to schools and Local Education Authorities, which means feeding back data in a manner that enables internal development.

A potential solution lies in the use of information and communication technology, not only for collecting data but for benchmarking and feeding back results in a format that enables an institution to privately compare the fine details of its performance against similar institutions. Whilst benchmarking is a powerful tool for continuous improvement, when combined with gap analysis, significant gaps in performance between similar institutions can be the catalyst for paradigm shifts in an organisation, particularly if a culture can be established in which institutions who perform well are prepared to be identified and share their processes with others.

Within the UK, IT is playing an ever increasing role in education management. The most popular education management information system (EMIS) is that developed by SIMS (http://www.sims.co.uk/) with a user base of approximately 85 percent of schools in England, Northern Ireland and Wales. This market penetration, resulting in over 21.000 schools using the system in 121 local education authorities, means that the company is well informed of user needs and is able to make representation to government agencies for the move to electronic forms of data collection. The SIMS system is an integrated suite of modules covering all of the business processes of schools and colleges. In addition, its education authority system (EMS) has the facility to transfer data to and from the school's system. Electronic forms of data capture are now becoming a reality. Each year, the Department for Education and Employment

(DfEE) and the Department of Education in Northern Ireland (DENI) issue forms for the collection of educational census data from schools. In the past, this paper exercise has taken a senior member of staff of the school up to two weeks to complete. Even then, staff at the DfEE have had to enter the data onto their computer systems, run validation checks and seek clarification from the school. SIMS now co-operates with the DfEE and DENI so that each year software is written to collect the relevant data from the school's EMIS. Where required processing of data is done locally and when the software has to use some intelligence to gain an answer the user is asked to confirm the entry. A major advantage of this approach is local validation and the ease with which data can be input at the centre. More than 250 validation checks are carried out, local users are informed of inconsistencies and asked to check their data. The resulting output can be sent to the DfEE either on disk or through electronic data interchange (EDI). In January 1996 it is estimated that over 14 000 schools returned their census data through electronic means. Whilst the saving in time for the DfEE and DENI is substantial, at the school level the time to complete the return can be as low as 20 minutes.

Similar exercises are now taking place with other government agencies, such as the collection of returns on students performance in public examinations and national curriculum assessments as well as the compilation of performance measures prior to the inspection of a school. All the required data can be drawn from the school's database, validated, processed locally and returned electronically. There are still challenges to overcome, particularly where schools have had the freedom to store data in formats of their own choosing, such as in the area of finance. One solution is to build into the software mapping processes which enable the school's ledger codes to be nested in or split between centrally defined codes. The software is given some intelligence to make guesses as to these mappings which can be confirmed by the user. The solution is not ideal, but the fact is that schools and local education authorities are unlikely to agree to give up their freedom to organise their data in a form most appropriate to them unless there is some pay off in return, such as valuable benchmarking information.

The move to efficient electronic data collection has been made possible by the fact that practically all schools in the UK now use an EMIS and the vast majority have chosen to use the same integrated system, thus providing resources to produce new versions of the software to meet the ever changing needs of Government. Secondly, the Government and its agencies have recognised that an IT solution is the only way in which they would be able to transfer data to and from a large number of schools and therefore agreed to inform software houses of changes in time for the new requirements to be coded and disks distributed. Finally, Government Agencies have set up internal systems to receive the data.

4 BENCHMARKING FOR INTERNAL REVIEW

Whilst IT has enabled central government to acquire the data it needs for measuring inputs, processes and outputs there is now a case for using the national data in a creative way to help schools and local education authorities in their strategic management processes. The challenge is to make the vast amounts of data collected by central government and its agencies available in ways that will enable schools to compare the detail rather than the headlines of their performance against similar schools. The process to make this happen is quite straightforward and has already been employed by SIMS to produce diagnostic and performance analysis software for benchmarking national assessments.

In one module, data from a large number of schools is statistically modelled to identify the relationship between students' performance at the General Certificate in Secondary Education (GCSE) and specific 'A' level subjects, which are taken by students two years later than GCSE. The resulting regression equations vary by subject and gender. By enabling schools to calculate their own regression lines it is possible to compare performance in a variety of ways. In another module, the school enters the marks gained by each student to each question in a national assessment. The software enables a diagnostic report to be produced of the student's performance as well as supplying tools to enable benchmarking against the national performance of students.

In the first module, SIMS acts as the collecting bureau. Schools in the project are supplied with software that automatically validates and collects, from the SIMS system, all the data that is required for creating the statistical model. The data is sent to SIMS, either on disk of through EDI. The incoming data is processed to determine all the relevant coefficients in the model. This "picture" of the national database is then transferred to a program which is sent to the schools and colleges in the project. On installation the program re-collects the local data to create equivalent local "pictures" of performance. The software then enables a variety of comparisons to made between or within the local and national 'pictures'. The software allows various forms of filters to be applied so that 'what if ...?' questions can be asked.

In the second module, national statistics are supplied to SIMS by the government agency responsible for assessment. Individual student data is entered by keyboard or through specially designed optical mark reader forms. Once data has been entered the school is able to analyse its performance using sophisticated statistical tools hidden behind simple graphical presentations. Both processes have a number of key features.

- Feedback is being given on data that has to be presented to the centre.
- Taking part involves minimal extra work.
- Feedback is quick so that performance can be analysed when the issue is alive.
- Schools can ask a variety of "what if" questions and even use the software as a basis for setting targets for future cohorts of students.
- Schools own their data; all analysis is undertaken by the school.

A further practical example where data is used for benchmarking is in the process of inspecting schools. Government Inspectors collect data from a variety of sources to form an extensive database of information about each school. Statistical modelling techniques are used to create various classifications of schools. Indicators are selected such as examination results, attendance, expenditure patterns, curriculum structures, staffing levels and so on and the expected range of performance is identified for each school that is to be inspected using the results of the national model but taking into account the context of the school. The resulting report provides background information for the inspection team which is also shared with the school.

5 CONCLUSION

As more countries move to decentralise their education systems, information technology can provide the solution for collecting accurate and validated data that does not place unrealistic demands on schools. However, increasing delegation also means that schools need to have access to information that enables them to fulfil their strategic management role. In delegated systems schools will begin to demand some return for supplying their data.

The two examples in this paper show that it is feasible to produce software that contains models of national data that can be used as benchmarks against which schools can compare their performance using a variety of interrogation techniques. As such, education managers, at all levels of the system can be supplied with information to help them formulate policies, plan strategically and measure performance. The availability of such information will provide the return that schools seek and recompense the cost of supplying data in the first place. At present it is necessary to create "pictures" that represent the national data and in so doing software designers determine the parameters to be analysed. With the advent of the superhighway it will be feasible for schools to directly interrogate national education databases, pulling down the results into local analysis generators. When that happens we can truly believe that we have moved from making census returns on paper, a time before computers (BC) to a time when the focus moves from simply adding data (AD) to the provision of information which is valued and used by schools.

6 REFERENCES

ICL (1992) *A Window on the future.* ICL, London
Liebfried & McNair (1994) *Benchmarking.* Harper Collins. London.
Office for Standards in Education (1996) On the *WWW* at http://www.open.gov.uk/ofsted/ofsted.htm
SIMS (1996) On the *WWW* at http//www.sims.co.uk/

7 BIOGRAPHY

John Warwick taught mathematics and information technology in a variety of schools before becoming an inspector of schools. From the position of Chief Inspector for Schools in Bedfordshire he moved to the post of Assistant Chief Education Officer. John has been involved in the development of educational management information systems for over 16 years and was a member of the original team that conceived of SIMS in 1981. Within the company John has specific responsibility for international developments and as such has also acted as a consultant for a variety of aid organisations. John also contributes to new product developments and identifies new opportunities for the company in the developing field of ITEM.

PART SIX

Learning Process Management

20

Support system for Chinese language teachers: a case of ITEM in support of teaching

A.C.W. Fung and S.S. Hau
Department of Education Studies, Hong Kong Baptist University
Kowloon Tong, Hong Kong
Phone: (852)-23395679 *Fax: (852)-23397894*
e-mail: alexfung@hkbu.edu.hk
andyhau@ctsc.hkbu.edu.hk

Abstract

Educational administrators in future schools unavoidably will have to face the challenge presented by IT in education. They have to be concerned not only with systems for school management information, or for decision support and the like. They also need to be prepared to manage IT holistically for school improvement and effectiveness. The impact of IT on teaching and learning has to be included on the agenda. It is necessary therefore that the scope of ITEM encompasses the managing of IT systems for teaching and learning support, in addition to IT systems within the school office. This paper reports a case of developing a 'Chinese Language Teacher Support System' in Hong Kong. The process of the innovation is described, together with discussion on the outcome and the future prospects for such a system.

Keywords

Database, information technology, teaching support, teleconferencing

1 INTRODUCTION

The rapid development of information technology (IT) has increased the popularity of computerised school administration and management systems. The term 'ITEM' was coined for the area of 'Information Technology in Educational Management' at the first IFIP International Working Conference on the subject in Israel, 1994. Its appearance is gaining in frequency in writings related to school information systems (SISs), computer-aided school administration (CASA), educational management information system (EMIS), and the like. In a broader perspective, as educational management would be meaningless when separated from teaching and learning, ITEM should have a place in issues related to curriculum, teaching, and learning activities where IT is, or can be, involved.

Gilmore (1995) has rightly observed that the focus of computers as a subject in itself in the educational field has been switched to their use as tools for learning and teaching. Transformational leaders in educational settings have to be aware that the impact of, for example, the Internet on education and schooling has only begun to appear as the tip of an iceberg. IT can do a lot more to support educational management and teachers, besides operational, administrative, and managerial processes.

This paper presents a case study of the development of a 'Chinese Language Teacher Support System' in Hong Kong. The concept of TSSs (Teacher Support Systems) where IT is used to support teaching is certainly not limited only to the subject of Chinese Language. A study by Gilmore (1995) shows that the use of computers in teaching increases teachers' confidence in addition to cognitive and social benefits for students. It is recognized that both CAL (Computer-aided Learning) and CAI (Computer-aided Instruction) have their importance in using IT directly in the learning and teaching process, but these are outside the scope of this paper. The focus of this paper is on a TSS that provides support and resource to teachers in their proactive planning in teaching.

2 NETWORKS TO SUPPORT TEACHING AND LEARNING

About a decade ago, the Education Department of South Australia set up a trial project, NEXUS, as an electronic information service to provide information to teachers and students (Leonard, 1990). NEXUS was later developed further to consist of electronic mailing, bulletin boards, and information databases. Users of the system can now share ideas of common interest, access materials and obtain experts' assistance through the network. Leonard (1990) remarks that schools are even willing to pay for the telecommunication service which can enhance the learning and teaching of their students. In the United Kingdom, the 'Campus 2000' project, launched in 1988, provides similar services of e-mailing, information retrieval, and teleconferencing to schools (Jones,1990). In Israel, the Ministry of Education initiated in 1995 a pilot project "The Israeli Informatics Teachers' Net" to provide personal mail, bulletin boards, discussion groups, and information banks using the Internet for teachers (Barta et al., 1996). In Japan, the NEC corporation has set up its own in-house education system for staff development even using satellite communication (Kurat et al., 1990). These activities in different places reflect that there is a demand for on-line support in teaching and learning, as well as in staff development.

In Hong Kong, there are two TSSs currently in development and access to both is limited to teachers from selected schools. The first TSS network is 'TELENEX'; this was started by the Teaching of English Language Education Centre of Hong Kong University in 1994 in support of English language teaching (Tsui, 1994). The other is 'CLTSS', for teachers of Chinese language; this began only in April 1995 at the School Administration and Management System Training & Research Unit of the Hong Kong Baptist University.

3 THE CHINESE LANGUAGE TEACHER SUPPORT SYSTEM

The CLTSS project is funded by the Language Fund of the Hong Kong Government. The Language Fund promotes research and development work in improving the language proficiency of people in Hong Kong. The aim of the CLTSS two-year project is to develop a computer-based information system network to support the teaching of Chinese language in local secondary schools. Technically the system is simply a computer network with a server at the support centre of the SAMS T&R Unit which can be accessed by teachers with computers and modems at their schools. The content database in the server stores Chinese Language teaching resources for secondary class-levels one to seven, including standard reading passages, teaching plans, teaching ideas, learning tasks, and test papers. Such contents, however, are not materials centrally developed by language experts. They are materials collected from front-line teachers in the schools. The CLTSS, in other words, serves as a pool of teachers' materials, experience, and expertise that are in the field. The system is basically only using IT as a tool to help with the sharing and dissemination of such valuable teaching resources. This may be a characteristic of the CLTSS which in a way distinguishes it from other similar networks.

CLTSS Project Management

Two aspects of the project are described in the following sections. The first focuses on 'user-participation' and linking up with schools and teachers. The second concerns the technical part of the system, including hardware and system design and development.

3.1 Link up with Schools and Teachers

The link up here refers to the 'soft' side of the connection with the people to be involved in the project. It is well recognised that user-participation and involvement are necessary elements to the success of the innovation. Getting commitment from school heads and teachers was the very first step taken care of in project. In view of the limited resources and capacity of the research team, only schools within one district in Hong Kong (the Tsuen Wan, Kwai Chung and Tsing Yi district with 43 secondary schools) were targeted. A lunch seminar was held for the principals and Chinese language department heads of the schools in that district to explain and discuss the project objectives and the contributions required from the schools to be involved. In the subsequent week the schools interested in joining replied to the research team after their internal discussion and decision. Twenty-three schools volunteered to join the scheme, which then began in May 1995.

Ten schools out of the twenty-three were chosen as a core group and the rest serve as support schools in the project. The distinction was only a matter of resource in that schools in the core group could each be given a set of computer, modem, and telephone line. Owing to the budget limitation in the project, the support schools did not receive these hardware items. Both groups of school, however, have to contribute teaching resources in Chinese language to be stored in the server located at the project centre. It has to be pointed out that, in this regard, the project has made an initial breakthrough in attempting to pool teachers' resources, because there is no such culture of sharing teaching resources among teachers in Hong Kong, not to say across different schools. The concept of the teacher as a continuous learner, the school as a learning organisation, and schools in the project as a learning network was 'sold' to the participants in the above-mentioned seminar and apparently it had some effect. At a later stage of the project, it is planned that the number of participating schools will be expanded to forty across the Territory.

In two subsequent meetings with representatives of the ten core schools, further details about the project were attended to - the vision, the benefits, communication structure and methods. The teachers understood that CLTSS is to be a joint venture, and not a 'centre-to-periphery' project where experts design and develop resources for users. 'Ownership' of the system is thus shared between researchers and participants. When successfully implemented, teachers can share their own teaching resources with others and learn from one another how to improve their teaching in Chinese language. They can be more efficient and effective in preparing their lessons, learning tasks and activities, compare notes, review past examination papers of others, and also get advice from colleagues or even professionals in higher education institutes. With such a support system, insights and creative ideas can be generated and teachers' professionalism will also be enhanced. Using CLTSS, teachers can also save up more time to work on their teaching methods, and to attend to individual student needs. Hopefully, the standard of students' Chinese language proficiency will be improved in the long run. This form of shared-effort can also create a bond between teachers with mutual support to meet new challenges in the currently quite turbulent Hong Kong education system. Support is a great sign of encouragement and relieves teaching stress. This may be more apparent among new teachers than experienced ones, and department heads equipped with CLTSS will be in a better position to help their colleagues in professional development.

3.2 Design and Development of CLTSS

Five teachers were identified as key people from the ten core schools. They took up the three major roles of (1) linkage with teachers in the twenty-three schools in collecting of teaching resources; (2) selection of materials to be stored in the system; and (3) feedback on the design and development of the software as to user-friendliness and integrativeness. While technical views are important in system design, experience of these front-line teachers are found to be most valuable in determining the user requirements, what contents to be included and how these should be categorised. Without such collaborative participation by the involved teachers, it would not have been possible to achieve any success with CLTSS - nor perhaps with any other system.

Most of the materials collected so far from the twenty-three schools are paper documents, with a small portion only in word-processed format. This reflects the fact that many Chinese Language teachers in Hong Kong are not yet accustomed to word-processing. Quite a lot of effort has been spent by the CLTSS support-centre to key-in the materials for the content database.

A system study was carried out in April 1995 and it was decided that a prototype should be produced as soon as possible for the ten core schools. Design and layout for the prototype were discussed with the five key teachers, and revised accordingly. Programming for this tailor-made prototype was completed in July 1995 and it was installed in the schools of the five key teachers for testing. The prototype consisted of a local searching system, and a connection facility to the CLTSS-database at the support-centre where five data lines had been installed.

The prototype provided a number of functions :

(A) Local operation -
Materials that have been inputed in digital form are classified into different categories of data for teaching or reference purpose. This forms the 'content-library' (see below) in the server at the support-centre, but a subset of the core content is duplicated also and stored as a database in the computer at each school. Teachers can search and retrieve from the local database documents they are interested in.

(B) Dial-up operation -
Functions provided under this category are commonly found on BBSs (Bulletin Board Systems) including E-mail, Teleconferencing, Special Interest Groups (SIGs are the same as discussion groups), and Information Exchange (for public messages from the centre to teachers, and vice-versa). In addition to these, a 'Content-Library' with all teaching resources currently available at the centre can be accessed. The data-set in this is bigger than that in the local drives at the schools.

Searching and retrieval from the Content-library is the same as from the local drive, except that the response and download time is longer.

There are several reasons behind the strategy adopted in the prototyping, with both local and dial-up operations. Firstly, as there were no suitable Chinese BBSs on hand at the time, it was necessary to use one operating on MS-DOS which was 'satisfying' only in terms of ease-of-use and response time. Secondly, to create early success in the project, the system had to provide users with some return in the shortest time possible; and this could be achieved through the use of the local database installed. Thirdly, the prototype also provided teachers an opportunity to learn about CLTSS, in preparation for future updates.

The CLTSS prototype was put into all the ten core schools in mid-October 1995, after testing by the five key teachers and with some minor modifications. By 31 December 1995, 68 teachers had registered as users and the system had answered 1,090 calls, accumulated 460 files uploaded and 483 files downloaded. This is on top of the local usage at the ten individual schools. (This local usage was not counted because it was only prototyping.) During that period of only two months in which two weeks were school holidays, 1,300 messages were exchanged including public messages and private e-mails.

Development continued on the content database and by the end of December, 15 different categories of teaching resource were built with a total of 372 files. However, the response time was, as anticipated by the system designers, not up to users' expectations. Fortunately a new Chinese BBS that operates on the Windows platform had already been identified and the prototype was superseded by the first regular version of CLTSS in April 1996. With this Windows-based version, even teachers with little computer experience will be able to make use of CLTSS more comfortably, and the response time has been demonstrated to be much faster than that with the prototype.

4 CONCLUSION

Much time and effort is required unavoidably in setting up a teaching support system. But such efforts will be rewarded in the longer term with time-savings on the teachers' part, with professional growth, and with improvement in teaching and learning effectiveness. Despite the explosion of information technology, there are teachers who are still using index cards and stencils, and who are still hesitant to follow the trend of information technology. Psychological effects and technical support are issues that can never be ignored. As Fung (1995) has said,

> "It would be very wrong to assume that given the hardware and software, information technology can be implemented into educational settings with automatic success. Using information technology in educational management, ITEM, irrespective of scope or scale, is an innovative process which needs managing." (p. 37)

With the advent of the Internet, the next phase of development for the CLTSS is naturally linkage to the World Wide Web. Besides development of the system, it is also planned that an evaluation research on the use of the system (e.g. the impact on the teaching behaviour of users) will be done. Although schools in Hong Kong are not currently provided by the government with the facility to access the Internet, it is likely that such access will be provided soon. The technology for building Chinese websites is already there; it is only a matter of time and resources before schools across and outside of Hong Kong would be able to login to a CLTSS website - with hypertexts and multimedia capabilities. It is also anticipated that similar websites for different subjects will be built in future, and such teacher-support systems will help to improve teaching and learning by the students in the schools.

5 REFERENCES

Barta, B.Z., Salant, A. and Telem, M. (1996) Internet support to school innovation management, in *Proceedings of the 2nd IFIP International Working Conference on ITEM*, Hong Kong Baptist University, Hong Kong.

Fung, A.C.W. (1995) Managing Change in ITEM, in *Information Technology in Educational Management* (eds. B.Z. Barta et al.), Chapman & Hall, London.

Gilmore, A.M. (1995) Turning teachers on to computers: evaluation of a teacher development program. *Journal of Research on Computing in Education,* **27(3)**, 251-269.

Jones, G. (1990) Communication for the curriculum, in *Proceedings of the IFIP TC3 Fifth World Conference on Computers in Education*, 983-987.

Kurata, M., Maekawa, Y., Nomura, Y., Matsushita, S., Inotsume, K. and Ohtake, Y. (1990) A networking educational system with NESPAC, in *Proceedings of the IFIP TC3 Fifth World Conference on Computers in Education*, 997-1002.

Leonard, R. (1990) Nexus III - Telecommunications beyond the classroom, in *Proceedings of the IFIP TC3 Fifth World Conference on Computers in Education*, 1003-1008.

Tsui, A. (1994) *The participant structures of TeleNex: a computer network for ESL teachers*. Paper presented at the International Language in Education Conference, Hong Kong.

6 BIOGRAPHIES

Alex C.W. Fung received a B.Sc. in 1970 from the University of Hong Kong and Cert.Ed., Adv.Dip.Ed., and M.Ed. in subsequent years from the same university. He received his Ph.D. in educational management and administration in 1992 from the London University Institute of Education. He was a secondary school principal in Hong Kong for more than twenty years before he joined the Department of Education Studies of the Hong Kong Baptist University as senior lecturer in 1994. He is currently an associate professor and also Director of the School Administration and Management System Training & Research Unit at the Hong Kong Baptist University.

S.S. Hau received a B.Sc. in 1989 from St. Francis Xavier University, Canada. He has been working in the Information Technology industry for 6 years. He is currently an M.Phil student in the Department of Education Studies of Hong Kong Baptist University.

21

An educational tool for planning and monitoring the teaching-learning process in Dutch secondary education

P. Hogenbirk
PRINT/VO
Plotterweg 30, 3821 BB Amersfoort, The Netherlands
Phone: (31)-33-4534343 Fax: (31)-33-4534353
e-mail: PRINT@XS4ALL.NL or P.Hogenbirk@Print.cps.nl

Abstract

Dutch higher secondary education is to be reformed in the next few years. The new system will be learner-orientated: it is intended that students will learn much more independently from teachers who will facilitate the learning process. This concerns a rather radical change in the view of learning, and therefore teaching, and students as well as teachers do need to transform their behavior. Both students and teachers will have new responsibilities in the educational process. To support these changes an educational tool for planning and monitoring the teaching-learning process will be developed. The tool consists of a database of activities, a planning module for students and a monitoring module for teachers. The tool should be linked to existing school management systems and to educational courseware and student assessment tools. An important aspect of the implementation of the system is that the coordinating body (PRINT) is preparing arrangements to make this system a nationwide standard for all educational parties involved.

Keywords

Information technology, secondary education, educational management, national policy, independent learning

1 INTRODUCTION

In the Netherlands we are in the middle of a process of reforming secondary education. In lower secondary education (age 12-15) the so-called "basic education" has been introduced in 1993. This innovation concerns general education for all students. The common objectives are aimed at:

- the application of knowledge rather than the knowledge itself;
- the emphasis on skills and abilities;
- the search for integration rather than separation of subject matter.

In 1998 this will be followed by restructuring higher secondary education (age 16-18). This reform will bring about an even more far-reaching change along two dimensions.

One dimension is that the content of all the subjects will be updated and redefined. The other dimension is that the organization of education will change from a teacher-oriented system into a learner-oriented system. This innovation is often referred to as the concept of the "study-house". It emphases the ability of learning to learn in the perspective of life-long learning and of learning more independently of the teacher. This second dimension of change will be the most difficult one, because it demands a total redefinition of the role of the teachers as well as the role of the learners. The teacher will more become an organizer of the learning-process and a companion of the students in their learning activities. The teacher is responsible for that element, but is not responsible for the learning itself. The latter responsibility has to be taken by the students. They have to plan their learning-activities according to their own abilities, preferences and interests.

It is our deepest belief that this new view of the learning process and on the organization of learning can only succeed if the teacher and the learners are willing to adopt new behaviors. To make that possible and more convenient, support from all available new technologies has to be provided. For that reason PRINT (Project for Implementation of New Technologies) is developing a new educational management tool. PRINT is aimed at the introduction, adaptation and implementation of using computers in secondary schools (age 12-18) at the levels of school management, teachers and learners. These goals have to be accomplished through providing information, organizing all kinds of courses for professionals, supporting teacher networks, developing courseware and instructional materials, cooperating with educational publishers and software-developers and advising the Dutch government.

2 BRIEF DESCRIPTION OF THE EDUCATIONAL TOOL

A school information system has several more or less independent subsystems. The core of the system is a database with, among others, students data: their names, addresses, school history and other relevant information. All kind of modules can be attached to this database, for example a module for budgeting, an attendance (or absence) registration module, a scheduling module and so on. (See figure 1.)

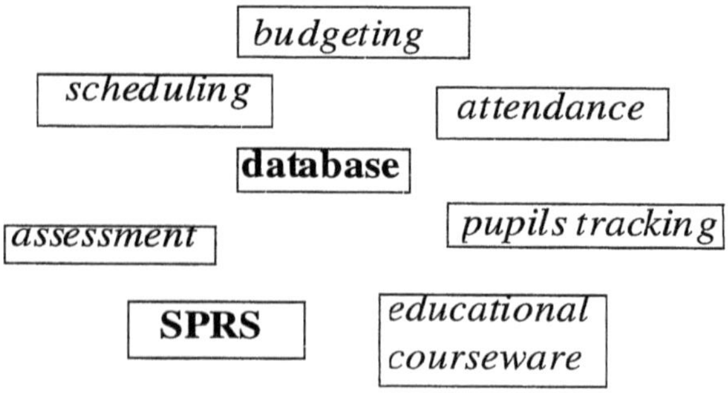

Figure 1 Modules of a school information system.

For lower secondary education an additional module is developed in the Netherlands to follow the students in their well-being at school. We call it a pupils tracking module. All kinds of test results about basic skills, behavior, physical and emotional well-being of pupils can be stored in this module, as well as short remarks on pupils from group counselors and teachers. By combining these results a so-called "student profile" can be generated, which gives the group counselors the opportunity to follow their students in their educational growth and satisfaction and to intervene if things are going wrong.

In order to support the described innovation process in higher secondary education a tool for planning and monitoring the teaching-learning process has been designed. The Dutch acronym for this module is SPRS. We will briefly describe the framework and starting points of this module. (See figure 2.)

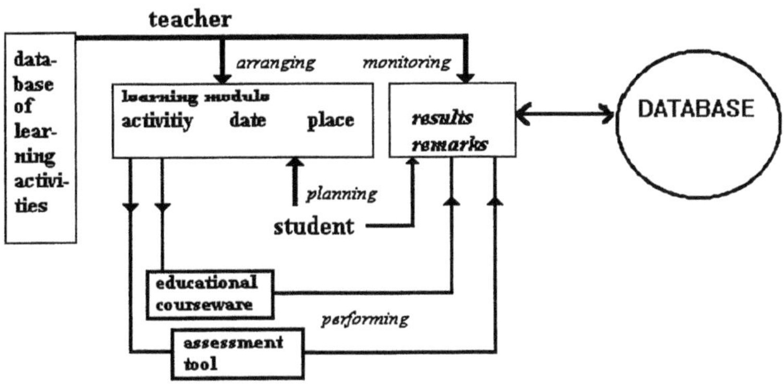

Figure 2 The tool for planning and monitoring the teaching-learning process: SPRS

Learning as an activity

The core of the module concerns a *database of learning activities*: These are descriptions of all kinds of activities to be carried out by students within a learning module. For example completing an assignment, studying some text, performing exercises, doing an experiment, making investigations, visiting a museum, an assessment, practising with educational software, and so on.

The database of learning activities should be provided by educational publishers in a well defined national standard and data-format. These learning activities are linked to the instructional materials the educational publishers provide. As part of a teacherguide a sequencing of learning activities can be proposed. The ultimate purpose is, of course, to enable the teacher to arrange and rearrange these activities to provide maximum benefit to the students. The teacher can also add remarks and hints, and the time and place for some or all of the activities. We could call this part of the SPRS the "*curriculum organizer*".

Planning the learning process

The schedule of learning activities is loaded into a *planning tool* for the students. They can add a date for every activity on which they plan to carry out the activity, and a date for actually having performed the activity. They can also input (in some cases) the result of an activity. Finally they can add remarks for the teacher. In that respect the system can also be a supportive instrument for communication between teacher and learner. This planning tool for the students is essential for the new vision of learning. The students are more responsible for their own learning path. They can skip some activity they do not consider necessary and they can add activities (like doing a diagnostic test, or performing more exercises) whenever they feel the need for that. The only constraint should be that their planning of the learning path fits with the constraints the teacher has given. These constraints can be the date and place of certain obligatory activities, for example a traditional instructional class for economics, an arrangement for an experiment in science or a summative assessment at the end of the learning module.

Monitoring by the teacher

The data in the student planning tool are also accessible by the teacher. In fact the teacher is watching the same screen, but with has another authorization. For the teacher this part of the system is a *monitoring and registration tool*. The teacher can add a result for a specific activity, especially when it concerns a general summative assessment; can also make remarks to be mailed to the students; and can generate reports for one student and reports on certain issues for a group of students.

The students can look at their results and to the remarks from the teacher, but then again via their planning tool. They are not authorized of course to change these data.
This monitoring tool is very important to allow the teachers to control the learning process and the achievements of the students. Without this source of information the independence of the students could easily develop into non motivation and dropping out. To encourage the adpotion of new vision of learning by teachers (and parents), these effects should be prevented.

Import and export of data

Besides these three described major components, the module should be able to exchange data with other educational and managerial tools. This is a demand for implementing the module in the existing educational environment. This means that there are two additional and essential starting points for the SPRS module.

The module has to be linked fully with the student-database of the school information system. The schools have invested a lot of time and money in the past few years to set up an information system for storing student data. If the SPRS module were to require a totally new implementation of the existing information system, this would not be accepted and it would not be very efficient.

The module can also be linked to educational software and assessment tools. The advantage is that name, class, level and other relevant student data can be imported from the general system and that results or remarks generated in the courseware and assessment tools can be exported to the general system. These results and remarks can be stored in the monitoring part of the SPRS and be read by students and teachers. This starting point is very important, especially for the publishers of educational software and assessment tools. They can develop new materials for use in the new higher secondary education without having to invest in a rather costly module like the one described here.

3 THE SYSTEM AS A NATIONAL STANDARD

Next to the design of the SPRS as a tool in the way described above, it is of the utmost importance that this system be standardized. This gives all the parties involved in supporting the educational system and in developing educational materials the opportunity to contribute to the new educational process in such a way that costs are reduced and effectiveness is maximized. It also means that all parties involved do have to commit themselves to the standard. Therefore the aim is to involve all relevant parties in defining, developing, distributing and implementing this system. These parties are the Ministry of Education, the developers of school management software, the educational publishers and software houses, the institutes for educational support and above all the schools themselves.

We try to build this commitment by involving all these parties in the development process. In the heart of this development there are four development networks of teachers and school managers, accompanied by members of educational support institutes and the software distributors. These networks will also be used for testing the prototypes of (components of) the system. The RAD-technique: Rapid Application Development, will be used. In this the different features of the tool will be built as prototypes, to be commented on and tested by future users.

The building of the system will take place in four phases. In the first phase a data-model will be made on the basis of a detailed interrogation of the schools and educational experts involved. The second phase consists of building parts of the system. The third phase will be an extensive evaluation of the system in the schools. Therefore the schools have to set up a testing environment in which the new ideas on independent learning and teacher guidance have to be implemented. The schools involved are prepared to do so in certain parts of the curriculum at certain levels of higher secondary education. In the final phase the system will be prepared for broad-scale implementation. In order to give support to all users of the school information system a helpdesk will be set up and the educational experts involved will define ways of implementing the SPRS in various types of schools. This implementation will start in 1998.

4 BIOGRAPHY

Pieter Hogenbirk started as a teacher in secondary education and was also involved in the development of innovative educational materials at the universities of Utrecht and Amsterdam. In 1987 he became project manager within the so-called NIVO-project, with a follow-up in the PRINT-project from 1989. He has been in charge of managing projects on the development of curricula, courseware and in-service teacher training and the implementation of materials and training for informatics and Computer Aided Learning. Since 1993 he has been director of the PRINT-management for secondary education. PRINT is carrying out more than 100 projects with respect to the development and implementation of the use of information and communication technology in Dutch secondary education. The SPRS-project is one of the topics that are being carried out for upper secondary education.

22

Electronic learning contract for the assessment of projects in information systems

R.C.W. Kwok and J. Ma
Department of Information Systems, City University of Hong Kong
Tat Chee Avenue, Kowloon, Hong Kong
e-mail: isron@msmail.is.cphk.hk
isjian@msmail.is.cphk.hk

Abstract

Assessment of students' learning is a crucial factor that will influence students' approaches to learning. This study investigates the effects of using electronic learning contracts on students' approaches to learning. An Electronic Learning Contract (ELC) is a continuously renegotiable working agreement between students and lecturers for assessing the outcomes of students projects. It focuses on group decision making through electronic meetings towards the learning outcomes. It specifies what students will learn, how this will be accomplished, within what period of time, and what the criteria of assessment will be. A Group Support System (GSS) is used to provide an environment for electronic meeting and to assist the processes for discussing, negotiating, formulating, re-negotiating and revising the content of the ELC among students and lecturers. Students' participation in the construction of the electronic learning contract will enhance their perception of assessment criteria. It will generate the backwash effects of assessment on learning, and thus encourage deep and achieving approaches to learning.

Keywords

Higher education, assessment, learning contract, group support system

1 INTRODUCTION

Students' approaches to learning can be classified into surface, deep and achieving approaches (Biggs, 1989; Biggs, 1991; Biggs, 1992). Recent studies (Biggs, 1992; Biggs, 1996) conducted in several tertiary institutions in Asia show that Asian students are committed to a low level, rote-biased (or surface) approach to learning. The students see university education, based on their extrinsic motivation, as a means to get a degree and to obtain a desirable job. They have a tendency to minimise their efforts but avoid failure. The strategy appropriate to meeting that intention is to limit the target to those essentials that may be reproduced through rote learning. Biggs (1989) shows that deep and achieving approaches to learning can be encouraged where the learning context encourages intrinsic motivation and attributions of ownership and self-efficacy, learner activity rather than passivity, and particular kinds of peer and teacher interaction.

Assessment methods have a strong effect on students' approaches to learning (Elton L. & Laurillard D., 1979). Current educational research focuses on the relationships between different assessment methods and students' approaches to learning (Biggs, 1992; Biggs, 1996; Imrie, 1995; Tompkins & McGraw, 1988).

This paper proposes the use of an Electronic Learning Contract (ELC) for assessing the outcomes of students' projects as well as the development and application of a Group Support System (GSS) for supporting the ELC. The ELC method has been tested in assessing the outcomes of students in the Department of Information Systems at the City University of Hong Kong. Quantitative data for comparing differences in students' approaches to learning have been obtained using Biggs' Study Process Questionnaire (SPQ) (Biggs, 1992). These data are used to analyse the impact of the new assessment method on students' approaches to learning.

2 ELECTRONIC LEARNING CONTRACT

Donald (1976) defines a learning contract as a document drawn up by a student and his instructor or advisor, which specifies what the student will learn, how this will be accomplished, within what period of time, and what the criteria of evaluation will be.

A learning contract is not just a document, it is the process that will encourage intrinsic motivation, active learning, and student-teacher interaction. Tompkins & McGraw (1988) also emphasise the importance of the process, including the relationship between the student and teacher and the negotiation that occurs throughout the learning experience.

In this paper, an Electronic Learning Contract (ELC) is a continuously renegotiable working agreement between students and teachers which focuses on group decision making processes through electronic meetings in relation to the students' learning outcomes. A Group Support System (GSS) is used to assist the processes for discussing, negotiating, formulating, re-negotiating and revising the content of the electronic learning contract among students and lecturers.

A conceptual model of the ELC is shown in Figure 1. The tasks can be carried out in the following eight stages:

Stage 1: The lecturers design and draft the list of assessment criteria based on the project objectives, the available resources and the assessment guidelines and policies of the institution.

Stage 2: Students and lecturers discuss and negotiate, based on their perceptions of the assessment requirements, the content of the proposed assessment criteria using the GSS.

Stage 3: The lecturers then filter the generated opinions and prepare a vote for students and lecturers to select the assessment criteria for the project using the GSS.

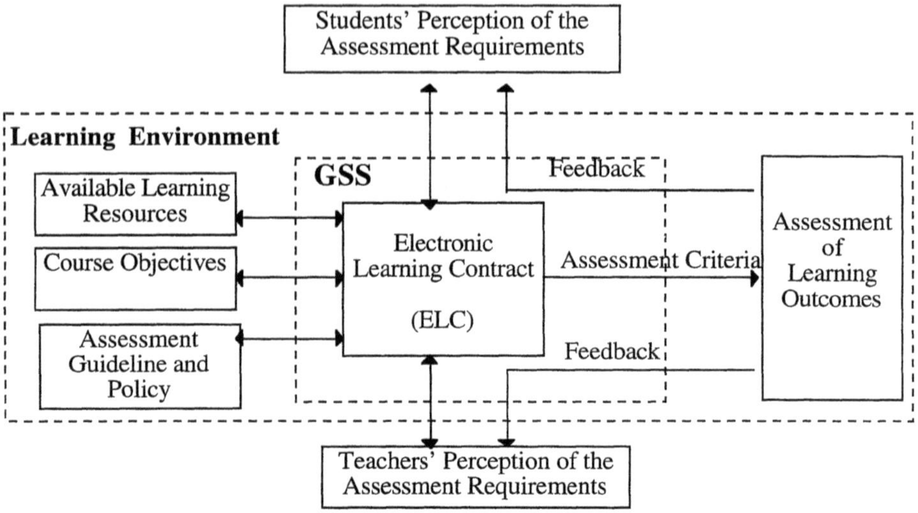

Figure 1 A Conceptual Model of the Electronic Learning Contract.

Stage 4: Students and lecturers select and rate the assessment criteria with respect to the objectives of the project.

Stage 5: The lecturers then process the result of the vote and formulate the final set of assessment criteria using the GSS. The final set of the assessment criteria will be announced and the students are allowed to enter their opinions on the results. Using the Delphi method, students and lecturers will then re-vote until most of the group is satisfied with the results, but the final decision is subject to the professional judgement of the lecturers.

Stage 6: Students and lecturers can express their opinion using the GSS on the agreed assessment criteria throughout the duration of the course. The list of agreed assessment criteria is subject to change if necessary. Students and lecturers can request revision of the assessment.

Stage 7: Lecturers will assess the students' learning outcomes according to the agreed assessment criteria throughout the course so that students get continuous feedback from the lecturers, and also students express their opinions on lecturers' comment on their performance.

Stage 8: Students also have the opportunity to self-assess their own performance and to peer-assess other students. Students can input their comment on their own performance and on that of other students.

3 A GSS FOR ELECTRONIC LEARNING CONTRACT

A GSS is an interactive computer-based system that facilitates the solving of unstructured problems by a group of decision makers. It supports more tasks than just decision making; it focuses on the processes used by working groups. It is an information technology based environment that supports group meetings, which may be distributed geographically and temporally (Turban, 1995). Group tasks include, but are not limited to, communication, planning, idea generation, problem solving, issue discussion, negotiation, conflict resolution and collaborative group activities.

A model of GSS is shown in Figure 2. These components are arranged to support the process of making a decision. The GSS includes a special decision model base for improvements of the decision making process, a database, an easy-to-use and flexible user interface, and a group facilitator procedure. The proposed GSS consists of all these components which will be discussed below.

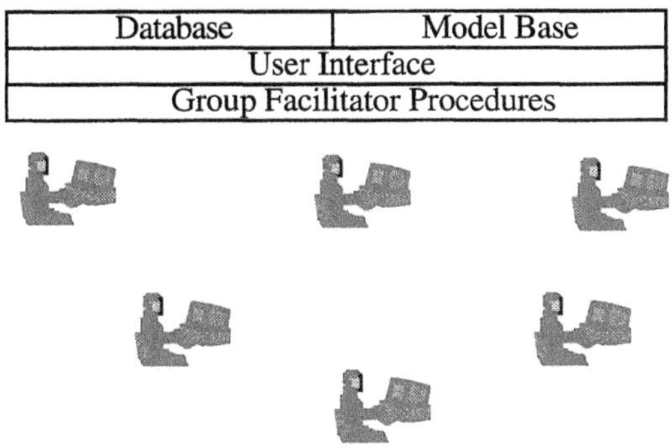

Figure 2 A Model of GSS (Turban, 1995).

The traditional negotiated learning contract is made between one lecturer and one student; it is quite easy to have the contract decided and agreed by both sides. It is more difficult to have a learning contract agreed by a number of students and lecturers within the proposed group facilitator procedure - the eight stages of ELC contracting processes previously mentioned. In order to smooth the contracting process and formulate a fair and non-threatening electronic learning contract, a fuzzy multi-criteria decision model (Chang & Chen, 1994; Grabisch, 1995) can be used for assessment criteria selection.

Suppose there is a group of *n* decision makers (D1, D2, ..., D*n*) who are responsible for evaluating the appropriateness of *m* alternatives of assessment criteria (A1, A2, ..., A*m*) under each of *k* decision criteria (C1, C2,..., C*k*) as well as the importance weight of the decision criteria. Let S*itj* be the rating assigned to alternative A*i* by decision maker D*j* under decision criterion C*t*. Let W*tj* be the weight given to C*t* by decision maker D*j*. The committee has to aggregate the rating S*itj* of *n* decision makers for each alternative A*i* versus each criterion C*t* to obtain the rating S*it*. Each pooled S*it* can further be weighted by weight W*t* according to the relative importance of the *k* decision criteria. Then, the final score F*i*, fuzzy appropriateness index, of alternative A*i* can be obtained by aggregating S*it* and W*t*. Finally, rank the final scores F*i*, (*i*=1, 2,..., *m*) to obtain the most appropriate alternative.

A database schema for the decision model of the proposed GSS is shown in Figure 3. The database schema is used to store necessary data for processing decision while the user interface is to allow the group to perform a joint function such as information entry, voting, or ranking alternatives through electronic meetings (Gray, Mandviwalla, Olfman & Satzinger, 1993). To the user, the system is the interface. One example of the public screens of the proposed GSS is shown in Figure 4.

PERSON(PID, Name);
LECTURER(PID, Appointment, Duty);
STUDENT(PID, Contribution, LearnAppr);
PROJECT(Proj-No, Total-Mark);
ASSIGN(PID, Proj-No);
A_ CRITERIA(ANo, AssessCriteriaName);
D_CRITERIA(CNo, DecisionCriteriaName);
RATING(ANo, CNo, PID, Rating-Score);
WEIGHT(CNo, PID, CNo-Weight);

Figure 3 A database schema for the GSS.

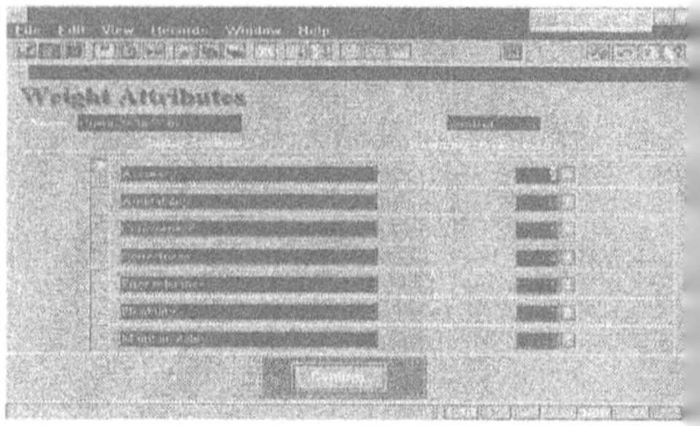

Figure 4 A screen for weighting the assessment criteria.

Finally, the goal of the GSS is to improve the productivity and effectiveness of electronic decision making meetings, either by speeding up the decision making process or by improving the quality of the resulting ELC. This is accomplished by providing support to the exchange of ideas, opinions, and preferences within the group.

4 CONCLUSION

In this paper, an electronic learning contract system is proposed for enhancing students' understanding of the assessment requirement and encouraging students to take the deep and achieving approaches to learning. This paper also suggests a fuzzy multi-criteria decision model for selecting assessment criteria. The concept of fuzzy sets is used in this paper because it can easily be used to describe the subjective selection of assessment criteria and the weightings of criteria. New methods of multi-criteria decision making need to be investigated to support the selection of assessment criteria and the weightings of criteria from decision makers of different importance.

Although the electronic learning contract in this paper is primarily designed to run on the university campus-wide computer network, it can be installed on Internet so that more stakeholders of the assessment policy in higher education, such as parents and future employers etc., can contribute their ideas in the assessment criteria decision processes. ELC can be applied for courses running on full-time, part-time or distance learning basis, at educational institutions or business organisations.

(The project work described in this paper was funded by the 1994 Strategic Research Grant of City University of Hong Kong and the 1994/95 Hong Kong Action Learning Project Grant).

5 REFERENCES

Biggs, J.B. (1989) Students' approach to learning in Anglo-Chinese schools. *Educational Research Journal*, **4**, 8-17.

Biggs, J.B. (1991). Approaches to learning in secondary and tertiary students in Hong Kong: some comparative studies. *Educational Research Journal*, **6**, 27-39.

Biggs, J.B. (1992). *Why and how do Hong Kong students learn? (Using the Learning and Study Process Questionnaires).* Faculty of Education, University of Hong Kong, Hong Kong.

Biggs, J.B. (1996). Assessing learning quality: reconciling institutional, staff and educational demands. *Assessment & Evaluation in Higher Education*, **21(1)**, 5-15.

Chang, P.L. & Chen, Y.C. (1994). A fuzzy multi-criteria decision making method for technology transfer strategy selection in biotechnology. *Fuzzy Sets and Systems*, **63**, 131-139.
Donald, J.G. (1976). Contracting for learning. *Learning and Development*, **7(5)**, 1-7.
Elton, L. & Laurillard, D. (1979). Trends in students learning. *Studies in Higher Education*, **4**, 87-102.
Grabisch, M. (1995). Fuzzy integral in multicriteria decision making. *Fuzzy Sets and Systems*, **69**, 279-298.
Gray, P., Mandviwalla, M., Olfman, L. & Satzinger J. (1993). The user interface in group support systems, in *Group Support Systems* (eds. L.Jessup & J.S. Valacich), Macmillan, New York.
Imrie, B. W. (1995). Assessment for learning: quality and taxonomies. *Assessment & Evaluation in Higher Education*, **20(2)**, 175-189.
Tompkins, C. & McGraw, M.J. (1988). The negotiated learning contract, in *Developing Student Autonomy in Learning (2nd Edition)* (ed. D. Boud), Kogan Page, London.
Turban, E. (1995). *Decision support and expert systems*. Prentice Hall, London.

6 BIOGRAPHIES

Ron C.W. Kwok received the Certificate of Education in Physical Education from the Northcote College of Education (HK) in 1986, the B.Ed. degree in Physical Education from the University of Liverpool (UK) in 1990 and the M.Sc. degree in Information Systems from the University of Brighton (UK) in 1994. He has been a member of the Department of Information Systems of the City University of Hong Kong since 1995, where he currently is a MPhil student. His current research interests are in the areas of technology based learning, student's approaches to learning, assessment methods and group support system.

Jian Ma is an assistant professor in the Department of Information Systems at City University of Hong Kong. He received his Doctor of Engineering degree in Computer Science from Asian Institute of Technology. His research interests are in the areas of group decision support systems, object-oriented systems, database management, business process reengineering, and assessment of problem-based learning in engineering and business education.

23

System modelling of ITEM: re-engineering of educational processes

Harald Yndestad
Aalesund College
Fogd Grevesveg 9, 6009 Aalesund, Norway
e-mail: Harald.Yndestad@hials.no

Abstract

IT in educational management is not merely a technical problem, but to a large extent a matter of understanding what effect IT has on organisations. IT has a great potential for making better schools, but at the same time IT introduces structural instabilities. System modelling may help leaders to get a holistic view of IT in schools.

Keywords

Information technology, management, system theory, structural instability

1 INTRODUCTION

IT in Educational Management (ITEM) has grown over a period of at least twenty years. Initially ITEM was introduced to keep records of students and to control finances. During the last twenty years, IT has been taken widely in use. Few questioned the importance of ITEM or studied what consequences this new technology has on organisations. Today ITEM seems to grow most rapidly as an information system on Internet.

If we stop for a moment and ask the basic question: Why are we using IT in educational management? The answer will vary, depending on whether you are a student, a teacher, a financial director or a principal. Today there is a new generation of fast-growing information technology. Integration technologies such as CD-ROM, virtual reality and Internet will change the way we get and use information. As far as I know, there has not been much research on how this new generation of IT will effects schools. System theory is a useful concept for better understanding fundamental aspects of organisations. We hope system modelling will be a helpful tool of choosing an IT strategy.

2 SYSTEM VIEWS ON SCHOOLS

2.1 General system theory

System theory is an organic view of understanding organisations (Bertalanffy, 1968). Systems are analysed with different perspectives in order to uncover different aspects of an organisation. Typical dual perspectives of systems are:

System = Ontology + Knowledge	Knowledge = Ethic + Learning
Ontology = Architecture + Dynamics	Dynamics = Structural + State
Architecture = Levels + Partners	Partners = Binding + Objects

Systems are analysed by dual elements and by levels of abstraction. Dynamics are studied by architecture and architecture by dynamics. Architecture is levels and partners. Partners are binding and objects. In system theory, the study of binding or relations between objects is of importance. By analysing the binding, we may know more about objects, architecture and the dynamics of organisations. In an organisation such as a school, binding between partners or objects is usually information. System theory should then be a suitable tool to analyse how a new generation of IT will effect schools as organisations.

2.2 System architecture

System architecture describes the relations between partners and levels of organisation. Level is an organisation that shares a common purpose. Partners are two or more organisations sharing a common purpose.

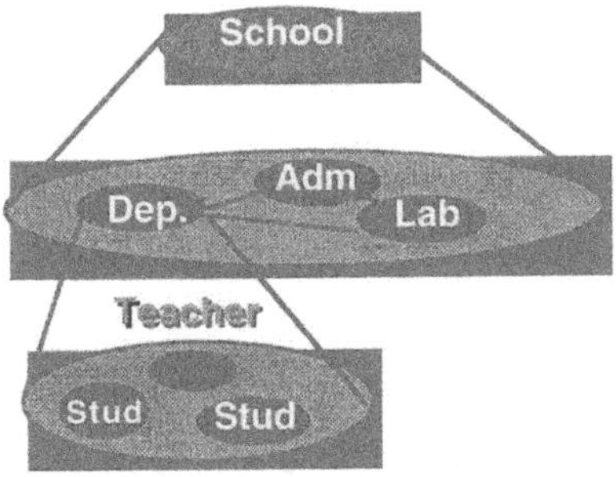

Figure 1 System internal partners

System partners in schools

Systems partners are partners because they are co-operating in sharing a common purpose. Sharing a common purpose needs some kind of binding between the partners. Typical internal binding in an organisation is communication, command, control and competence (C^4). In a school the situation is essentially the same. There is a need of communication, command, control and competence at each level of the organisation. This may be between students, teacher, administration and the external society.

IT is a tool for faster communication between organisations, command in scheduling, control of finances, control of student records and so on. Faster communication changes the binding between partners. Changes in binding will introduce changes in the organisation knowledge and dynamics. Faster information between the management, library, laboratory and so on, has made schools more flexible and efficient. On the other hand, the school has changed in the way it organised and solve its problems. From the theory of systems dynamics we know that this may lead to instability problems in the organisation (Forrester, 1967).

System levels in schools

School usually have 3-5 organisational levels dependent on the type of school. We have the student level, the teacher level, the department level, the school and the governmental level. Since each organisation level has a special purpose, the different levels have different information needs. At a low organisation level the information focus is on the product, and at higher levels the focus is more on running the business. This means that even if all information in a school are carried on a single network, information must be adapted to each level. The teacher must be responsible for how to manage information in respect of teaching; the head of department must be responsible for the integration of information in his department, and so on.
The introduction of new IT such as Internet will radically change how the information is organised and distributed. Increase in information speed, relations and openness is equivalent to less binding between partners. Less binding between partners will expand the partners' purpose in the organisation. The effect of this is less specialised partners, a more decentralised organisation and fewer organisation levels. In schools we may expect that the management of students will be decentralised from a specialised student administration to an educational department and even to the teacher. The same effect will occur in relation to other parts of the organisation. The library is bypassed by direct search for information world-wide on the Internet. Integration of multimedia, simulation models, virtual reality and electronic instrumentation will open for a world-wide laboratory testing. This is a structural change of education processes. Such changes in education will undermine mass production of education and open for specialisation of education.

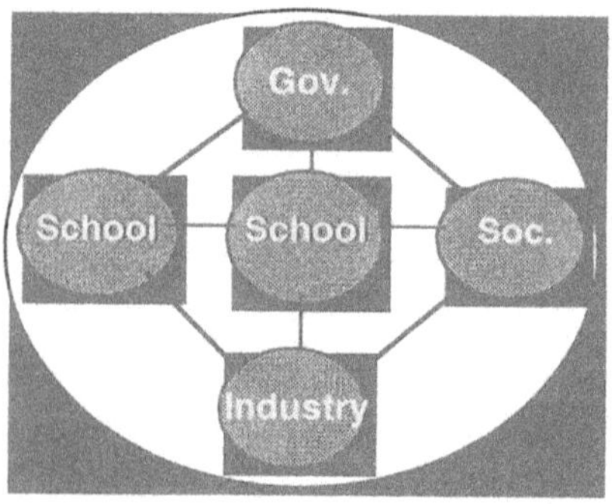

Figure 2 School and external partners

External partners

A school is related to external partners. This may be another school, the industry or other parts of the society. Together they are a system on a higher level sharing a common purpose. Fundamental aspects of systems are independent of system levels. Then changes in external binding, will have essentially the same effect as changing internal binding.

IT already is in use through the Internet for better communication between schools and the society. The government is using IT for better student records. Students already seek information world-wide by Internet. Soon they will do this from their homes. This is an fantastic world-wide opportunity to get information online cheap and updated. But on the other hand: What is ITEM in a global campus ?

2.3 System Dynamics

If there are no dynamics in an organisation, management is an easy task. System dynamics has two perspectives, viz state dynamics and structural dynamics. Management has to control both of these perspectives at the same time. Thus, from a management point of view, ITEM is using IT for better control of dynamics of schools as organisations.

State Dynamics
State dynamics are the dynamics of partners based on stable relations. This is a well known paradigm from science and planning where the dynamics of organisation has a flow perspective. State dynamics provide a perspective where IT may easily be used. We may use IT to get an optimal estimate of future needs of recruitment, costs, teachers, employment of educated students and so on. Most schools are already using IT for optimising resources and this is probably the ITEM state of the art today.

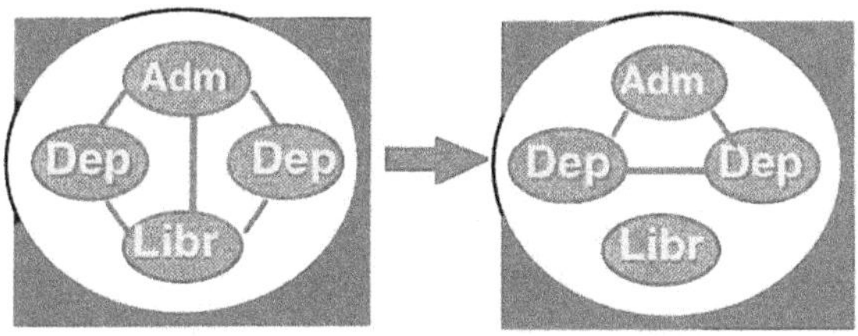

Figure 3 Structural dynamics

Structural dynamics refer to dynamic binding between partners. This is the same as changes in relations between partners. Structural dynamics have a relational perspective and thus we may discover the life cycle of objects. Examples of life cycles in schools are information, lectures, knowledge, staff and so on. ITEM is based on the ability to modulate the reality. There is no easy theory of understanding structural dynamics. The nearest is probably chaos theory and catastrophe theory (Zeeman, 1977). This type of dynamics is not controlled by IT but by management.

A value theory
The value of systems is judged by the strength of binding to its context. Structural dynamics thus is a critical problem leaders of schools should look out for.

Total Quality Management of schools
Schools need changes in a wanted direction like any other organisation. Understanding the importance of correct binding between partners is the key to influencing the direction. Analysing the relation between partners is essentially the same as the essence in Total Quality Management. Following this doctrine, an important management task is adapting the right relations between internal and external partners. The question is: How may we use IT for better relations with partners ?

A simple advice here is to follow the ISO 9004-2 standard for quality assurance of service organisations. In this standard schools are labelled as service organisations. Following the guidelines in the standard, we have a functional specification of ITEM. The standard will help us to select where to introduce IT inside schools and where to use IT in relation to external partners.

2.4 System knowledge

System knowledge is something more than the sum of knowledge for each individual person. Knowledge reflects the culture of the organisation. It affects how the organisation behaves, solves its problems and how it survives. The behaviour of the organisation affects the paper flow in the organisation, where the decision is taken and what information is used for decision making. Knowledge based ITEM is therefore not an automatic decision system. It is the ability to select the right IT-system and to predict how the introduction of IT will affect the organisation.

System ethics

Systems as organisations have a tendency of striving for immortality (Heylighen, 1991). We know school lectures, courses, departments and even schools have a life cycle. The "genes" of schools are however in what they represent. Such "genes" materialise themselves in libraries, research papers, symbols and more. Today schools actively present their appearance and values on the Internet. This means that IT is the most important tool for accumulating historical information and to show the world its values. Thus the schools are moving their binding from local relations to more international relations. When most schools in the world are visible to each other on the Internet, this will have a dramatic effect on how these schools behave, how they define their identity and knowledge.

System learning in schools

System learning is the ability to predict, control and adapt the dynamics of the organisation. The dynamics of organisations are influenced by binding to internal and external partners. Binding between partners has a level perspective and a relational perspective. Learning organisations choose the right levels and relations. Traditionally schools have stable partners. Stable partners has open for schools as an stable organisation. The planning horizon has been 3 to 10 years. This is a typical state dynamic situation where ITEM may be used for prediction and control of recourses. The new generations of IT change the relation between internal and external partners. Learning in this perspective is choosing the right relation. This is the same as re-engineering the organisation.

Optimising resources

Systems tends to optimise their energy and resources. Schools are hardly a profitable business in strict financial terms. Nevertheless there is the same need as in business organisations to optimise their resources. Optimising resources is not necessarily the same as doing things faster. Optimising resources may be doing the right thing, using the full potential of the organisation or adapting the organisation in new ways to its context. Introducing ITEM in organisations opens for a more flat and flexible organisation. Schools are no exception. By introduction IT schools may be more open, flexible and decentralised. The schools may then be better adapted to the society.

2.5 Structural instability

There is no question that most schools will take the opportunity to use IT to provide better education and improve their own functioning. But is IT always something positive for a school ? Is there a dark side of IT ? If we go back to a basic doctrine of systems, it tells us that the value of systems is dependent on binding to its context. It is obvious that IT rapidly makes new relations. If new loose relations grow faster than robust stable relations, the school may be isolated because it looses its binding to its context. In this case ITEM is not a tool which will make stable partners on a higher system level. It will be a tool for fragmentation of organisations or structural instability. In a rapid internationalisation process, this may be a price we have to pay.

2.6 Education processes re-engineering

If new generations of IT lead to structural instability, then IT will be more of a threat than a new opportunity. Such a threat may be solved by a re-engineering of the organisation as an education process. To reengineer an education process is to strive for a new kind of structural stability. This may by a closer vertical integration of schools in the value chain of education and it may be a closer integration between schools and the society.

3 CONCLUSION

New generations of IT such as CD-ROM, virtual reality and Internet will have a decisive influence on schools. Most schools will easily pick up the opportunity of using these new tools for cheaper and better education. At the same time this new generation of IT will introduce structural instabilities in schools as organisations. System theory is an holistic concept for understanding complex organisations. By using system theory we may be better prepared to understand how IT will influence schools and how to choose a right IT-strategy.

4 REFERENCES

Bertalanffy, L. (1968) *General systems theory: foundations, development, applications.* George Braziller, New York.

Forrester, J.W. (1967) Industrial dynamics. *Productivity System Dynamics series.* Portland, USA.

Heylighen, F. (1986) Towards a general framework for modelling representation changes, in *Proceedings of the 11th International Congress on Cybernetics*, Assoc. Internat. de Cyberne'tique, Namur.

Heylighen, F. (1991) An evolutionary system about evolutionary systems: introducing the Principia Cybernetica Project, in *Workbook of the 1st Principia Cybernetica Workshop*, (ed. F. Heylighen), Principia Cybernetica, Brussels-New York.

Senge, P. M. (1990) *The Fifth Discipline.* Century Business, UK.

Sterman, J.D. (1994) *Modelling for learning organisations.* Productivity Press, USA.

Yndestad, H. (1995) *Generell Systemteori.* HIÅ. [*General System Theory,* Aalesund College], Norway.

Zeeman, E.C. (1977) *Catestrophe Theory: selected papers 1972-77.* Addison-Wesley, Reading, Mass.

5 BIOGRAPHY

Harald Yndestad received has a degree in cybernetics from the University of Trondheim. He has worked for 10 years researching on complex IT systems, 6 years as principal at Aalesund College and 7 years as assistant professor at Aalesund College. For the last two years he has been engaged in research on IT and system theory.

PART SEVEN

Panels and Discussions – Summaries

24

The preconditions for computer-assisted decision-making in tomorrow's schools

P. Hogenbirk and R. G. Taylor

with B. Davey, F.R. Tarrago, and J.D. Warwick

Abstract

This paper is a summary of a multi-session group discussion among the listed authors in which they deal with three broad questions: What sorts of decisions need to be made in schools? What kinds of computer assistance would be helpful? What are the barriers to obtaining this assistance? Several general conclusions are reached, touching on the importance of the articulation of agreed-upon objectives, developing confidence in the assistance computers can give, the need for collaboration and group decision support, and the need for rigorous research.

Keywords

Decision-making, decision support systems

1 OPENING NOTES

For the purposes of this paper, and in the context of education, Computer-Assisted Decision Making (CADM) is defined as follows: "CADM is the use of information and communications technology to support decision-making at all levels of the school: managers and management, teachers and teaching, and students and learning." In this context, management should be defined broadly and should include both the management of the classroom and the learning process.

The starting point for any analysis or discussion of CADM must be with the sorts of decisions that need to be made, and not on the methods or the technologies related to CADM. The temptation is to embrace the technology without first being clear about the purposes for doing so. By focusing on the nature of the decisions first, CADM becomes an important subset of the broader topic of Decision Support Systems.

Once the decision or decisions are articulated, there is a continuum of ways information and communications technology can be supportive:

- by facilitating the process by which a person or group approaches and reaches a decision;
- by retrospectfully justifying the decision;
- by making the decision;
- by taking the decision.

The above-mentioned issues can be organized and discussed around four basic groups of questions:

- What kind of decisions need to be made in schools?
- What kind of computer-assistance would be useful?
- What are the barriers to obtaining such assistance; how can they be overcome; what resources are needed?
- What overall conclusions can be reached; what suggestions can be given?

2 KINDS OF DECISIONS

Rather than attempting to provide a typology of decisions, a short list of examples is given below. This list serves to illustrate the range of decisions that must be made by those who manage education, either individually or within a group. By no means is this list exhaustive or even comprehensive.

- Perhaps the most general and most enduring problem in school management is having to choose among alternatives in the absence of good information. This kind of decision-making context presents itself everyday and at every level of the school's organization.
- Another problem is discerning a pattern within a complex set of data. For example, given a rather complete pupil tracking system, are there any patterns within the data to suggest that an intervention by the school counselor into a particular student's school life might save the student from some indesireable consequence?
- Without understanding or analyzing the inner mechanisms of certain complex situations, when is it possible to come to a conclusion or make a decision based strictly on prior evidence or experience? This problem is akin to evidence-based diagnosis as used in the medical profession. If I make a certain decision, what is the probability that I have done the best thing? Or, put differently, given past experience, what is the most likely outcome for each alternative, and how severe is the down-side consequences if I am wrong?
- Clearly, the context of some decision-making situations are better structured than others. Contexts that are low in structure often present a mix of data types, from well-behaved quantitative variables, to qualitative variables, to variables with missing and/or fuzzy values. Add to these complications the typical additional demands of low resources and competing priorities, and the decision-making environment is about as difficult as it can get. For example, what is the best allocation of instructional time to each of several subject areas for children in a given class?
- At the other end of the continuum of structure, are problems that are largely quantitative and have an easily agreed-upon objective. Usually, setting a master schedule (rooms, teachers, courses, time periods) is representative of such a problem.
- Some decisions may be relatively easy to make once there is consensus on which inputs are important and which are not. Such consensus may be hard to obtain because the individuals involved will suffer or gain substantively by the outcome. Many human resource management policy decisions fall into this category.
- Other decisions may also be relatively easy to make once there is consensus, but they carry the burden of being regarded as irrelvant by some or nearly all of the persons who are asked to make them. Adopting a mission statement and a set of institutional objectives is illustrative of such decisions.

- Some problems are well-structured but are based largely on social utilities that may be very hard to measure reliably. For example, how are decisions regarding the measurement of student progress, teacher effectiveness, and student promotion to be made?

3 CADM

There are many possible criteria for deciding when and how CADM should be used within a Decision Support System. The follow are examples:

- Is the problem structured or non-structured? Or, to restate the question, how well is the problem structured? Arguably, the appropriateness and the utility of CADM are positively correlated with the degree of structure.
- How efficient is the use of CADM likely to be? Or better, what is the benefit-to-cost ratio and is that ratio attractive?
- Are the inputs measureable? Generally, the more measureable the inputs, the more easily CADM can be employed.
- Is there really a decision to be made? There are many situations in education where it appears as though a decision is being made by a certain leader or group, but, in fact, many other individuals actually make the decision for themselves. How many curriculum committees, for example, have spent hundreds of man days making pedogogical decisions, only to have every teacher (including members of the curriculum committee) close the door to their classrooms and do whatever they want?
- Is the decision well-articulated? If not, how are we to know what decision needs to be made? Neither CADM or any other tool is useful if the decision cannot be expressed unambiguously.

4 BARRIERS

There are numerous barriers to the full implementation of CADM in schools, even for those decisions which are clearly amenable to such an approach. These barriers run the gamut from purely psychological constraints to limits on the state-of-the-art in computing to such practical matters as cost. The following is a brief list of such impediments to progress:

- On both a theoretical and practical level there is often a paucity of empirical models appropraite for a given situation.
- Or, when such models exist, they are not well understood by the persons using the CADM system. Thus, the need for training and cross disciplinary communication is a substantial constraint.
- CADM is confronted by all the usual attitudinal barriers customarily associated with organizational change and the adoption of technology.
- What is not well understood, is often feared or distrusted. Thus, the lack of training and experience feeds lack of confidence towards the models used. An addition, there is often a healthy distrust of the quality of the data, especially in environments where there has been no long-standing and rigorous standards for the collection and recording of information.
- Although in the long run, the costs of CADM may clearly offset the development costs, the initial investment may be prohibtive to the institution. Thus, the economic issues relate both to the cost-to-benefit ratio and initial capitalization.

- CADM deals with decisions and, only peripherally, helps with the formulation of goals. Thus, in the absence of goal congruence among the decision makers, CADM is not relevant. An institution that lacks well-articulated goals, congruent among the major players or constituencies, is not a good candidate for CADM.

5 CONCLUSION

- Do not use decision-making or decision-taking systems when there are no clear institutional goals, or even when the goals and purposes of the support system are unspecified. CADM is a tool for people and organizations which have a reasonably clear idea of where they are trying to go.
- Adopt a sensible and conservative implementation strategy. For exmple, install well-tested and trustworthy CADM applications into schools, let the people there get some experience with these CADM components, and let confidence grow, before adding complexity to the support system. Perhaps it would be best to start with decisions that are reasonbly well-structured.
- Although it is always approprite to suggest additional research, CADM in schools is a radically under-research area. In the case of hard deterministic data, the outcomes of CADM are likely to be somewhat predictable. However, for soft and probabilistic data, the likely outcomes are much harder to anticipate. Thus, reserach needs to include this latter more-difficult area.
- For many problems and in most organizational structures, group decision-making is more effective than top-down or one-man decision-making. CADM is an ideal tool when mixed with group work, becuase it adds data richness to people richness. A manager that does not care to tap into the reserves of knowledge and skill held by people, is unlikely to want help from a machine.

25

Impact of information and communication technology on the management of future schools

M. Mäkelä, A. Tatnall, P. Nolan, and C. Fulmer

with F. Frank, A.C.W. Fung, H. Gorsler, T. Okamoto, A.J. Visscher, H. Yndestad, and W. Yongmanitchai

Abstract

Future schools will involve participants (students, teacher tutors and the school community) working in collaborative environments. Members of the working group discussed the possible influences of IT on learning in and management of future schools, looking at some recent trends from the countries represented. They concluded that changes will occur in schools, but not without difficulty and change in the mindset of all concerned.

Keywords

Information technology, future schools, networking, communications

1 SCHOOLS IN THE FUTURE

The aims of education may be more achievable in the future with changes in both schools and technology - the question is whether IT (Information Technology) will make a difference. Will IT make it easier to achieve these goals? Schools of tomorrow could be different from today's schools for the following reasons.

- Society is changing from a labour and capital intensive mode of production towards an information intensive one.
- Outside demands (labour markets, development of information technology and the information industry, pressure of parents and society, etc) will set new goals for the schools and for their curricula.
- The new technology is already available and there is a demand from students to use this technology. Furthermore, students are motivated to learn with this new technology.

However, in spite of promises offered by prior technologies (such as TV and video), fundamental changes in the processes of schooling have not been realised. The issue is whether IT will follow this same path, or achieve a more enduring and effective impact in schools. The task involves both changes in schools and the appropriate application of IT tools.

The permanent skills relevant to lifelong learning are the skills of communication and cooperation (team work), and a capability to search for, and find relevant information from different sources in a changing problem solving situation. It will be more important to learn permanent skills and to learn to learn new things than to mechanically remember given facts.

Recent research results from learning psychology and pedagogical experience have led to the modern concept of active learning, and teaching must change according to these precepts. Students must control their own learning process actively participating in cooperative working teams and solving interdisciplinary problems together with teachers. Learning results should lead to generalisations and abstractions that are transferable to other experiences. The curriculum will thus be custom designed, interdisciplinary, fragmented, flexible, and capable of meeting specific need and demands.

As learning will happen any time and everywhere, the school of the future is a larger concept than the present one. It will be a distributed system with a fragmented netlike structure and without any clear hierarchy. The most important parts of the system are:

- the people involved - students, teachers as tutors or facilitaters of learning, administrators and managers of the system, and members of the "outside" world,
- space - school buildings, homes, libraries, museums, working places, etc and
- communication networks - computer networks, telecommunications, etc

People are working in collaboration together. They are distributed flexibly in time and space. The system is in continuous change, and adaptation to the change is vital.

2 'IT' IN THE FUTURE

Based on the evolutionary trends in IT one could forecast that continued improvements will be achieved in the following areas: networking connectivity, user interface, information accessibility and productivity tools. Recent advancements in technology offer the potential for asynchronous communication, integration of applications data sources, remote access to systems and large quantities of information. Multimedia technology and video conferencing allow group participation 'on the screen' from remote sites. Another thing that makes this different is that there is a multimodal interface nature to the technology - we have more and different ways of getting information and of communicating.
Specific examples for some countries are listed below:

- Hong Kong - with SAMS (School Administration and Management System), schools will be getting Internet accounts supported by the government: the Education Department is being computerised
- Thailand - School Net links 200 schools. The reason this is being done is to better utilise resources and to provide distance education and resource sharing. IT Campus resource sharing also occurs between specialisation areas (eg agricultural science and

medical science) with a video center at each university to use these resources. Web pages are used to interconnect to people and other schools and to provide distance education.

- Japan - a 100 school networking project is being scaled up to 1000 schools. The Ministry of Education will make plans to foster innovation in education in schools with a new integrated curriculum and will conduct a new curriculum incorporating integrated problem-based, cooperative, integrated subjects and communication skills.
- Victoria, Australia - two seemingly contrary trends are apparent: networking between schools and with the Department of School Education, and individual school governance. This centralisation and decentralisation represents both top-down and bottom-up trends.
- Finland - a yearly conference on this matter has been held for the last four or five years.
- Norway - started ten years ago. The 'Uninet' network of universities and colleges provided an integrated easy step to go into the Internet - a gateway was open already. This consisted of a satellite-based system for a total quality management program - all students know which school they will go to in the first year.
- U.S. - public schools have satellite uplinks and use video conferencing, schools are communicating around the world using satellites and are hiring information analysts. Students in some schools talked to the astronauts.
- Netherlands - 'study house' concept, student-centred learning, more decentralisation. Schools have become more independent and they do more on policy development now, and the government doesn't make as many decisions.

3 IMPACT OF THE NEW TECHNOLOGIES

Information and communications technologies will assist new schools to be functional. They will offer a means to distribute huge amounts of information in hypermedia form. They offer a total working environment for the learners and their tutors as well as for others, and can work together at different places and at different times seeking information in order to solve their problems. IT is a tool for integration and for problem-oriented learning in research teams.

Networked computing helps daily work, improves contacts and contents, broadens views. It is a basis for management of the changing system. Administration and management of the system will be impossible without a suitable management information system supporting decision making.

IT also offers new possibilities: distance learning using satellites and Internet access gives students the opportunity to learn at home or at remote places where it is not possible to reach school otherwise. IT offers huge amounts of information. Schools should also be able to help students to choose the 'proper' information and to evaluate it.

We must remember that IT is only one tool to make things possible, easy and flexible, and to increase productivity. IT cannot replace the human aspects, and other tools should be used when appropriate. Teachers will still be needed, but in a new role.

One concern of the impact of IT on schools is that individuals may become isolated with changes in traditional schools as schools evolve to use the networking technologies. The socialisation goal of schooling could be compromised. Opportunities for students, teachers, and other educational stakeholders to meet in groups should supplement this individualised learning mode.

Some learning control is needed. We must be sure that the students have learned the generic skills and capabilities required. Also management will need measures to control costs and ensure effectiveness of the system.

IT better enables the analysis of data and therefore enhances rational decision making. It also facilitates use of the data at a higher level for activities like decision making rather than for routine information retrieval. These tools facilitate collaborative work which reduces compartmentalisation of both content and work, through integration.

The traditional organisation of schools will be redefined, and schools may possibly evolve into smaller organisations. This will be painful, or even bad, if school management cannot manage the learning. Students will have the power, and schools must rise to the occasion.

4 CONCLUSION

The following conclusion are suggested:

- Participants in the group often used different words for the same ideas - there were communication difficulties, and this will be common in future schools also.
- A clear framework for management of the future system is needed.
- Technology should not be allowed to become dominant.
- Implementation and utilisation require time - perhaps one or even two generations, and at least several years. There are severe problems in the introduction of IT.
- Teacher education will be crucial.
- It is difficult to separate the features of the future schools from the impacts of IT. They will belong together.
- Change is hard to make. Technology provides the opportunity to make these changes but the decision to proceed must be a human one, taking into account the effect it will have on individuals. Change will not occur without some pain.
- The trends of changes in both schools and technology are similar: cooperative, interactive, connective, centralised/decentralised, resource sharing.
- Changes in schools and technology will not occur without a change in the mindset of all those concerned with schools and information technology.

26

Evaluation strategy for ITEM quality

C.D. O'Mahony, P. Wild, I.D. Selwood, L. Kraidej, and M.G. Reyes

Abstract

To produce a quality ITEM system, the essential process of evaluation must not be ignored. Within an existing framework, this paper discusses how we should evaluate ITEM systems and considers what objective and subjective measures are possible. Instruments are proposed for evaluating both individual school systems and systems used by groups of schools. The paper concludes with recommendations for future ITEM research.

Keywords

Educational management, evaluation, methodologies, future developments.

1 INTRODUCTION

Around the globe, those responsible for education delivery, be they government agencies or private foundations, are seeking ways to maximise their effectiveness, as measured against both external and internal criteria. In schools, an era of economic rationalism has dictated that educational managers must do 'more with less', and school decision-makers are more than ever calling for ways to measure and evaluate both curriculum and administrative programmes.

In any field of endeavour, future performance can be improved by learning from experience. The process of learning is more effective if it is properly organised rather than being haphazard and left to chance. Panic learning of lessons resulting from a painful and public disaster is insufficient (CCTA, 1994). In this context, evaluating the quality and effectiveness of IT systems for educational management is of great importance. As schools make greater investments in their IT/IS portfolios, evaluating the quality of this function has become a major concern. Evaluation assists to inform designers, programmers, installers, trainers and support teams so that barriers to system use are removed and promoters are used to encourage system use (Wild & Fung, 1996).

Tools for performing such evaluations are, however, not easily found or generated. Commenting on ITEM in seven nations, Visscher (1991) has noted:

> *"None of the countries has studied in a systematic way the quality of the available information systems. This is a universal problem; in fact, very little empirical data on system quality are available. ...*

This is regrettable since insight into variables that determine system quality can help to build better systems."

During the 1996 International Conference on ITEM for the Schools of the Future, ITEM evaluation was identified as a major theme for discussion. In particular, discussion addressed the following questions:

- How should we evaluate the quality of IT systems for educational management?
- What problems have been identified?
- What objective measures are possible?
  What subjective issues are relevant?

Each of these questions requires further decomposition. During the Conference, discussions built on the focus questions, and this paper encapsulates the concrete proposals and recommendations presented to the Working Conference in the closing session. The following pages develop the focus questions in further detail, highlighting some of the issues relevant to the evaluation of ITEM.

2 HOW SHOULD WE EVALUATE THE QUALITY OF ITEM SYSTEMS?

The development of appropriate evaluation measures is still pre-scientific. The intrinsically qualitative nature of such measures requires agreement on clear and concise terms of reference. One strategy for developing appropriate evaluation measures is offered by Fitzgerald (1993), as follows:

1. Identify / validate determinants of success;
2. Identify / validate the dimensions of ITEM that influence their success;
3. Devise measurement instruments for each of the constructs identified in steps 1 and 2;
4. Link each of these constructs with its operational indicators;
5. Select appropriate methodologies for data collection and analysis.

Members of the Discussion group used this strategy to frame and stimulate debate. The Discussion Group believed that constructive and useful evaluation must be guided by an underlying framework. To this end, previous research by DeLone & McLean (1992) was considered appropriate in providing a model of ITEM success (Figure 1).

This model proposes a framework of six variables which lead to success with information systems. These variables are System Quality, Information Quality, Use, User Satisfaction, Individual Impact and Organisational Impact. However, each of these 'variables' hides a complex interconnection and interweaving of influencing factors. The DeLone & McLean framework, originally developed as a taxonomy of research reports, has received informal support from the information systems research community. Such an underlying framework parallels the first point of the strategy suggested by Fitzgerald (1993).

3 WHAT PROBLEMS HAVE BEEN IDENTIFIED?

The experiences and observations of group participants assisted in developing this theme. Problems were perceived both with IT in Educational Management, and with evaluations themselves.

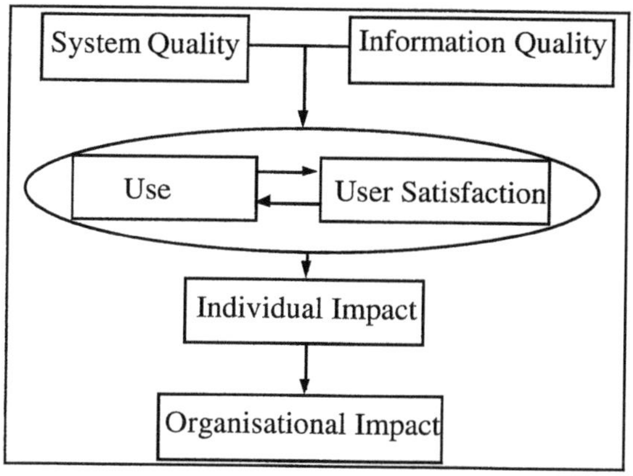

Figure 1 IS success model (DeLone & McLean 1992).

Problems with ITEM include use and usability, staff training, staff awareness and resistance to change. These issues, and others less predictable, were identified in a small scale research project which aimed at contextualising industrial based evaluation tools for the education sector (Wild et al., 1992). Rapidly increasing information needs have meant that systems have been developed reactively rather than proactively to improve organisational efficiency and effectiveness (Wild & Fung, 1996). Another issue explored at the conference was the influence of organisational culture on ITEM effectiveness (O'Mahony, 1996; Reyes 1996).

Problems with evaluations themselves include such issues as agreement on criteria, agreement on quantitative and qualitative methods, and the politicising of the evaluation process (Hirschheim & Smithson, 1987). The Discussion Group noted that evaluation often became a low priority in ITEM development and maintenance efforts, and recognised that useful evaluations must be continuous and cyclical in nature Wild & Fung, 1996). The evaluation process must necessarily be time-consuming, but is crucial to achieving success throughout many parts of educational organisations. Formal feedback mechanisms are required, which are user-focussed, throughout ITEM development as well as at all levels of use.

4 WHAT OBJECTIVE MEASURES ARE POSSIBLE? WHAT SUBJECTIVE ISSUES ARE RELEVANT?

Both the ITEM literature and mainstream information system literature bemoan the lack of appropriate objective, quantitative methods for evaluating IS quality (O'Mahony, 1995; Visscher, 1991). Quantitative approaches include measurement of IS in terms of return on investment (Willcocks, 1994), but this has limited application in a schools context.

Objective measures worthy of further exploration include Critical Success Factors and Benchmarking (Rolstadas, 1995). The use of educational outcomes to justify ITEM investment

Table 1 Dimensions of success variables

Variable	*Quantitative Measures*	*Qualitative Measures*
System Quality	Cost Speed Capacity Robustness, reliability, consistency Mean time between failures Upgradability Security, control Validation, verification Support (training & technical) Compatibility	Flexibility, function User Friendliness Maintainability Documentation (User, task, technical)
Information Quality	Compatibility	Accuracy Relevance Recency Completeness
Use	Keying, error handling, navigation, output Utilisation Frequency of use	Avoidance of use
User Satisfaction	Stress	Stress Ease of use Task match Support Perceived consequences of use / removal of use Task variety Empowerment / influence
Individual Impact	Productivity Working environment (EEC directive 90/270/1992) Reskilling, competence Attendance	Productivity Working environment Motivation Job descriptions
Organisational Impact	Staff turnover Marketing effectiveness Accounting flexibility Cost benefit analysis EDUCATIONAL OUTCOMES	Management culture Management practices (eg Communication, Control, Command Accountability Responsibility Quality of decision making EDUCATIONAL OUTCOMES

has so far not been validated. Inter-school, inter-system and inter-national comparisons may well assist in the development of objective measures.

Subjective measures are also highly relevant. The influence of soft systems methodologies on qualitative research is a growing trend. Work by such researchers as Sauer (1993) has offered alternatives for IS evaluation. The concept of information systems failure is a valuable insight into the importance of ITEM evaluation. Variables identified by Visscher (1991) in the development of computer assisted school administration (CASA) show a marked similarity with the DeLone & McLean framework. They are Design & Development Strategy, IS Quality, Other Factors That Affect Use, Use of IS and Impact. Relationships between these components are still subject to debate among ITEM researchers.

Although useful for individual schools, the key value of subjective measures is ultimately their generalisability.

Using DeLone & McLean's model of IS success, the discussion group identified the measures shown in the following table (Table 1). The identification of these measures parallels the second point in the strategy suggested by Fitzgerald (1993).

It should be noted that the dimensions identified in Table 1 are not intended to be exhaustive. Many constructs can and should be decomposed. For instance, 'individual impact' varies depending on the individual's position within the school. Some stakeholders use ITEM in an administrative mode, whereas others utilise ITEM in a management mode.

5 MEASUREMENT INSTRUMENTS

One instrument that incorporates many of the above constructs is the User Acceptability Audit (Wild et al, 1992). Originally developed by Richardson (1987), the User Acceptability Audit has already been successfully trialled in UK schools. Within an individual school it represents a qualitative measurement instrument. Across groups of schools, however, the User Acceptability Audit becomes a powerful instrument for collecting data which can then be analysed in a more quantitative way.

Instruments for measuring qualitative variables include the following:

- Questionnaire
- Logged data collection
- Structured interview

Action research methodologies also show potential for gathering rich qualitative data on ITEM. Despite overlap between instruments, each appears to make a unique contribution to the evaluation process. A multi-method strategy will yield more reliable data (Henderson et al 1995).

6 CONCLUSION

The evaluation of ITEM is clearly an issue that requires further investigation. In many ITEM development projects evaluation is performed ad hoc, and results from evaluations are frequently ignored in project reviews. The authors have proposed the use of an existing framework for the identification of appropriate evaluation variables. This framework considers ITEM evaluation from six different perspectives, making use of both objective and subjective measures.

Appropriate methodologies for data collection have been proposed in this paper. The development of rigorous measurement instruments for each of these constructs should be the subject of future research. Only through the development of valid evaluation techniques will ITEM projects achieve success.

7 REFERENCES

CCTA (1994) *PRINCE project evaluation.* London: HMSO.

DeLone, W.H., and McLean, E.R. (1992) Information systems success: the quest for the dependent variable. *Information Systems Research*, **3(1)**, 60-95.

Fitzgerald, E. (1993) Success measures for IS strategic planning. *Journal of Strategic Information Systems*, **2(4)**, 335-350.

Henderson, R., Podd, J., Smith, M. and Varela-Alvarez, H. (1995) An examination of four user-based software evaluation methods. *Interacting with Computers*, **7(4)**, 412-432.

Hirschheim, R. and Smithson, S. (1987) Information systems evaluation: myth and reality, in *Information Analysis: selected readings* (ed. R.D. Galliers). Addison-Wesley, Wokingham, UK.

O'Mahony, C.D. (1995) *Improving school information systems management: the quest for quality*. Australian Catholic University, Sydney.

O'Mahony, C.D. & Dampney, C.N.G. (1995) Trends in the management of school information systems, in *Proceedings: 6th Australasian Conference on Information Systems,* Sept 1995, Curtin University, Perth, W. Australia.

O'Mahony, C.D. (1996) IS effectiveness and organisational culture: an underlying model for ITEM evaluation, in *Proceedings of the 2nd IFIP International Working Conference on ITEM*, July 1996, Hong Kong Bapist University, Hong Kong.

Reyes, M.G. (1996) The impact of organisational culture on success of information projects, in *Proceedings of the 2nd IFIP International Working Conference on ITEM*, July 1996, Hong Kong Bapist University, Hong Kong.

Richardson, S. (1987) Operationalising usability and acceptability: a methodological review, in *New methods in applied ergonomics* (eds. J.R. Wilson et al.), Taylor & Francis, London.

Rolstadas, A. (1995) *Benchmarking: theory and practice*. Chapman & Hall, London.

Sauer, C. (1993) *Why information systems fail: a case study approach*. Alfred Waller, Henley-on-Thames.

Selwood, I.D. (1995) The development of ITEM in England and Wales, in (1995) *Information technology in educational management* (eds. B.Z. Barta et al.), Chapman & Hall, London.

Visscher, A.J. (1991) Computer assisted school administration and management: the state of the art in seven nations." *Journal of Research on Computing in Education*, **24(1)**, 146-168.

Wild, P. & Fung, A.C.W. (1996) Evaluation of ITEM for proactive development, in *Proceedings of the 2nd IFIP International Working Conference on ITEM*, July 1996, Hong Kong Bapist University, Hong Kong.

Wild, P., Scivier, J. and Richardson, S. (1992) An Evaluation of a LEA's Secondary Schools IT system for LMS Support. *Education Management and Administration,* **20(4)**, 40-48.

Willcocks, L. (1994) *Information management: the evaluation of information systems investments*. Chapman and Hall, London.

INDEX OF CONTRIBUTORS

KEYWORD INDEX